PATSY NEAL
Brevard College, Brevard, North Carolina

# coaching methods for women

ADDISON–WESLEY PUBLISHING COMPANY

Reading, Massachusetts

Menlo Park, California · London · Don Mills, Ontario

This book is in the

ADDISON–WESLEY SERIES IN PHYSICAL EDUCATION

Consulting Editor
KATHERINE LEY

## about the author

Patsy Neal is an assistant professor in the department of physical education at Brevard College in North Carolina. She received her B.S. degree from Wayland College (Texas) and her M.S. degree from the University of Utah. Although she is an accomplished tennis player and coach, Miss Neal is best known for her achievements in basketball. She was an All-American for three years, the 1957 National free-throw champion, a member of the American basketball team at the 1959 Pan American Games, captain of the United States team at the 1964 World Tournament in Peru, on the United States team that toured Europe and Russia in 1965, and an instructor at the Fourth National Institute on Girls and Women's Sports. In addition, Miss Neal was selected as one of the Outstanding Young Women of America in 1965 and was included in *Who's Who of American Women* in 1967. The author of the book *Basketball Techniques for Women* and numerous articles in magazines and anthologies, she is a member of the American Association for Health, Physical Education, and Recreation, the United States Lawn Tennis Association, and the Basketball Subcommittee of the United States Collegiate Sports Council.

# preface and acknowledgments

This book was written to encourage sound coaching principles and training methods for women. The information herein will help the woman coach, the man who coaches a woman's team, the physical education major who will be dealing with skilled athletes, the leader of a recreational program, the physical education instructor, and the player herself.

The trend toward competition for skilled women athletes has created a need for textbooks, classes in coaching techniques, and qualified leaders in the field of women's sports. This book is designed for use in college classes on coaching techniques for women. This is the first book written specifically for the woman coach, and the first book geared exclusively to the needs of the girl and woman athlete. It includes the latest findings on strenuous competitive programs for women as well as up-to-date training and conditioning methods. (Of course, new material is being printed every day; there is still much to be learned about women and competition.)

The chapter on The Role of the Coach should help a person to formulate a philosophy of coaching and to gain a concept of the relationship between coach and player.

The section on Factors to Consider in Coaching Women should be invaluable to anyone who has had to rely on the research that has been done in the field of men's sports. There has been a lack of information about the woman athlete; it is hoped that this book will help fill the gap.

The chapter on Advanced Techniques and Strategy covers most sports that women are engaged in on a competitive basis today, and will help the coach deal specifically with skilled woman athletes. Competitive programs for women would greatly improve if an expert in each sport would write a book geared to the expert female performer. But until such books exist, the suggestions given here should prove useful, both to the beginning coach and to the experienced one.

For the coaches and administrators of schools that are just beginning to initiate girls' sports programs, reading the chapter on Standards and Guidelines for Athletic Programs for Women will help them to give the participants the full benefits of competition.

Because of traditional cultural and social attitudes toward women in sports, some women have been limited in their opportunities and their outlook. Many girls have not reached their full potential in sports simply because they have been defeated psychologically before they even competed. The participation of women in competitive sports has been hampered by myths and superstitions. Today, however, because we are becoming aware of the fact that women have a much greater capacity for physical activity and a much greater desire for sports programs than we gave them credit for in the last half century, more women are developing their talents in this field.

Woman's role in society has changed greatly in the last few decades. This change has been accompanied by a change in the public's attitude toward the woman who wishes to engage in sports. At one time, people's feelings about women athletes were so negative that a woman who considered herself a lady wouldn't think of competing in sports and risking being thought masculine, unladylike, or low-class. But with today's more sensible attitude toward sports for women, a girl can participate in competitive sports without losing her image of herself, or having it mangled by a narrow-minded public.

Our sports programs for women must of course be geared to women's abilities, both as performers and coaches. Nevertheless, in our efforts to open up the field for women, we must be careful not to pass over qualified men coaches in preference to less-well-qualified women coaches, just to get a woman coach. Our women should have the *best* possible coaching, whether the coach is a man or a woman. Few women have had enough experience and training in competitive sports in the past few years to qualify them to do an outstanding job of coaching skilled women athletes. The better coaches today, in most cases, are men, simply because men have grown up with competition and sports, and thus their background for coaching has been more extensive. During the years when women hesitated to take on this responsibility, men have been carrying on many of the women's programs, and they deserve full credit for their willingness to do so, and their competence in their jobs.

So, although we need women to be in control of the women's programs (especially with respect to administration and chaperonage), until women can do as good a coaching job as men, they should not replace them in coaching positions.

One of our biggest problems as coaches is to enforce standards and principles that will safeguard girls who participate. However, our girls also need adequate training in the basics of human movement. If, because of poor coaching, they do not get this training, this can eventually lead to an even larger problem: failure to achieve their full potential.

If our athletic programs for women are to prosper, we must have programs that are planned by intelligent leaders who are interested in the welfare of the participants; and we must of course have good coaching. Standards such as those published by DGWS ensure women of their right to compete while giving them the chance to maintain their femininity.

Naturally no one has all the answers to the problems of competition for women; so we must be willing to keep our eyes open to new possibilities in the field. And, as we seek to provide a challenging program for the highly skilled girl, we must try to motivate average players as well to reach their full potential. Therefore, we must be careful that we do not swing our programs from one extreme to another. We cannot afford to ignore the average girl and give preference to the highly skilled girl, or vice versa.

This book does not set forth a day-by-day coaching plan, but it does present the basic information a coach needs in order to work with the skilled girl.

In writing this book I have often slipped into using the feminine pronoun when referring to the coach. However, this book is intended for men as well as women; feminine connotations are only a matter of simplification in writing.

I wish to thank Dr. Katherine Ley of the State University of New York at Cortland, for her help with the manuscript. Her suggestions and comments were invaluable. I am also greatly indebted to the physiologist at Cortland, Wayne Tomik, for his advice and help with research for chapters two and four.

Special thanks go to Susan Zehrung, a student at Brevard College, for drawing the original illustrations, and to George Guzzi and the art staff at Addison-Wesley for the final work.

I am grateful to the members of the Health and Physical Education Department at Brevard College, especially Leighton W. Martin, for help and encouragement during the writing of the book. I also wish to thank Dr. Dean Summers of Indiana University for her contributions to research, and Miss Anne Priest and Miss Carla Lowry for their help during the typing of the manuscript.

Some individuals and publishers have been very cooperative in allowing me to use material from copyrighted sources. I am indebted to Dr. Laurence E. Morehouse and the W. B. Saunders Company for permission to paraphrase from *Sports Medicine for Trainers*, and to the American Association for Health, Physical Education, and Recreation for permission to use the DGWS guideline statements for junior high school, high school, and colleges.

Others who have contributed valuable material to this book are Carolyn Osborn Bowers, Dr. John Cooper, Sharon Peterson, Frances Schaafsma, JoAnne Thorpe, Betty Jane Trotter, and Jane Ward.

Help with photographs was given by Mrs. Mary Carol Bagwell, Mr. Joseph C. Bowles, Miss Helen Briwa, Miss Carol House, Miss E. J. Howard, Mr. Dick Lowy, Mr. Keichi Nakamoto, Miss DeDeOwens, *Ski* Magazine, Sundby Publications, United States Track and Field Federation, and the Women's Recreation Association at Colorado State University.

So many people have played a part in my background in competitive sports and in my appreciation of the values of sports that I cannot name them all. Nevertheless, I am grateful to all these people, and especially to my family.

The teachers and administrators of Wayland College, the University of Utah, and Brevard College have not only given me opportunities to compete, but also time away from the institutions so that I could participate in competition and professional activities. They have contributed to my philosophy of sports and have encouraged me to write this philosophy.

My earliest competitive experiences took place in the school system of Elberton,

Georgia, and I am thankful that Georgia offered a well-rounded competitive sports program for women at a time when few states paid attention to the needs of women as well as men.

To those people in the profession who have worked toward better understanding and cooperation between AAU and DGWS, and who as a result have opened up a new era in women's sports, go my special thanks and respect.

This book is simply a written expression of appreciation for the many, many opportunities that have been made available to me through the medium of sports.

*Brevard, North Carolina*                                                    P. N.
*March 1969*

# chapter two  factors in coaching women

If the misconceptions about the effects of strenuous activity on women are to be dispelled, research findings on the subject should be accessible to everyone interested in women's athletics. Toward this end, I have based this chapter on research in this area, hoping that by citing this research, I can help to clear away negativism and misunderstanding of the effects of competition and exercise on women.

Since women do not have the same body build that men have and thus do not have the same physical potential, we must carefully consider those factors that may influence a training program designed for women: (1) health/medical factors, (2) genetic/morphological factors, (3) physiological/metabolic factors, (4) developmental/emotional factors, and (5) environmental factors. One area that needs more research is the subject of psychological factors.


## HEALTH AND MEDICAL FACTORS

It is only in the last few years that we have realized that physical activities and participation in sports are not harmful to a woman. On the contrary, they can be a factor that contributes to her overall health, provided that she has no physical defects prior to engaging in strenuous exercise. Laboratory and field research point to many benefits. Let us review some of these.

### BENEFITS OF EXERCISE

Exercise, and the health benefits that can be gained from it, is as important to the woman as it is to the man [26]. Thus the healthy woman who participates in athletics need not fear danger to her health because there are no significant risks involved [70].

The American Medical Association has pointed out that sound sports programs can contribute a great deal to a woman's total fitness. Participation in sports activities can make her more aware of health factors, and promote in her a sense of satisfaction and achievement. The motivation provided by participation in sports reinforces self-discipline in carrying out good health practices, and can lead to a more "dynamic womanhood" [2].

Observation of athletes themselves underscores the benefits of strenuous activity. Regardless of the wear and tear on their bodies, the tremendous demands on them, and the physical and emotional stress during competitive events, very few athletes miss practice or scheduled events because of illness. To use my own case as an example, during 15 years of competition I have missed only one game because of illness; and among the thousands of people I have competed with, I have known only a few who missed a competitive event because they were ill. It is true that many athletes compete while suffering from colds and other illnesses that would keep the average person in bed. This is probably due to a combination of factors: a high degree of motivation, self-discipline in enduring discomfort, and an ability to bounce back quickly because of good physical fitness. Undoubtably it is also due to the health benefits derived from strenuous exercise.

Regardless of reasons why the well-trained athlete can continue to compete when the untrained person would be unable to cope, it appears that top women athletes do not suffer any bad effects in later life from illnesses or injuries occurring during competition, either with respect to health, number of children, or ease of childbirth[1].

## EXERCISE AND THE HEART

Misconceptions about the effects of sports on women have persisted not only with regard to women's health in general, but also with respect to the function of the woman's heart and its ability to withstand the strain of strenuous activity.

A study by Tuttle[78] showed that the normal heart rate of women athletes was slower than that of non-athletic women, and that they had a higher degree of physical efficiency. In a three-minute step test, Skubic and Hodgkins [72] found that trained women swimmers performed the second and third minutes of the test with slower heart rates, and that they had a slower heart rate during recovery, than women who were not conditioned.

To draw a comparison with men: Studies of men athletes by J. B. Wolffe [84] indicated that strenuous physical activity did not cause abnormal cardiac enlargement or myocardial damage so long as the person was normally healthy to begin with. As a result of his studies, Wolffe feels that the expression "athlete's heart," in its usual sense, should be redefined, since the athlete has a heart that is better developed, stronger, and that operates more economically than the heart of a person who is physically untrained.

It is now generally known that one of the three main factors in preventing coronary heart disease is regular exercise [87], and that both young and old benefit from physical activity that demands an efficient heart.

## EXERCISE AND THE MENSTRUAL PERIOD

Ignorance of the effects of exercise on a woman's menstrual period has led to another unfounded fear. Two studies of women athletes have helped clarify the effects of athletic competition on the menstrual cycle: Jokl [38], in a study of 543 women participants in track and field, hockey, tennis, gymnastics, and swimming, failed to find a single case of serious menstrual disability.

Erdelyi [23], in a study that involved 729 Hungarian women athletes, found that, during participation in athletics, 85.1% of the women noticed no change in the menstrual cycle, 5.6% noticed favorable changes, and 9.3% noticed unfavorable changes. (By way of comparison, consider the fact that approximately 10% of nonathletes experience unfavorable changes during the normal course of their daily lives. Thus, before blaming sports activity as the cause of unfavorable changes in the menstrual cycle, one should consider other factors as well.) Erdelyi found that the highest percentage of menstrual disorders occurred among young athletes between 15 and 17 years of age (18.0%), while only 7.4% of the adult group (18 years and older) experienced unfavorable changes during the menstrual cycle. Erdelyi concluded that women may safely continue to participate in sports activities during their menstrual periods, provided that there are no unfavorable changes in their cycles and provided that their performances don't suffer.

Other observers [3, 33, 60] also feel that women who have no menstrual disorders should be allowed to participate, during menstruation, in all types of physical activity and competition, including swimming. Pros [63] feels that if a girl is used to athletic competition, then she can continue to compete during menstruation.

Some medical people disapprove of intensive athletic competition during the first two days of menstruation [80], while others disapprove of participation in certain sports such as swimming, diving, tennis, skiing, and gymnastics at any time during menstruation because of the intense effort these sports demand and the high percentage of menstrual disorders associated with them [23].

My own belief is that participation in sports can improve a woman's general physical fitness to such a degree that participation during the menstrual period does not entail discomfort, either psychological or physical. Ordinarily, the woman athlete who has followed a sound conditioning program and has trained for competition simply forgets that it is "that time of the month." I have never known a topnotch woman athlete who missed a competitive event because she was menstruating, or one who blamed poor performance on this factor alone. If a woman does experience discomfort or poor performance, it may be due to social and psychological conditioning over a period of years rather than an inability to perform well during menstruation.

Some studies [23, 47] have indicated that if a woman's performance does sag during the menstrual cycle, the sag occurs during the premenstrual period or the first two days of menstruation, with the best performance coming during the postmenstrual phase. However, there is usually no letdown in performance, and most women athletes are capable of performing at their average level during menstruation [1, 23, 62, 66].

Far from having an adverse effect on a woman's menstrual habits, participation in sports, by strengthening her abdominal muscles, can eliminate many symptoms of dysmenorrhea [18, 29, 30] and thus one by-product of a sports program is often an improved menstrual cycle.

The sport that is most controversial with respect to competition during menstruation is swimming. Studies [3, 5] indicate that swimming is not generally a causative factor in menstrual disturbances, and that women who have been ardent swimmers usually go through life relatively free of obstetrical and gynecological difficulties. If a girl does complain of pain, a change in the menstrual cycle, or a lag in performance while she is participating in swimming (or in any other sport), she should be given a thorough physical examination to rule out other possibilities before one assumes that these bad effects are a result of swimming or strenuous activity. If the results of these tests indicate that the girl has trained too hard, then she should not practice or compete during her menstrual period.

Top-flight women athletes compete every day, many of them while they are menstruating. No one watching them compete could point out which ones are menstruating, because their performances and their psychological attitudes toward competition do not vary with the time of the month. In fact, women can not only compete while they are menstruating, but can excel in their performances. In the 1956 Olympics in Melbourne, six gold medals were won by women who were menstruating at the time they competed [16].

### EXERCISE AND CHILDBIRTH

Another common worry connected with women engaging in competitive sports is that it may adversely affect a woman's child-bearing function. The few studies that have been done in this area indicate that women athletes have fewer complications during pregnancy and childbirth than nonathletes [23], possibly because of women athletes' strong muscles (especially in the abdominal and pelvic region), overall physical fitness, and ability to relax in the face of pain and discomfort.

Generally, women athletes have no more trouble than non-athletes in adjusting to marriage and motherhood, although they may marry at an older age [23]. A study by Astrand [5] supports findings that women athletes have a normal desire for marriage and children, and that sports training has no adverse effect on fertility.

During the early months of pregnancy, a woman can usually continue to participate in sports, except those that involve body contact or bumps [16]. However, she should not participate in those sports that involve unnecessary risks, although spontaneous abortion as a result of strenuous exercise is rare [47]. (Another interesting fact about the 1956 Melbourne Olympics is that three women participants were pregnant [16].)

After a woman athlete has had a baby, she should allow some time to elapse before continuing her training and competition on a serious basis. Charles [16] suggests a 3-month interval, while Pros [63] advocates a wait of 4 months.

### GENETIC AND MORPHOLOGICAL FACTORS

Evolution and heredity have resulted in a woman's having certain physical traits and structure that make her ability to perform different from a man's. Before we plan sports programs for women, we should consider these differences.

DIFFERENCES BETWEEN MEN AND WOMEN

The differences in body type and body composition of men and women are probably not as great as some would believe. However, let us list some of them, based, of course, on men and women of average size.

1. The woman has a narrower shoulder than the man [43, 50, 80].
2. The male is taller than the female [80].
3. The female's center of gravity is lower than the male's [50, 51, 80].
4. The woman's arms and legs are proportionately shorter than the man's [51].
5. The woman has a smaller lung capacity than the man [50, 80].
6. The woman's pelvis is wider and shallower than the man's [43, 50, 51, 80, 83].
7. The female's heart is smaller than the male's [80].
8. Some skeletal differences begin at birth, with some bones in the female ossifying before those in the male [50, 80].
9. The angle of the female's arm is slightly different from the male's [43, 51, 80].
10. The male has a longer growth period than the female; therefore the female matures earlier [50, 71, 80].
11. Women have more fat or adipose tissue than men [51].
12. The woman's thumbs are proportionately shorter than the man's, while the index fingers are longer [77].
13. The femur is more oblique in the female than in the male [83].
14. The female has approximately 36% muscle [51, 77], the male 43% [51].

These differences do have some implications for athletic programs for women. Since the woman does have narrower shoulders, broader hips, and an inward inclination of the arms, most women find it hard to engage in activities in which the body must be supported for any length of time by the arms. The angling of the arms may also make throwing more difficult for the woman than for the man.

Having broader and heavier hips may also mean that the woman may not be able to run as well as the man. The obliquity of the femur may also lead to a mechanical disadvantage for the woman in running when compared to the male.

Since the woman is generally not as tall as the man, she is at a disadvantage in jumping and in running events, in which speed depends on length of stride. However, this shortness gives her an advantage in events that rely heavily on stability, since her center of gravity is lower than a man's.

The fact that the woman's hands have thumbs that are shorter and index fingers that are longer than a man's gives her an advantage in activities that demand dexterity. One often reads about women's ability to play better golf than men around the greens, where touch is more important than power.

The woman's earlier maturation makes her less susceptible than the man to bone and joint injury during adolescence, while the extra fat adds protection against bruises and helps keep her warm in a cold environment. However, a woman's adipose tissue forces her to expend more energy to gain the same results a man does, since she must move a greater amount of dead weight because of tissue that consists of fat rather than muscle.

DIFFERENCES AMONG WOMEN

Women vary greatly among themselves in their traits and structure. Therefore, in guiding a program of women's athletics, one must also consider each woman's overall body type. The bounds within which any athlete has to work are set to some degree by heredity. Some physical characteristics may limit a person severely in one specific sport, while other characteristics may greatly help the person perform well in another sport. Height is an advantage to the basketball player, but a disadvantage to the gymnast and the tumbler. The woman who is overweight or proportionately fatter than average may be at an advantage in swimming great distances or in throwing events that demand power, but at a disadvantage in activities in which the body weight must be supported or which involve jumping and running.

One of the better-known classifications of men's bodies was formulated by W. H. Sheldon, whose classifications may also be applied to women. According to Sheldon, there are three basic body types: (1) *endomorphs*, characterized by roundness and softness of body, (2) *mesomorphs*, who are muscular, with large bones, and (3) *ectomorphs*, who are slender and relatively thin and small-framed. It should be remembered that these body types can overlap.

Generally, endomorphs excel in the one sport in which weight is an advantage rather than a disadvantage: long-distance swimming. Most swimmers who can cover great distances, such as the English channel, are obese or of stocky build, with fat concealing the muscles. The insulating property of adipose tissue enables the fat person to maintain body temperature in cold water over a long period of time. In addition, the specific gravity of adipose tissue is less than that of muscle, so that the buoyancy of the swimmer is increased [51]. Mesomorphs can usually excel in events that demand speed, strength, and endurance. People who are a combination of endomorph and mesomorph are usually good at sports that require strength and a certain amount of speed and endurance, such as the shot put and discus throw, as well as middle-distance runs. The ectomorph, though at a disadvantage in events demanding strength and stability, may do well in endurance events and jumping events, since there is a limited amount of body mass to move, and in running events in which length of stride is important.

The tall person can successfully compete in basketball, badminton, tennis, golf, softball, swimming, most track and field events, and volleyball, if she can control her body well and if she has adequate strength to move her long limbs. Long legs and arms not only help the person in activities in which reach is important, but allow a greater range of motion and a greater coverage of a specific area. Long arms can also improve one's performance in sports that require throwing (for example, the discus and the javelin) or batting and hitting (for example, tennis and softball), since the longer the arm used as a lever, the greater the speed and velocity of the object thrown or hit.

The tall volleyball player not only gets more power from the hitting action on a spike, but she also has an angle advantage as a result of her longer reach. A fencer has a definite advantage if her arms are longer than the opponent's, and a high jumper has an easier time clearing the bar if her legs are longer and her center of gravity higher than average.

The short girl can compete well in tumbling, diving, hockey, skiing, and ice skating. The fact that her short limbs enable her to tuck her body in tight helps the tumbler and diver to execute movements, somersaults, and spins with speed and overall body control. A low center of gravity and greater stability helps the short hockey player by enabling her to maintain balance and to start, stop, and change direction quickly, and also aids her hand-eye coordination, since her body is low and close to the ball. The low center of gravity is a definite advantage in skiing, in which speed and sharp turns as well as body balance are imperative. The short ice skater has the same advantage.

This is not to say that a short girl cannot excel in a specific sport such as basketball or tennis, or that a tall one will never be any good in a sport such as tumbling or skiing. Some of our greatest athletes do not fit the expected mold: Billie Jean King is one of the world's best tennis players, yet she is relatively short. She counteracts her height disadvantage with skill, quickness of reactions, hustle, and determination. In golf—in which height gives extra leverage and consequently more power and distance—Sandra Haynie does exceptionally well and yet weighs about 107 pounds and is petite.

One can't say that selection of an athlete for an activity is more important than training, or vice versa. Ideally, a coach could select an athlete who had all the qualifications for a specific sport and then train her to be a top competitor. But desire and interest can be such great motivating factors that an athlete with lesser physical attributes can compete on even terms with one having all the physical characteristics, but less motivation.

The woman who *does* choose a sport in which her height, weight, or overall body type put her at a disadvantage must accept the facts and be willing to face up to the options open to her. First, both the coach and the athlete must realize that there are limitations to what the girl can accomplish when she is competing with someone else who is equally motivated and who in addition has physical characteristics that are an advantage in the given sport. Second, the girl must be willing to work harder to counteract the disadvantages of body type. For instance, the heavy basketball player may have to work very hard on endurance and speed in order to keep up with the slender girl, while the thin girl may have to utilize speed and try to develop additional strength in order to compete with the muscular, stocky girl in the shot put or some other event that depends on strength and body weight. Third, the person must have extraordinary determination and hustle. Motivation and mental attitudes play a tremendous part in athletics, and often psychological factors outweigh physical ones.

Some studies, in fact, have even shown that body type is not a large determining factor in some performances. Patterson [57], for example, found no significant correlation between women's success in swimming and their height and weight. Watson [81] found that the relationship between college women's body measurements and their ability to throw a baseball was low, with respect to both accuracy and distance. Perbix [58] indicated that there was no relationship between women's somatotype ratings and their trunk extensions, although the same study found that there seem to be significant relationships between mesomorphy and strength and power, and that women physical education majors have more dominant mesomorphic traits than women in other fields. In a study of men, Pierson [61] found that there seems to be little relationship between speed of reaction and height, weight, body fat, or lean body mass.

DO SPORTS MASCULINIZE WOMEN?

Another subject of contention is whether women lose their femininity if they are athletes. The natural desires of women in the past for play activities and athletic competition have been inhibited because of this misconception, and even today there are evidences that the myth persists that girls who participate in a sports program acquire masculine characteristics.

Participation in sports does not masculinize women [43]; the belief that it does has no foundation, since the great majority of women who participate in athletics show no signs of masculinization even after competing for years [23].

True, there are always a few women to be found engaging in sports who have masculine characteristics; these characteristics may give them some advantages because of the structure of their bodies. However, Carpenter[11] measured the factors that influenced the athletic performance of college women, and found that the two most important ones were power and muscular strength, while the third factor measured—masculine type of build—had less influence. This study indicated that there is no significant correlation between a woman's athletic performance and femininity of body type.

However, Cress and Thorsen [19], in a study of college women, found a higher correlation between androgyny ratings and motor performance than between androgyny ratings and somatotype ratings. They also found that masculinity of physique showed a significant positive correlation with pure speed, the 50-yard dash, the Sargent jump, arm strength, and the Humiston test.

For some time there have been rumors that certain countries entered men, disguised as women, on some of their women's Olympic teams. In the 1968 Olympics, to ensure that women would be competing against women, female participants had to pass not only a visual checkup, but they also had to pass the buccal smear and the karyotype (chromosome patterns) tests. These tests are based on the theory that masculinity and femininity are determined by the characteristics of chromosomes. However, as pointed out in an article in *Sports Illustrated* [88], the reliability of these tests has been questioned, on the basis that more than one criterion must be involved in determining the sex of an individual.

When women athletes do show evidences of masculinity, there is no proof that participation in sports is the cause of it. It is more likely that the athletes already had these characteristics before they began to take part in athletics. After all, there are ex-

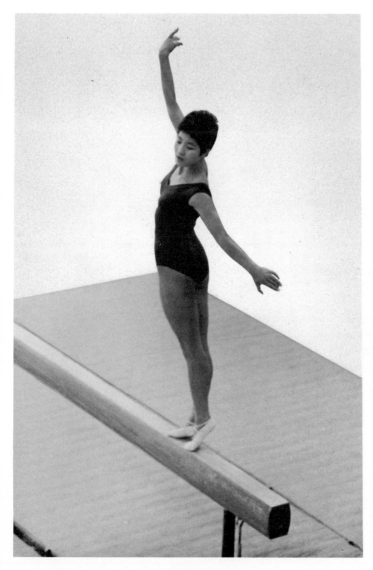

Beam balance (courtesy Sundby Publications).

ceptions to the norm in any field of endeavor. The feminine women participating in sports—and they are in the majority—should not be judged on the basis of the few exceptions who are masculine. One has only to look at some of the women who have won medals in the Olympic Games to see that a woman can be feminine and talented in sports at the same time. Wilma Rudolph, Peggy Fleming, and Debbie Meyer are examples (to name but a few).

Participation in sports, therefore, does not seem to masculinize women. It is just that our culture has imposed its own code of conduct on both women and men, and when anyone exhibits behavior that varies from this code, a false label is attached to that person. In most cases, this code of conduct is based on scant knowledge of the physiological, morphological, or psychological workings of the male or female. The code has assigned cultural roles on the basis of sex, and reinforced them over the years until people have generally accepted certain traits as being masculine and certain others as being feminine. Yet confusion is arising because, although society at large accepts one role as feminine and another as masculine, science has led many people to question the cut-and-dried division between these roles. And women themselves are reaching out and seeking a more vital role that will allow them greater development professionally, socially and physically. The age-old limitations on women, aptly defined by the Germans as *Kinder, Küche, Kirche,* are beginning to fade. And there are many questions that need to be answered as to the real meaning of masculinity and femininity.

Are strength and endurance purely masculine traits, or can women engage in activities that require these two factors and still remain feminine? Does aggressiveness belong only to a man, grace only to a woman? Are courage and the ability to endure pain strictly masculine traits, or can women be courageous and train themselves to continue physical exercise in spite of discomfort? Is it feminine to bear pain with fortitude only during an involuntary experience like childbirth, but masculine to do so under voluntary, competitive athletic conditions? Steinhaus [76], for one, feels that women should be allowed to compete, within their own limits, without being labeled masculine or unladylike, and raises the important question of whether our "forced, false, male-made standard of femininity" isn't preventing women from developing their personalities fully.

Men and women *both* are capable of kindness, aggression, physical and mental self-discipline, strength, and endurance. Men and women *both* can be strong, can endure, can run, jump, laugh and cry. These capabilities are not sex-dependent, although the degree of accomplishment may be limited by sex. But, to women as well as men, the development of one's physical potential is as necessary to well-being as the development of the mind or spirit. It is time society banished the pejoratives "tomboy" and "sissy."

Women should be encouraged to be athletes—not to emulate men athletes—but so that women too may enjoy the benefits of health and the psychological satisfaction of competition as part of a full and a satisfying life.

## PHYSIOLOGICAL AND METABOLIC FACTORS

There are some physiological and metabolic differences between men and women: At every age the woman's metabolic rate is lower than the man's [33, 50]. Her heart is smaller, and thus the rate of her heartbeat is faster than a man's, both at rest and during exercise, with a slower return to normal during the recovery period following strenuous activity [51].

Women have lower systolic and diastolic blood pressures than men [33, 80] and their smaller thoracic cavity and lungs seem to make women's respiratory movements faster than men's [80]. The average woman has 25–30% less lung capacity than the average man, although physically trained men and women appear to utilize the anaerobic processes to the same extent [9]. The male has more red blood corpuscles and a greater supply of hemoglobin than the female [33, 50, 51, 80].

STRENGTH

The female has only about 78% as much muscular strength as the male [52]. Furthermore, she has less muscle in relation to her size than the male. Yet there does not seem to be any impairment in the workings of her muscles because of her sex [80]. These differences simply mean that women do not have as much total strength as men. But women's muscles function with the same efficiency, the difference being not in the ability to perform but in the proportion of muscle to body mass.

SPEED AND ENDURANCE

Klafs and Arnheim [43] believe that before puberty girls can equal—and in some cases surpass—the performances of boys in the same age group, in athletic feats that involve speed, strength, and endurance. Shaffer [71] contends that girls and boys respond about the same until approximately 14 years of age, and then the girls tend to drop off in both endurance and caliber of performance. Whether this decline in girls' performances after puberty is due to cultural restrictions and the role expected of the female or to morphological or physiological limitations is an unsolved question. A study by Jones [41] indicates that this drop in performance is not due to physical limitations, since, according to his findings, postmenarcheal girls have more strength than premenarcheal girls of the same age.

Jokl [39] believes that for most girls the peak of endurance comes at age 14, and that, to develop their potential to the utmost, girls should start training for endurance events *before puberty*. He feels that training during this period, when physiological development is at a maximum, would give better results, and that the effect of this conditioning would be to improve performances over a period of years.

Skubic and Hodgkins [73] feel that younger girls do better than older ones in situations that involve endurance. In their study, junior high school girls did significantly better on a cardiovascular test than high school or college women.

Shaffer [71] points out that since endurance, strength, and coordination seem to be related to maturation, the age of girls excelling in sports will become even lower because of the fact that girls are maturing at a younger and younger age.

Because of their physiological and metabolic makeup, girls seem better equipped to compete in activities that involve endurance than in ones that rely greatly on strength and power [33]. A fundamental principle of the physiology of exercise is that training produces similar physiological responses in men and in women [33], although there is a difference between them in the degree of potential which can be

developed through training [9]. The training program for women should not be no-
ticeably different from that for men except for the degree of intensity and the level of
achievement sought.

People over the years have been concerned that too much strain and stress might
be placed on the female during training and competition. I believe that the makeup of
the human body, especially the woman's, is more capable of adjusting to intense demands on it during conditioning and competitive situations than many realize. This
view was also taken by Dr. Allan J. Ryan when he was questioned about the matter
[66]; he replied that we shouldn't worry because he didn't feel we were even close to
the point of too-great strain yet.

PERFORMANCE AND AGE

As the athlete ages, some physiological changes may affect his or her ability to perform. After 30, maximum oxygen intake declines progressively as the athlete gets
older [9, 51, 56], making it more difficult to engage in strenuous activity for long
periods. There also appears to be an increase in lung ventilation while the athlete is
participating in submaximal work [56]. Strength and the ability to keep up performance demanding a high degree of coordination seems to decline with age [51, 56].
However, as pointed out by Brouha [9], the ability to perform well and to reach maximum performance is dependent more on the physical fitness of the athlete than on a
set chronological age.

This view is supported by Morehouse and Rasch [51], who believe that if training
is continued, there may be very little decline in physical fitness in later years. They
also point out that the ability to do light work stays at a high level beyond 60 years of
age, although an athlete past 30 can maintain a high level of athletic performance only
if he or she progressively increases the amount of training and conditioning. This
means that older athletes can successfully compete with younger ones provided they
are willing to spend more time and effort to achieve the same results.

An example of what conditioning can do is Dr. Thomas K. Cureton of the University of Illinois, who is in his middle sixties, and who often gives demonstrations
involving two hours of running, swimming, etc., that wear down younger participants
[87].

Men athletes taking part in the Olympics seem to turn in their best performances
when they are between 17 and 30 [42]; athletes engaging in events that demand speed
and agility are younger than those taking part in events that demand endurance [37,
42].

Of course, there are exceptions to these generalizations about age and performance. Some athletes with great motivation and self-discipline can maintain a high
caliber of performance in events that involve both strength and endurance well beyond
30. Others lose interest and drive before 30, and therefore do not reach their maximum potential. One of the young champion swimmers, Chris von Saltza, retired before the age of 20.

Christine Gortschel of France during International Ladies Races at Grindelwald, Switzerland, in January, 1963 (courtesy Ski Magazine).

## DEVELOPMENTAL AND EMOTIONAL FACTORS

Girls today mature at an earlier age than ever before. The average age for the onset of the menarche has dropped almost a year and a half over the past hundred years [79], while the average adolescent has gained approximately 1/2 inch in height and 3 pounds in weight per decade [71]. Better living conditions and improved nutrition and health are thought to be contributing factors, but perhaps increased protein in the diet and changes in endocrine functioning brought about by added psychological stress may also be causes of earlier maturation [79].

## MATURATION

The girl's pattern of growth is much faster than the boy's, with the girl's prepubertal growth starting 2 to 3 years before the boy's. The male has the greatest acceleration in his growth pattern in his fourteenth or fifteenth year and the girl in her twelfth [50], or before the menarche [71].

The onset of the menarche marks a change in the physical growth and development of the girl. Her strength improves, but her motor ability begins to taper off [25, 41, 71]. Espenschade [25] maintains that girls' development in motor performances changes little after puberty, although boys' continues to improve, but stresses the fact that adolescent sex differences have other causes besides capacity, such as training, previous experience, and motivational factors. Jones [41] found that the increase in strength brought about by growth acceleration starts approximately a year before the menarche in girls and reaches a peak about the time of the menarche, with all girls eventually attaining similar levels of strength at a late age, even though their growth patterns differed.

## MOTOR ABILITY

Motor ability in activities that require strength and power seems to be closely related to body size and build at all ages, while motor ability in activities that involve balance and coordination seems to have little relationship to a person's physique or body strength at a particular age, although the ability to perform them does improve with age [25].

A study by Phillips et al. [59], which used the Kraus-Weber test to determine the muscular fitness of elementary school children, showed that girls scored higher than boys at all age levels, partly because of the flexibility items. They also found that flexibility for both sexes decreased as age increased, and that the flexibility of girls decreased to a greater extent than that of boys; thus the older children were closer to the same flexibility level.

Hanson [86], in testing students in grades 1 through 6, found that boys scored higher than girls in motor performance except in two categories: rope-skipping and balance. Generally, girls and boys in one grade level were superior in performance to girls and boys in the grade below them.

Although boys continue to increase their performance scores in running, jumping, and throwing from childhood to the last year of high school, girls' improvement continues only until they are about 13; at the same time, even though girls generally exhibit no further improvement in motor ability, there is an increase in their physical size and strength beyond the age of 13. This lack of motor improvement may possibly be due to changes in the body build brought about by adolescence, but it is more likely due to a lack of interest and motivation on the part of the girl, due to cultural pressures [24, 25].

## SOCIAL AND CULTURAL INFLUENCES

It is possible that as cultural influences, psychological attitudes, and the expected roles of the male and the female become less constricting, we may discover that girls exhibit a greater variation in range of motor skills than one finds in a comparison between boys *and* girls.

Women can reach a higher degree of achievement in sports than thought previously, as shown by the accomplishments of the Russian women athletes. Some of the greatest gains in the Soviet Union's international competitive standing have resulted from the performance of its women athletes. Recently, because of the interest in the U.S. in our record in international competition, the United States has also improved its records in some areas. This interest has given women more motivation to engage in athletics and to strive for their maximum potential.

The main reason that American women have had scant interest in sports in the past is that cultural taboos have choked out any natural motivation they might have had to engage in competitive activities, and have forced them to assume the protective coloration society demands: marrying, raising a family, and being a good homemaker. Although for centuries men have been urged to show their courage, endurance, strength, skill, and aggressiveness in sports activities, girls who showed an interest in running and jumping, or in strenuous physical exercise, have been labeled tomboys. This area was thus off limits to any feminine girl. Over the years, the conflict between girls' natural capacity and desire for physical activity and the socially acceptable role for women was so great that many people believed that competitive activities endangered a woman's health and femininity.

In 1957, the Sixth National Conference on Physicians and Schools [64] made public a statement that the physical makeup of girls was such that they could take part in sports just as readily as boys, if it weren't for the social mores that had imposed limitations on girls.

Cassidy [13] observed that the girl has been deprived of the chance to reach her highest potential because of the belief that girls should be protected from the "evils and stresses in competitive athletics."

Jokl [38], in a survey of Olympic athletes, pointed out certain social implications that are beyond the limits of the sports world. He remarked that those countries which did not enter women in the Olympic games also had high child mortality and higher overall rates of morbidity and mortality. Countries such as the United States, Russia, and the British Commonwealth nations had a high participation and success ratio, which paralleled the social advancement and industrialization of these countries.

Several studies involving male athletes have indicated that high school athletes are better adjusted and exhibit more leadership ability than nonathletes [8, 12, 20, 68], while at least one study [28] indicates that high school girls who participate in athletics are personally and socially better adjusted than those who do not.

In a 1954 study of college extramural and varsity programs for women, White [82] found that in 61% of extramural programs and in 39% of varsity competitions, women experienced no undesirable results from the sports program. When the programs proved to be unsatisfactory, the problem most often mentioned was demand on faculty and/or student time.

A society's sociological, philosophical, and psychological concepts determine the direction of the sports programs for its women at a given time and place. Since these concepts have changed greatly in Western society in the past few years, it is likely that a truer concept of the male's and female's roles in the sports world may be evolving, although the evolution will continue for generations.

Once the social mores have been examined and scientific evidence replaces superstition and myth, sports and competition for girls may prove to be a powerful tool for educating them. It is not hard to identify the biological and psychological differences between men and women, but the sociological, philosophical, and psychological limitations imposed by society invoke more subtle reactions, and conceivably play a greater part in the public apathy toward women's sports than the biological differences between the sexes.

## ENVIRONMENTAL FACTORS

Any athlete's performance can be greatly affected by changes in the environment. Going from one climate to another or from one altitude to another forces the body to adjust to the different external stresses on it.

In order for the body to maintain a state of homeostasis, it must keep a balance between the heat being produced internally and the heat being lost externally. Metabolic processes, such as the working of muscles during exercise, cause an increase in internally produced heat. The body can also gain heat from contact with the environment, such as playing on a warm day or swimming in a pool that is overheated. The body can regulate this accumulation of heat in several ways; for the athlete, most of the heat is lost through the evaporation of perspiration during strenuous activity. Therefore humidity plays a role in the performance of the athlete, because when humidity is high, perspiration does not evaporate as quickly, and the body is not able to regulate its temperature as easily, as when the humidity is low.

### ADJUSTMENT TO CLIMATE

It is easier for an athlete to adjust from a hot climate to a cold than from a cold to a hot. In a cold climate, the heat dissipated from the working muscles is partly counterbalanced by the cool environment. At the same time, the athlete competing in a cold environment can regulate body temperature by increasing or decreasing the amount of clothes worn, while in a hot environment a certain minimum of clothing must be maintained. If an athlete wears too much clothing during competition under cold conditions, such as skiing, the body must get rid of excess heat just as it does in a warm climate.

The real problem arises when an athlete must compete in hot weather. When the external temperature is above 80°, the body undergoes certain physiological changes in order to cope with the added stress caused by heat. The body metabolism rises, there is a water loss through perspiration (some marathon runners lose as much as 4 to 5 liters of water through sweating), there is a salt loss, the pulse rate becomes higher, and the heart's output of blood per beat is lower [42]. There is an increased load placed on the cardiovascular system, as it must keep the blood supply going to three different areas simultaneously: (1) surface blood vessels, which are dilated to aid in cooling the body, (2) muscles that are being used during the exercise, and (3) the brain [10]. The athlete has problems during competition when, either because of a lack of conditioning or a lack of acclimatization, her heart is unable to supply these three areas adequately.

When the body is unable to cope with the heat load placed upon it, the athlete may suffer from cramps, exhaustion, or even have a heat stroke. Ordinarily, an athlete suffering from heat cramps can help the body in its effort to maintain a balance between heat production and heat loss by replenishing the fluids and salt that have been lost through competition and by resting and cooling off when the heat load is too great. If the athlete continues to play, exhaustion may follow; the athlete may suffer dizziness and, in extreme cases, unconsciousness. Fainting is the body's way of preventing extensive harm to itself, since the body becomes inert and has a chance to regain a homeostatic condition. However, if an athlete is highly motivated and has an intense drive to compete, the preliminary signs of cramps, dizziness, and even momentary fainting spells may be ignored, and a heat stroke may result which can be fatal.

Women seemingly cannot handle heat stress as well as men [21, 27, 32] because physiologically it takes more effort for them to maintain a heat balance in a hot environment [32]. However, since heat acclimatization helps keep the body temperature lower, allows the heart to work more efficiently, and keeps the blood pressure more stabilized [10], women as well as men can benefit from acclimatization to heat.

Buskirk and Bass [10] believe that acclimatization to heat can be accomplished by working out in a heated room 2–4 hours every day for a period of 7–10 days before a competitive event in a hot climate. They state that once this acclimatization to heat is reached, the body is able to maintain this state of acclimatization for one to two weeks, even though there is no further exposure to heat.

The coach and the athlete should remember that if conditioning has been done in a cool environment, the athlete is not conditioned for competition in a hot environment, since the body is under more stress to balance the heat load.

If the athlete will take adequate fluids and salt before and during competition, wear light clothes that allow maximum evaporation of perspiration, work out under similar heat conditions 7–10 days before the meet or game, and pace herself to allow cooling periods when possible, she should be able to perform well even in unaccustomed heat. The coach can help the athlete by scheduling events early in the morning or in the evenings to avoid the worst part of the heat during the day.

ADJUSTMENT TO ALTITUDE

Another environmental problem is performance at high altitudes. Although much more research needs to be done in this area, it now seems that while athletes in events such as sprints (which can be done anaerobically) and other events that require effort of less than a minute are not affected by altitude, athletes performing distance runs and events that demand endurance or effort for more than a minute *are* affected [6, 15].

Changing from a lower to a higher altitude presents problems to the athlete because of the decrease in total barometric pressure as one goes to higher altitudes. As a result of the lower pressure, there is not as much oxygen in the blood, and consequently, the working muscles and other active tissues do not get an adequate supply of oxygen. This makes it impossible for the athlete to carry on intensive effort over a long period of time. Short periods of effort can be accomplished anaerobically, so that performance at the time does not suffer from the low oxygen content in the blood, but the recovery period takes longer. During recovery, the oxygen debt is not repaid at the same rate as it is at lower altitudes, and the lower barometric pressure thus results in a slower recovery period. When work is done over a long period of time aerobically, an oxygen debt builds up, even at sea level. This results in a less efficient performance because of the inadequate oxygen supply.

An athlete's body *can* become acclimatized to altitude [6, 7, 15, 42], resulting in more oxygen being carried in the blood and greater efficiency of the lungs and cardiovascular system, which leads to a greater working capacity and therefore a better performance.

The best results come when physical training is combined with acclimatization [6, 42]. Although there is a difference in opinion as to exactly how long it takes an athlete to become acclimatized, it has been shown that changes in the blood which can limit endurance are brought about shortly after the athlete goes to a higher altitude [6]. Thus if an athlete (or team) doesn't have time to become acclimatized before competing at a higher altitude, the trip should be so planned that the athlete can compete as soon as possible after arrival.

Balke [6] advocates a minimum of one week for acclimatizing purposes for an increase of 3000 feet in altitude, while Cervantes and Karpovich [15] believe that an altitude such as Mexico City should require 9–13 days of acclimatization for sprinting events and approximately 3 weeks for endurance events, such as swimming 400 meters.

Although all the facts and research concerning the 1968 Olympics in Mexico City have not been published at the time this is written, some things do seem to be evident. Competition at high altitude does have its dangers, as shown by the high number of athletes who collapsed during and after exertion. One of the most frightening cases of exhaustion was that of Ron Clarke of Australia, who collapsed at the end of the 10,000-meter race and had to be given oxygen for 10 minutes before he regained consciousness [89].

A second fact that seemed to be brought out by the 1968 Olympics is that, if a competition is to be held at some place that has a high altitude, anyone who lives at high altitude the year round has a definite advantage over a person from a sea-level environment, even though the sea-level athlete may train at high altitude for months before he competes. The Kenyan runners, who came from an altitude comparable to that of Mexico City, surprised the sports world with their domination of the distance events [90, 91].

Roger Bannister feels strongly that a sea-level athlete can never become completely acclimatized for competition at high altitude, and feels that it is unfair to the majority of athletes to hold the Olympics or similar competitions at high altitude, such as Mexico City [92].

Sheeler-Winton Invitational Swim Meet (courtesy Dick Lowy, Hialeah, Florida).

ADJUSTMENT TO WATER

Another environmental problem arises in swimming. Swimming presents a different adjustment to heat regulation, since the athlete cannot lose heat as easily through perspiration evaporation. The problem is intensified because water temperature varies greatly from pool to pool. When the water is too warm during endurance events, the inability of the body to balance heat production and heat loss can affect performance just as in any other environment in which overheating occurs. If the water is too cold, the body has to expend energy to maintain normal body heat, thus depleting the energy that could be used for optimum performance. Standarized pool temperatures, based on research dealing with the best temperature for optimum performance in speed and endurance events, would certainly help swimmers' performances.

Swimming poses another problem for the girl who is menstruating and who does not ordinarily use tampons. Certainly, as far as comfort and hygiene are concerned, internal protection during swimming is best. According to Anderson [3], most girls can use tampons without difficulty and without impairment to their virginity. Therefore swimming during the menstrual period should not hamper the girl.

SUMMARY

1. Most physiological research indicates that sports competition for women is not detrimental to their health, normal function, or well-being. When a sane conditioning program precedes a sane competitive program, the normal woman may participate in vigorous athletic competition. The average woman can be happier and healthier as a result of sports activities.

2. There are differences between men and women morphologically, physiologically, metabolically, and psychologically. However, these differences are not as great as they were once thought to be. It is possible that there are greater differences between the performances of different girls than there are between the performances of girls and boys.

3. There have been, and still are, cultural and social influences that greatly handicap the performance of the woman athlete. The strength of these influences changes with the times, but we seem to be emerging into an era in which women's participation in athletic events does not carry as much negative connotation as in the past, although women still are not now—and may never be—encouraged to the extent that men are.

4. Because of the biological differences between the male and the female, most women are incapable of equalling the performances of most men in strength, power, and endurance events. Therefore women's achievements in sports should not be compared with men's, although there are some activities in which women can hold their own against men. Competition should not pit men against women, and when coed competition involves pitting a man and a woman against another team consisting of a man and a woman, care should be taken to equalize the teams.

5. Educators should be careful that they do not set up inflexible programs on the basis of the "average." As a result of regional, educational, social, philosophical, psychological, and cultural influences, as well as biological differences, the difference between the performances of one woman and another can be tremendous. Coaching the woman athlete should thus be done on an individual basis, taking into consideration the ability and potential of each person. At the same time, coaches should be selected on the basis of their qualifications, not on the basis of their sex.

6. Physiologically, women react to training in the same way that men do. The differences are basically those of capacity, with the woman having a lower level of performance. Training programs for men and women, therefore, may differ in degree and intensity, but not necessarily in technique.

7. Participation in sports does not have a harmful effect on the normal function of the reproductive system. Although opinion is not unanimous, the medical profession generally maintains that women can take part in physical activity during menstruation without harm. Some authorities feel that a woman who is menstruating should avoid events in which maximum effort is demanded of her, and avoid swimming, for which training involves long exposure to water. Others feel that there need be no restriction placed on the woman during menstruation. So long as the woman does not experience any abnormal change in her cycle, however, she should feel free to train and to compete during menstruation. There is no evidence that participation in stressful competition has a detrimental effect on the normal processes of pregnancy and childbirth; on the contrary, there is evidence that they are aided by participation in sports.

8. The belief that participation in sports tends to masculinize women is a myth. A person's body size and structure is regulated by the endocrine glands, and although muscles may increase in size because of a program that requires much high-resistance exercise, women seldom engage in this type of training program. Some people mentally associate all women athletes with the image of the huge Russian shot putter or discus thrower. However, the Russian woman is a product of her heredity and genetic background rather than the sport. The large body frame and potential for power were there long before she started training for the event; otherwise she would never have chosen an activity demanding strength. Or, even if she had, she would never have attained Olympic caliber without this large body build. For every Tamara Press, there are hundreds with the grace and beauty (though not necessarily the skill) of Wilma Rudolph, Maria Bueno, and Penny Pitou.

9. We still don't know everything there is to know about women and competition, or for that matter about men and competition. The area of sociological and psychological factors is a relatively unexplored one, in which we definitely need more research.

**BIBLIOGRAPHY**

1. AAU, *Study of the Effect of Athletic Competition on Girls and Women.* New York: AAU, n.d.

2. AMA, "Sports Opportunities for Girls and Women," *Journal of Health, Physical Education, and Recreation,* **35**, 46, November–December, 1964

3. Anderson, Theresa W., "Swimming and Exercise During Menstruation," *Journal of Health, Physical Education, and Recreation,* **36**, 66–68, October 1965

4. Astrand, I., "Aerobic Work Capacity in Men and Women, with Special Reference to Age," *Acta Phisiologica Scandinavica* **49**, Supplement 169, 1960

5. Astrand, P. O., *et. al.,* "Girl Swimmers, with Special Reference to Respiratory and Circulatory Adaptation and Gynaecological and Psychiatric Aspects," *Acta Paediatrica Supplement,* 147, 1963

6. Balke, Bruno, "Work Capacity and Altitude," in *Science and Medicine of Exercise and Sports,* edited by Warren R. Johnson. New York: Harper, 1960, Chapter 18

7. Balke, B., and J. G. Wells, "Ceiling Altitude Tolerance Following Physical Training and Acclimatization," *Journal of Aviation Medicine,* **29**, 40, 1958

8. Biddulph, Lowell G., "Athletic Achievement and the Personal and Social Adjustment of High School Boys," *Research Quarterly,* **25**, 1–7, 1954

9. Brouha, L., "Physiology of Training, Including Age and Sex Differences," *Journal of Sports Medicine and Physical Fitness,* **2**, 3–11, March 1962

10. Buskirk, Elsworth R., and David E. Bass, "Climate and Exercise," in *Science and Medicine of Exercise and Sports*, edited by Warren R. Johnson. New York: Harper, 1960, Chapter 17

11. Carpenter, Aileen, "Strength, Power, and 'Femininity' as Factors Influencing the Athletic Performance of College Women," *Research Quarterly*, **9**, 120-125, May 1938

12. Carter, Gerald C., and J. R. Shannon, "Adjustment and Personality Traits of Athletes and Non-Athletes," *School Review*, **46**, 127-130, February 1940

13. Cassidy, Rosalind, "Critical Issues in Physical Education and Athletics," *Journal of Health, Physical Education, and Recreation*, **35**, 16-17, June 1964

14. Cearley, Jess, "Linearity of Contributions of Ages, Heights, and Weights to Prediction of Track and Field Performances," *Research Quarterly*, **28**, 218, October 1957

15. Cervantes, Jose, and Peter V. Karpovich, "Effect of Altitude on Athletic Performance," *Research Quarterly*, **35**, 446-448, October 1964

16. Charles, A. H., "Women in Sport," in *Injury in Sport*, edited by J. R. Armstrong and W. E. Tucker. London: Staples Press, 1964

17. Coffey, Margaret A., "The Sportswoman—Then and Now," *Journal of Health, Physical Education, and Recreation*, **36**, 38, February 1965

18. Connolly, Olga, "Let Them Participate," *DGWS Track and Field Guide, 1964-1966*, Washington, D.C.: AAHPER, 1964

19. Cress, Carolyn L., and Margaret A. Thorsen, "Morphological Bisexuality as a Factor in the Motor Performance of College Women," *Research Quarterly*, **35**, 408-417, October 1964

20. Derian, Albert Steven, "Some Personality Characteristics of Athletes Studied by the Projective Method," unpublished master's thesis, University of California, Berkeley, 1947

21. de Vries, H. A., *Physiology of Exercise for Physical Education and Athletics*. Dubuque, Iowa: Wm. C. Brown Company, 1966. Chapter 26, "The Female in Athletics."

22. Edwards, H. T., "Lactic Acid in Rest and Work at High Altitude," *American Journal of Physiology*, **116**, 367, 1936

23. Erdelyi, G. J., "Gynecological Survey of Female Athletes," *Journal of Sports Medicine and Physical Fitness*, **2**, 174-179, September 1962. (Also called "Women in Athletics" and distributed at the First National Institute for Girls' and Women's Sports, Norman, Oklahoma, November 1963.)

24. Espenschade, Anna, "Development of Motor Coordination in Boys and Girls," *Research Quarterly*, **18**, 30-44, March 1947

25. Espenschade, Anna, "Motor Development," in *Science and Medicine of Exercise and Sports*, edited by Warren R. Johnson. New York: Harper, 1960, Chapter 22

26. *Exercise and Fitness*, special report of the Joint Committee of the American Medical Association and the American Association for Health, Physical Education, and Recreation. *Journal of Health, Physical Education, and Recreation,* May 1964

27. Folk, G. E., *Introduction to Environmental Physiology.* Philadelphia: Lea and Febiger, 1966

28. Hale, Creighton J., "Athletics for Pre-High School Age Children," *Journal of Health, Physical Education, and Recreation,* **30**, 19, December 1959

29. Hamer, M. C., "Dysmenorrhea and Its Relation to Abdominal Strength," *Research Quarterly,* **4**, 229-237, March 1933

30. Harris, Ruth, and C. Etta Walters, "Effect of Prescribed Abdominal Exercises on Dysmenorrhea in College Women," *Research Quarterly,* **26**, 140-146, May 1955

31. Henry, F. M., and W. E. Berg, "Physical and Performance Changes in Athletic Conditioning," *Journal of Applied Physiology,* **3**, 103, 1950

32. Hertig, B. A., *et al.,* "Artificial Acclimatization of Women to Heat," *Journal of Applied Physiology,* **18**, 383-386, March 1963

33. Heusner, William W., "Basic Physiological Concepts as They Relate to Girls' Sports," Proceedings of Second National Institute on Girls' and Women's Sports, Michigan State University, September 26-October 1, 1965. (Published by AAHPER, 1201 Sixteenth St., N.W., Washington, D.C.)

34. Houston, C. S., and R. L. Riley, "Changes During Acclimatization to High Altitude," *American Journal of Physiology,* **149**, 565, 1947

35. Johnson, P. B., *et al., Physical Education: A Problem-Solving Approach to Health and Physical Fitness.* New York: Holt, Rinehart, and Winston, 1966

36. Jokl, Ernst, *Nutrition, Exercise, and Body Composition.* Springfield, Ill.: Charles C. Thomas, 1964

37. Jokl, Ernst, *et al., Sports in the Cultural Pattern of the World*, A Study of the Olympic Games of 1952. Helsinki, Finland: Institute of Occupational Health, 1956

38. Jokl, Ernst, "The Athletic Status of Women," *Amateur Athlete,* **33**, 14, May 1962

39. Jokl, Ernst, "The Athletic Success of Young Girls," *Amateur Athlete,* **34**, 20-21, January 1963

40. Jokl, Ernst, "Youth and Swimming Records," *Amateur Athlete,* **34**, 24-25, October 1963

41. Jones, Harold E., "The Sexual Maturity of Girls as Related to Growth in Strength," *Research Quarterly,* **18**, 135-143, May 1947

42. Karpovich, P. V., *Physiology of Muscular Activity*, sixth edition. Philadelphia: W. B. Saunders, 1965

43. Klafs, Carl E., and Daniel Arnheim, *Modern Principles of Athletic Training.* St. Louis: C. V. Mosby, 1963

44. Koenig, Fran Becker, "Conditioning and Competition Related to Postpubescent Women," unpublished paper, Michigan State University, 1965

45. Ladell, W. S. S., "The Effects of Water and Salt Intake Upon the Performance of Men Working in Hot and Humid Environments," *Journal of Physiology,* **127**, 11–46, 1955

46. McCurdy, J. H., and Leonard A. Larson, *The Physiology of Exercise.* Philadelphia: Lea and Febiger, 1939

*10* 47. "Menstruation and Sport," *British Medical Journal*, December 21, 1963, 1548

48. Metheny, E. L., *et al.*, "Some Physiologic Responses of Women and Men to Moderate and Strenuous Exercise," *American Journal of Physiology,* **137**, 318, 1942

49. Meyer, Margaret H., and Germaine Pella, "The Effect of Hard Laboratory Exercise on the Total and Differential Leucocyte Count of Young Women," *Research Quarterly,* **18**, 271, December 1947

50. Moore, Roy B., "An Analytical Study of Sex Differences as They Affect the Program of Physical Education," *Research Quarterly,* **12**, 587–608, October 1941

51. Morehouse, Laurence E., and Philip J. Rasch, *Sports Medicine for Trainers.* Philadelphia: W. B. Saunders, 1963

52. Morris, Carrie Belle, "Measurement of the Strength of Muscle Relative to the Cross Section," *Research Quarterly,* **19**, 295–303, December 1948

53. Morton, Henry W., *Soviet Sport.* New York: Collier Books, 1963

54. Neal, Patsy, "Personality Traits of 1959 Pan-American Athletes as Measured by the Edwards Personal Preference Schedule," unpublished master's thesis, University of Utah, 1963

55. Neilson, N. P., and F. W. Cozens, *Achievement Scale in Physical Education Activities.* Sacramento: California State Department of Education, 1934

56. Norris, Arthur, and Nathan W. Shock, "Exercise in the Adult Years, With Special Reference to the Advanced Years," in *Science and Medicine of Exercise and Sports,* edited by Warren R. Johnson. New York: Harper, 1960, Chapter 24

57. Patterson, Jane K., "The Effects of Competitive Swimming Training on Girls in Relation to Selected Anthropometric and Strength Measurements," *Swimming Techniques,* **2**, 14, April 1965

58. Perbix, Joyce, "Relationship Between Somatotype and Motor Fitness in Women," *Research Quarterly,* **25**, 84–90, March 1954

59. Phillips, Marjorie, *et al.*, "Analysis of Results from Kraus-Weber Test of Minimum Muscular Fitness in Children," *Research Quarterly,* **26**, 314–323, October 1955

60. Phillips, Marjorie, Katherine Fox, and Olive Young, "Sports Activity for Girls," *Journal of Health, Physical Education, and Recreation,* **30**, 23, December 1959

61. Pierson, William P., "Body Size and Speed," *Research Quarterly,* **32**, 197–200, May 1961

62. Pierson, William R., and Aileen Lockhart, "Effect of Menstruation on Simple Reaction and Movement Time," *British Medical Journal*, 796–797, March 23, 1963

63. Pros, J. R., "Current Literature; Some Errors in Engaging Women in the Physical Education," *Journal of Sports Medicine and Physical Fitness*, 4, 192, September 1964

64. *Report of the Sixth National Conference on Physicians and Schools.* Bureau of Health Education, Chicago: American Medical Association, 1957

65. Research Committee, DGWS, "Recommendations from Women Doctors and Gynecologists About Sports Activities for Girls," *Journal of Health, Physical Education, and Recreation*, 30, 23, December 1959

66. Ryan, Allan J., "Consultants Answer Questions," *Values in Sports*. Washington, D.C.: AAHPER, 1962

67. Ryde, D., "Effect of Athletic Competition on Girls and Women," *Practitioner*, 177, 73, 1956

68. Schendel, Jack, "Psychological Differences Between Athletes and Non-Participants in Athletics at Three Educational Levels," *Research Quarterly*, 36, 52–67, March 1965

69. Scott, Gladys, and W. W. Tuttle, "The Periodic Fluctuation in Physical Efficiency During the Menstrual Cycle," *Research Quarterly*, 3, 137, March 1932

70. Shaffer, Thomas E., "Misconceptions in Athletics and Physical Education," *Journal of School Health*, 33, 349, October 1963

71. Shaffer, Thomas E., "Principles of Growth and Development as Related to Girls Participating in Track and Field Gymnastics," Proceedings of First National Institute on Girls' and Women's Sports, Norman, Oklahoma, November 1963. (Published by AAHPER, 1201 Sixteenth St., N.W., Washington, D.C.)

72. Skubic, Vera, and Jean Hodgkins, "Cardiovascular Efficiency Test for Girls and Women," *Research Quarterly*, 34, 191–198, May 1963

73. Skubic, Vera, and Jean Hodgkins, "Cardiovascular Efficiency Test Scores for Junior and Senior High School Girls in the United States," *Research Quarterly*, 35, 184–192, May 1964

74. Smith, Lafayette, "The Girls in the Olympics," *Today's Health*, 42, 28, October 1964

75. Steinhaus, Arthur, "Exercise and the Female Reproductive Organs," *Toward an Understanding of Health and Physical Education*. Dubuque, Iowa: Wm. C. Brown, 1963

76. Steinhaus, Arthur H., "What Are We Doing to Our Girls?" (letter to the editor), *Journal of Health, Physical Education, and Recreation*, 35, 6, November–December, 1964

77. Tuttle, W. Gerald, "Women *Are* Different from Men," *Science Digest*, 14, 69–72, September 1943

78. Tuttle, W. W., and H. Frey, "A Study of the Physical Efficiency of College Women as Shown by the Pulse-Ratio Test," *Research Quarterly,* **1**, 17–25, December 1930

79. Ulrich, Celeste, "The Tomorrow Mind," *Journal of Health, Physical Education, and Recreation,* **35**, 17, October 1964

80. Ulrich, Celeste, "Women and Sport," *Science and Medicine of Exercise and Sports,* edited by Warren R. Johnson. New York: Harper, 1960, Chapter 26

81. Watson, Katharine G., "A Study of the Relation of Certain Measurements of College Women to Throwing Ability," *Research Quarterly,* **8**, 131, October 1937

82. White, Christine, "Extramural Competition and Physical Education Activities for College Women," *Research Quarterly,* **25**, 344–363, October 1954

83. Williams, Jesse F., *The Principles of Physical Education.* Philadelphia: Wm. B. Saunders, 1932

84. Wolffe, J. B., "Heart of the Athlete," *Journal of Sports Medicine and Physical Fitness,* **2**, 20–22, March 1962

85. Youngen, Lois, "A Comparison of Reaction and Movement Times of Women Athletes and Non-Athletes," *Research Quarterly,* **30**, 349, October 1959

86. Hanson, Margie, "Motor Performance Testing of Elementary School Age Children," Ph.D. dissertation at University of Washington, Seattle, 1965

87. *The Healthy Life,* a Time-Life special report. New York: Time Incorporated, 1966

88. Underwood, John, "Games in Trouble," *Sports Illustrated,* **29**, 45, September 30, 1968

89. Bannister, Roger, "A Debt Was Paid Off in Tears," *Sports Illustrated,* **29**, 22, November 11, 1968

90. "The Olympics' Extra Heat," *Newsweek,* October 28, 1968, pages 74–80

91. Underwood, John, "A High Time for Sprinters—and Kenyans," *Sports Illustrated,* **29**, 19, October 28, 1968

92. Bannister, Roger, "A Debt Was Paid off in Tears," *Sports Illustrated,* **29**, 22, November 11, 1968

# chapter three organizing and selecting the team

One of the most important duties of a coach is to choose the personnel he or she is to work with. Selection of players is no easy job. Some people, when they report to practice early in the season, are out of condition. Because of fatigue and lack of timing, they don't look good in the first sessions. Others look great early, but improve only slightly as the season wears on. Still others are intent on personal goals and do not work well toward team objectives. Thus a determining factor in any season's record is the coach's ability to choose players wisely and mould them into a working unit. If there are personality problems—either between the coach and certain players or between team members—they should be resolved at the beginning of the season. If these problems persist, they can multiply and destroy what would otherwise be a good team.

Unless the coach knows the players well, psychological factors may show up only late in the season. A coach has to seek just the right tone of voice or the right words to bring out the best in some people. Some players can't perform in a relaxed and confident way until a certain amount of rapport has been established between themselves and the coach

In selecting players, the coach must look to the future as well as the present, remembering to work not only for the season at hand but for the following season as well, and must bear in mind the following factors: (1) organization of the team, (2) practice sessions, (3) determining players' potentials, and (4) cutting the squad.

## ORGANIZATION OF THE TEAM

The coach who wants the best opportunity to select players must organize workouts so that all interested persons will know what is expected. Publicity should include the details of practice time, place, who is eligible to try out for the team, etc. For the best results, one should utilize all the usual media: boards, assemblies, school papers, and posters. The first notice should be given several weeks in advance, followed up by other publicity, right up to the day of beginning workouts.

The first meeting should give the girls a chance to become familiar with each other and with the coach. It is important that each girl know right from the start what the coach will expect of the team during the season. Things that should be stressed are:

1. Importance of attending practice
2. Training rules
3. Conduct and attitude
4. Teamwork, individual and team pride, and individual effort
5. Eligibility requirements: grade point average must be maintained, players must carry so many hours, etc.
6. Tentative season schedule

One should allow time for questions and answers about anything that is not clear to the participants.

### PRACTICE SESSIONS

A definite time should be set up for practice each day. Since time and facilities are usually limited, each team member should be ready for practice on time. Any tardies or absences should be cleared through the coach.

Although there is disagreement as to the effects of warm-ups, most coaches feel that they are worth while, and include them both in practice sessions and before games. Drills and exercises should be chosen to develop the timing, coordination, endurance, and strength needed for the specific sport being engaged in. One should aim at a *gradual* increase of endurance and strength, so that the peak of development is reached at the end of the season.

The players' mental attitude in these first practice sessions can set the pace for the rest of the year. If the coach is enthusiastic, has a positive attitude, and instills confidence and desire in the players from the start, there will be no problem of having to "get the team up" for each game or meet. Unless players are overworked or become stale during the season, the morale established at the beginning will rise with each new accomplishment.

Although the coach must be aware of each player and her abilities, and must be approachable by each player, at the same time she must be in control; what she says must go. A team has to be committed to the authority of the coach. However, this dedication must be earned. The coach who is prepared each day, who is professionally qualified, and who has had experience in the coaching field (or at least understands skills and strategy) is one who has earned the right to speak with authority and who can guide her team well. This doesn't mean that the coach should not listen to suggestions from the players. Open discussion should be invited, but the final decision is the coach's responsibility.

Practice sessions should be used wisely. During rest periods, the coach or a skilled player should give oral instructions and demonstrations. Chalk-board talks and walk-through drills often clarify questions and eliminate confusion later, when players have to execute a maneuver at full speed. If players must sit on the bench during scrimmage or games, they should always be taking part in the action mentally, preparing themselves for the moment when they will go in as substitutes.

Loafing should not be permitted. A player who "goofs off" in practice also tends to slack off in actual competition, or else will not be able to play the entire game at full speed. If a player becomes too tired to continue hustling during practice sessions, she should be encouraged to ask for a substitute rather than loafing through the rest of the practice.

Where applicable, isometric exercises, weights, and other devices should be used to increase the strength of the players. For sports that require endurance, practice should include running, jumping rope, and drills to increase the efficiency of the cardiovascular system.

Fine skills that demand precision, timing, and quick reflexes should be practiced at the beginning rather than at the end of the workout because of the fatigue factor, although in most cases these skills also need to be used when fatigue has set in. If a player attains perfection in these skills when she is fresh and rested, she will be able to execute them better when she is tired.

The amount of time allotted to workouts should depend on the skill level and the age of the group being coached.

Most skills should be practiced under actual competitive situations. To a hockey player trying to perfect her dribble in a congested area, practice against one or two opponents is much more effective than dribbling for hours by herself. Practice makes perfect only if skills are performed correctly and under the right circumstances.

Drills and practice techniques should be varied in order to prevent monotony and eventual staleness. Preseason practice sessions should provide motivation that will keep players on their toes until the actual competition begins. When staleness does set in, a few days of rest or a change in scenery is often enough to snap a team back into top form. For instance, if a track team becomes tired from running laps around the stadium, the coach can renew motivation by holding practice sessions on a beach or in another area.

Preseason workouts should allow all participants an equal chance to show what they are capable of doing, as well as giving the coach an idea of each girl's potential. After the coach has cut the squad, she should use practice sessions to perfect systems of play, improve individual and team skills, and develop mental and physical fitness.

## DETERMINING PLAYERS' POTENTIALS

It is always hard to gauge a person's potential accurately. Some girls are late starters; others look great at the beginning but fail to improve later on.

When deciding whether a girl has the skills or the potential to make the team, the coach must consider several aspects of the girl.

1. Mental attitude
2. Dedication and willingness to sacrifice

3. Physical development

4. Health

5. Capability for teamwork

6. Love of the game

7. Skill

In most cases, mental attitude makes or breaks the athlete. Many who start out without much skill become champions purely because of desire and positive attitudes. Others must overcome tremendous physical handicaps: Ben Hogan and Glenn Cunningham are just two who have proved the power of having "heart," or the desire to compete.

A person who will not quit, even against big odds, and who will scramble and scrap down to the wire is often preferable to a person with more skill but less desire to compete. The girl whose attitude is "I can" has the potential of being a better player than the girl whose attitude is "I will if I feel like it."

A person's dedication and willingness to sacrifice in order to perfect her skills is usually what makes the difference between a good athlete and a great one. Training for a sport is hard, time-consuming work, and the great athlete must be willing to forgo many pleasures in order to excel. The girl who prefers late parties, smoking, and drinking to achieving her top potential as an athlete will never reach this goal. The self-discipline necessary for constant conditioning is impossible to anyone who is not dedicated to the game; if she is, then the goal outweighs the work.

In junior high and high school, the physical development of the girl must be taken into consideration. Because the growth of each individual varies, some junior high school girls may already have reached the peak of their growth spurt, while others may not even have started. A girl who is gaining rapidly in height and weight needs time to learn to control her new size. Many girls who are experiencing a spurt in growth may appear awkward, uncoordinated, and unskilled, but these same girls may turn out to be the best athletes after their growth has leveled off and they have learned to control their bodies.

The overall health of a girl is of course a vital factor. Many great players and teams have been weakened by re-occurring injuries or illnesses. And any girl who is a hypochondriac naturally has a demoralizing effect on the team. Therefore all girls should have medical exams before the training period, and the coach should keep an eye on their health as the season advances.

In team sports, the importance of teamwork is immeasurable. A girl who is a "ball hog," or who risks making the big play herself rather than giving the opportunity to someone who has a better chance will hinder a team. The best shooters and spikers are not always the best players; for every shooter and spiker, there must be someone who can get the ball *to* them. A team composed of girls who work together well, and who are intent on winning and looking good as a team, is much more effective than a team composed of girls working as separate units and striving for outstanding individual performances rather than an outstanding team **performance.**

Love of the game involves many things: the thrill of being able to control the body and mind while competing in tense situations; the joy of running, of jumping and throwing, of using strength and coordination; the satisfaction of knowing oneself in many different situations and moods. To take part in a sport after one has stopped loving it is no longer rewarding. Love, dedication, and sacrifice must be a significant part of competition.

Skill, though often overemphasized, is nevertheless necessary. Regardless of how much a player wants to excel, unless she has perfected the fundamentals of her sport, she can't go beyond a specific point in her development. The champion has usually perfected both her skill and her mental attitude; and one without the other is a handicap. The coach should encourage both aspects of her athletes.

## CUTTING THE SQUAD

Once a coach has had a chance to see what each girl can do, and has tried to assess the potential of each, she must cut the squad. This can be one of the hardest jobs she encounters, because often her judgments about a person's potential will turn out to be wrong. Even so, the coach must have enough faith in herself to act in accord with her judgments until they are proved wrong.

The squad should be cut down to a number that can be worked with easily. In most cases, this means two complete teams plus a couple of substitutes to ensure that enough players will be available for game situations. When travel is necessary, the coach may have to cut the squad down even further. The traveling squad should be subject to change, dependent on the improvement of individual players as the season progresses.

In cutting the squad, the coach must evaluate not only individual performances, but team performance as well. Play combinations should complement each other, and girls selected for the squad should fit the play of others on the team. The effectiveness of having several good players on a squad is decreased if they are like so many mismatched parts of a whole.

Telling a girl that she has not made the team requires tact and sympathy. A coach must decide whether to make the announcement in front of all the girls, or to take each girl aside individually. Sometimes a written announcement posted on the bulletin board is the easiest for the coach (but not always for the girl who has been cut from the team).

It should be stressed that any girl who is cut from the team for one particular season should be encouraged to try again next year. The coach should also try to tell each girl what skills she needs to work on in order to improve her chances of making the squad next time. In this way the coach, even while cutting the team, helps the potential athlete rather than dampening her love for the sport.

# chapter four training, conditioning, and reduction of injuries

Training and conditioning are the only ways to build up the stamina, endurance, strength, speed, and flexibility that the body of the athlete requires. Training demands not only the sweat and pain of physical exertion, but the mental trait of self-discipline. For most athletes, exercise is performed under a controlled program in which the discipline is imposed by the coach; but the finer points of conditioning, such as getting enough sleep, eating the right foods, and abstaining from drugs, smoking, and drinking rest with the individual's self-discipline and motivation.

First, before any type of training program, each girl must have a thorough medical examination and must be pronounced fit for strenuous activity. Second, every coach should understand the principles of athletic training and conditioning and their results, and be familiar with up-to-date methods. Especially should the coach realize the importance of gradual conditioning over a period of time rather than a crash program of a few days or weeks.

## PRINCIPLES OF TRAINING AND CONDITIONING

Training produces physiological changes in the athlete which enable her to perform more efficiently. Brouha [5, 6] and Morehouse and Rasch [34] have pointed out these changes:

1. An athlete's muscles become larger, stronger, and more efficient than the non-athlete's.
2. The athlete's **heart beats** more slowly, and there is a greater volume of blood circulated with each stroke.
3. There is a retarded progressive fall of systolic blood pressure.
4. The athlete needs less oxygen for moderate loads of work, but consumes a greater amount of oxygen during exhaustive work.
5. The athlete has lower pulse rate and blood pressure during submaximal exercise.
6. The exchange of oxygen and carbon dioxide between lungs and the blood is more efficient in the athlete.

7. Pulse rate and respiration of an athlete return to normal more quickly after exertion.

8. There is less lactic acid formed in the muscles of an athlete for a given amount of exercise, which enables athletes to perform more work both aerobically and anaerobically and to perform longer before exhaustion.

9. The dissipation of body heat during submaximal work is more efficient in an athlete.

10. For an athlete, there is less pulmonary ventilation for a given load, resulting in slower breathing rate and deeper breathing.

All these physical advantages enable the athlete to exert less effort than the nonathlete to produce the same amount of force; the athlete also displays better neuromuscular coordination and has more efficient cardiovascular function and increased pulmonary ventilation. As a result, the athlete's body uses energy and handles waste materials more efficiently than the nonathlete's. Her muscles have more oxygen and her blood circulates better (this aids in heat control). The coach's duty is to so train the athlete that these plysical changes do take place.

The fundamental aspects of training and conditioning which the coach must bear in mind are: (1) demand, (2) sequence, (3) regularity, (4) maintenance, (5) specificity, (6) retrogression, (7) staleness, (8) rest and sleep, and (9) individual differences.

## DEMAND

A person in good physical condition adapts to the demands placed on his or her body either adequately or poorly, depending on the training stimulus. The more the athlete does, the more she will be capable of doing, and vice versa, although some factors such as heredity, previous training, nutrition, and so forth do set a limit to her ability to perform. Once she reaches this limit, there will be no improvement in her performance *regardless* of how much training she undertakes. Someone who is in excellent condition may maintain her level of fitness with less effort than it took her to attain it. However, if training stops, she drops back to a lower level of ability.

After a few weeks of training, the athlete reaches a plateau where there is no longer an improvement in performance. Regardless of the time spent in practice, improvement will result only if there is an increase in the work rate [5]. There is also a fine line in training beyond which continued stress can either improve performance or lead to the state known as staleness.

Many coaches use the principle of overload in order to increase the demands on the players, and therefore to improve their performances. That is, the coach makes the athletes adapt to additional stress in order to develop strength and endurance by demanding that their bodies do more than they have previously.

If the athlete wants to build up strength, she must work with a heavier load (one that offers greater resistance) and fewer repetitions. If she wants to build up muscular endurance, she should use a light load (little resistance) and many repetitions [39].

SEQUENCE

Some athletes try to do a whole season's work in one day. But to eliminate injuries and get the best results, the athlete should start on a level that is within her capabilities, and then increase the work load slightly each day until she attains the fitness she feels is necessary to perform at maximum efficiency.

Many athletes become discouraged when they reach a plateau and seem to level off. Yet if the athlete just sticks to her planned program and continues to increase her exercises gradually, she will find that self-discipline and perseverance pay off, and that she will attain a new level of skill. Training should not be done haphazardly, but should follow an orderly progression so that the body has time to adapt to the demands on it.

Doubles action (courtesy Joseph C. Bowles, Brevard College).

REGULARITY

If an athlete wants to do well in competition, she must train continuously. A person who trains faithfully one week and takes the next week off can rarely reach a peak performance. The frequency of workouts depends on the person's goals. An Olympic competitor may find that two or three practice sessions a day are required, while the college athlete may find that daily workouts suffice. For the person who just wishes to be generally fit for daily living, three workouts a week may be adequate.

Whatever the conditioning program is, the athlete must perform her exercises regularly to get the desired results, for irregular practice periods result in erratic performance.

MAINTENANCE

The effects of exercise are reversible if the conditioning program is stopped. However, when the athlete has achieved the desired level of conditioning, she does not have to expend as much effort or time in order to maintain this level, provided that she engages in her conditioning program regularly and does not decrease the intensity or decrease the work load.

SPECIFICITY

When an athlete is conditioned for one sport, this does not necessarily mean that she is in condition for another, even though both sports may require endurance or strength. Timing, efficiency of movement, and physiological adjustments geared to badminton, for example, may not enable one to play tennis with the same effectiveness. To operate with a minimum of wasted motion and a maximum of coordination, the athlete must train specifically for a particular sport.

RETROGRESSION

Shortly after her training has started, an athlete may feel that she is losing ground rather than improving. However, this is a normal reaction, because the body may be unable to adapt itself immediately to the demands placed on it. And if the body has to cope with other handicaps such as inadequate sleep or poor eating habits, the athlete may experience other periods of retrogression. These slumps should not be confused with a normal difference in performance from day to day, nor should they be confused with staleness. Environmental stimuli and internal changes, as well as psychological factors, can cause variability of performance. The coach and the athlete must expect that some days will be better than others; but good athletes keep variability in performance to a minimum.

STALENESS

Staleness is a steady decrease in performance. Some symptoms of it are continuous fatigue, irritability, sleeplessness, possible loss of appetite and weight (though some may overeat and gain), increased tendency to worry, indigestion, and in some cases, headaches and nausea. Physiological changes occurring during staleness include a higher heart rate and a higher lactic acid concentration than that normally resulting from a given amount of exercise [6], though only rarely does a coach have the time or the means to measure this. If the coach finds that the conditioning program is resulting in staleness, she should decrease the work load for a few days. If this does not help, she may need to stop training completely for a couple of days. Participation in an entirely different activity during this time can give players the fresh mental outlook and physical rest needed to eliminate staleness.

REST AND SLEEP

If the athlete is to cope with the added stress on her body resulting from an intensive training program, adequate sleep and rest are very important. Schoolwork, practice, and social life together take up a great deal of time; usually the thing that gets short-changed is the time set aside for rest and sleep. People vary as to the amount of sleep they need. One girl may get along fine on six hours, another may need ten. If a person can go to bed and get up each morning without any trouble, and with a rested feeling, then she is probably getting an adequate amount of sleep. Irritability, a need for afternoon naps, excessive fatigue, etc., should be taken as signs that the person may not be getting enough sleep. Most athletes should allow 8 to 10 hours for sleep, to allow their bodies a chance to recover from the tremendous demands placed on them. Loud noises, excessive light, extreme room temperatures, and uncomfortable beds are impediments to sleep, and should be avoided. Regular hours for going to bed and getting up help one to sleep well. If the athlete is tense or overtired, she should take a hot bath before going to bed; and of course, she should try to put aside all worries before going to sleep.

INDIVIDUAL DIFFERENCES

Each person differs in capacity to engage in strenuous activity at the beginning of a conditioning program. Therefore programs should be flexible enough to meet the needs of the individual. If the coach cannot arrange for highly individualized programs, the beginning point of the conditioning program should be such that even the most out-of-condition girl can handle the overload without harmful effects; or the coach should match each girl with others of similar ability for workouts.

TRAINING THE ATHLETE

In training and conditioning athletes, the coach must think about four main elements: (1) strength, (2) endurance, (3) flexibility, and (4) speed.

STRENGTH

The coach can use three types of exercises to improve athletes' strength [38]: (1) the lifting of body weight, with several repetitions, (2) adding external weights to specific parts of the body being moved, with fewer repetitions, or (3) isometric contractions. All these methods utilize tension in the specific muscle group to be developed.

*Isometric contraction** is contraction that produces partial or maximum tension in a muscle *without* movement in a joint, and takes place when antagonistic muscles work against each other with equal force, or when a muscle group works against a stationary external object. In most isometric exercises, muscles contract for a maximum of six seconds, then relax. The contractions and rest periods are continued for a specific number of times. Isometric exercises can be used to increase strength in specific

---

* Research on isometric contraction was first published by Dr. Theodor Hettinger and Dr. Erich Müller in 1953.

muscles of the body and to maintain muscle tone, but their value in increasing total physical fitness is probably not as great as some coaches believe.

*Isotonic contraction* is contraction that produces partial or maximum tension in a muscle *with* movement in a joint. For instance, pushing against an immovable weight causes isometric contraction, while pushing against a movable one causes isotonic contraction.

Isotonic exercises are better utilized in circuit training because of the range of motion possible when there is movement of the joint. Neither isometric nor isotonic exercises are sufficient in themselves for general conditioning purposes, but they have their place when combined with other methods.

Muscles become stronger only when they must do more than they have done before. Repetition, without overloading, has little effect on strength. The best results seem to come from using about 75% of maximal force in isotonic exercises, and about two-thirds maximal force in isometric exercises.

People used to think that girls would become muscle-bound if they used resistance and overload exercises to build up their strength. Women especially were apprehensive about this method of training because they did not wish to lose their femininity while competing, or look like Amazons because of their muscle development. Nowadays people realize that this fear has no basis if the exercises allow a complete range of motion, or if extensive weight-training is not used over a long period of time. Many women athletes are now improving their performances by weight training.

If the athlete is to develop strength rapidly, the muscles must work against a heavier resistance or overload than usual. To do an exercise many times with a light resistance will result in increased endurance but not increased strength. As strength increases and the athlete finds the work load easier to handle, the work load should be progressively increased [3].

ENDURANCE

Endurance is the ability to engage in activity for a long time without undue fatigue. If a girl's endurance is low because she is not conditioned for the activity, her performance may suffer, since fatigue impairs one's ability to maintain a high level of work. If she continues to play after fatigue has set in, she may eventually get to the point we call exhaustion. When that happens, she can no longer keep going.

Exhaustion, or neuromuscular fatigue, results from an accumulation of acid waste materials, lack of adequate oxygen in the working muscles, or failure or inefficiency in the neuromuscular (nerve-muscle) junction [3]. It seldom occurs during competition unless the girl has failed to follow a sound conditioning program, or else is so "up" for the event that she continues to compete even though she is highly fatigued. Intense motivation or psychological factors can force her to overcome physical fatigue through mental determination. Exhaustion, or the body's inability to meet the demands placed on it, is a safety valve that prevents the athlete from going beyond a point that would result in harmful effects if the exertion were to be continued.

There are two kinds of endurance: muscular and circulatory–respiratory (better known as *wind*). Several factors can affect endurance. A strong girl can naturally perform work for a longer period than a girl who lacks tonus or strength in her muscles. When the athlete competes in an event that requires the lifting of heavy loads—such as tumbling, free exercise, or routines on uneven parallel bars—her endurance depends greatly on her strength. When a muscle is strong, its fibers may not all have to contract to perform a movement; this enables some of the fibers to rest. When certain muscle fibers can relax while others are contracting, the resting fibers get a richer blood supply and more oxygen, allowing the athlete to continue movement over a longer period of time. Thus the athlete with strong muscles can work longer than the athlete with weaker ones. So when an event demands endurance and allows the athletes no chance to rest, strength is a definite advantage.

Another factor in endurance is the skill of the performer. Good athletes use less energy in a given activity than less-skilled ones because the skilled athlete's movements are more efficient and relaxed. Established patterns of movement that have been used over and over are easier to execute and are done with a minimum of waste motion. This means that, when endurance is a factor, the skilled athlete has an advantage over the less-skilled one.

A third influence on endurance is the efficiency of the athlete's circulatory and respiratory systems, since an increase in waste products in the blood can result in fatigue. The amount of oxygen debt (see page 28) the athlete can tolerate limits her endurance, because the oxygen debt is related to the amount of lactic acid built up in the muscles. Therefore an athlete's muscular endurance depends on her ability to adjust to the buildup of waste products in her body, and her ability to dispose of these waste products. Of equal importance is the ability of her heart, blood vessels, and lungs to take in and use oxygen.

The reason that records are being broken today is that athletes are conditioning themselves to go full speed for a longer period of time than they used to. However, because of the limitations of the body, no one can go full speed for a long time. The less effort the athlete has to use in a certain sport, or the slower she has to move during competition, the longer she can participate in that activity.

Work that requires brief but maximum effort, such as lifting a heavy weight, can be repeated only three or four times before fatigue sets in. If the exertion is less intense, a reduction in performance does not occur so quickly. For sports such as running, swimming, bicycling, and skiing, maximum effort can be exerted for only approximately 30 seconds. Most runners can give their maximum effort and maintain their top speed for about 300 yards, but then the speed must be reduced or the runner may become exhausted [34].

In order to develop endurance, the athlete must be willing to sustain effort even when she is tired. However, for psychological and sometimes physiological reasons, there must be a balance between work and rest. The more time the athlete has to recover, the more blood is pumped to the muscles to supply oxygen and other needed materials and to remove waste products; this enables the athlete to continue work without as much fatigue as she would have had if there had been no rest. Muller [35] pointed out that it is what the body does during rest periods that is important because as long as the body is able to recover at a rate that keeps pace with the fatigue, then the athlete is able to continue. Now if a girl increases the work load and goes beyond the point of comfort while she is training, she improves her endurance, because physiological changes take place to meet the stress on the body. These changes speed up the rate of recovery, so that the highly conditioned athlete needs less rest or recovery time than the poorly conditioned one. Therefore, when a person is striving for a higher level of endurance, rest is important, but so is the acceptance of pain or discomfort.

An athlete can build up endurance by repeatedly taking part in a specific event. However, if the event does not always demand a great deal of the athlete, her physiological systems are not all forced to perform at maximum efficiency, and thus she may not be able to build her endurance to its peak by this method. In order to improve her endurance (and also her performance), she should not only participate in her chosen sport, but she should include special overload exercises in her practice sessions.

Regardless of pace, endurance depends primarily on the intake of oxygen and the ability of the circulatory system to carry oxygen to the muscles. When an athlete is using up energy faster than she can take in oxygen to meet her body's demands, she builds up an *oxygen debt*. If she is unable to rest or slow down long enough to replenish this oxygen, she will eventually become exhausted and unable to perform. When the body has an inadequate oxygen supply during intense effort, it uses *anaerobic* energy sources. If, on the other hand, the athlete slows down and has enough oxygen coming in to supply the muscle tissues and to get rid of waste products (lactic acid), she is said to be working *aerobically* and within her steady-state capacity. An athlete who has an adequate oxygen intake can continue to participate in the sport for a long time without undue fatigue.

*Pace.* In endurance events, the athlete must conserve energy in order to finish the event; therefore a basic objective of the coach in training the athlete is to develop the best pace for her. Good athletes have a steady pace, worked out to provide a rhythm that will conserve energy and avoid fatigue too early in the competition. In a running event, for example, the athlete should distribute the work output evenly except for the closing moments, when she should give the final "kick" and go all out in the finish. She uses the greatest amount of energy at the beginning of the race when she must overcome the inertia of starting from a standstill to build up to the maximum speed she wants to hold throughout the race. This acceleration from a standing start to a maximum speed takes approximately 6 seconds, or 30–40 yards, and once the girl hits the desired speed, she expends energy to maintain momentum and to carry out the physiological changes going on in her body. It is more economical to maintain a steady pace than to decelerate and then accelerate, for any energy saved by slowing down is quickly used up when the athlete speeds up again [34].

The beginning athlete often starts out at a fast pace in hopes that she can get a big lead before she tires, but her rapid expenditure of energy leads to a high oxygen debt early in the race, forcing her to run the last part in a fatigued state. The same thing happens when the athlete suffering from butterflies expends her excess energy by en-

Out of the blocks (Photograph by Audio-Visual Center, Indiana State University, courtesy United States Track and Field Federation).

gaging in the warm-up session too strenuously, or by unnecessary movements at the beginning of the contest. It pays to budget one's energy and channel it constructively throughout the competition.

## FLEXIBILITY

Flexibility concerns the range of motion in the joints. The good athlete needs not only strength and endurance, but average or above-average joint movement.

A person's flexibility is limited by the bony structure of his or her body, but the range of motion is also influenced by the elasticity of muscles, tendons, and ligaments. This elasticity can be improved by means of stretching exercises.

The range of motion in a given joint depends on: (1) the length of ligaments and other tissues around the joint, (2) the length and elasticity of muscles and tendons concerned with flexion of the joint, (3) muscle and fat that may limit movement in the joint, and (4) the bony structure of the joint. To improve flexibility, the athlete should use progressive exercises in which force is gradually increased and the duration of the held position is lengthened [3].

To maintain a desired level of flexibility, a girl should perform each exercise through a full range of motion. To increase flexibility, she must continue to perform the exercise until she can actually feel the muscle or muscles being pulled. During warm-up periods most athletes do stretching exercises, because they know that having a full range of motion leads to greater ease of movement during competition.

When a person stops activity, either by choice or because of injury, the muscles and tendons tend to lose their elasticity and ligaments no longer have their normal extensibility. The athlete who gains weight may also lose some flexibility due to the added body fat, because fat can restrict flexibility if it reduces the internal elasticity of the muscle or if it limits movement at the joint. The same thing can happen when muscles are overdeveloped.

McCue [28] found that a girl can improve her flexibility to a significant extent within 3 weeks by engaging in mild exercise. She also found that people who could jump better had a higher mean score in flexibility of the hip and trunk during flexion, and that the underweight person had a greater mean in hip flexion than the overweight one, although the overweight person had a greater mean for lumbar extension.

## SPEED

Is there such a thing as building up speed? Naturally, there is a limit to the speed any given person can attain, but a girl certainly should be able to build up her speed to her maximum potential, just as she builds up strength, endurance, and flexibility.

Youngen [49] found that women athletes were significantly faster than women nonathletes in speed of arm movement and reaction time, and that—although tennis players, fencers, and field hockey players differed significantly in speed of movement—there was not a significant difference in their reaction times.

One might assume that the speed of performing specific movements can be improved through training, but that the initial reaction or reflex time does not differ significantly among trained, skilled players.

One could describe speed in running as being due to a combination of reflex time (reaction to starting gun or signal), strength (especially in the legs), endurance, and flexibility. All these factors together give a person a specific response within a given time. Since running speed depends on the length of the stride and the number of strides in a given amount of time, the person must work on flexibility of the legs and ankles, and must also increase strength in order to make the thrusts against the ground more forceful.

## CONDITIONING METHODS

There are many methods for training the athlete, but *fartlek*, interval training, circuit training, and weight training seem to be the methods most widely used at present.

### FARTLEK*

This type of training is used widely to build endurance in the athlete. *Fartlek* is a Swedish word, which is usually translated "speed play." It allows the individual a certain amount of freedom, since it consists of the athlete running at a pace that she decides on, the pace being adjusted according to her feeling that she should speed up or slow down.

---

* Originated by Gosta Holmer of Sweden.

*Fartlek* is simply a pace that becomes slow or fast depending on the athlete, and consists of jogging, sprinting, jogging, walking, sprinting, etc., as the athlete varies her running to develop endurance. Usually the athlete trains while running cross-country, partly because it does not get so monotonous, and partly because of the space needed for running. However, any area with adequate space—such as a golf course, football or soccer field, or a standard track—may be used.

The disadvantage of this method lies in the very fact that the pace, distance, etc., are controlled by the athlete. If this method is to be effective in building up endurance, the athlete must force herself to run while she is tired. Therefore some people don't gain as much from using this system as they should. It is very hard to exert oneself to the point of pain; it takes great motivation and self-discipline.

### INTERVAL TRAINING*

Unlike *fartlek*, which is regulated by the athlete, *interval training* is controlled by the coach. In this type of training program, the athlete takes a fast lap for a preset distance, then a slower lap to allow time for recovery, then another fast lap.

To increase endurance, the athlete can: (1) run the first lap at a greater speed or go a longer distance, (2) run a shorter distance for the interval or recovery lap, and (3) run a greater number of fast and slow laps. Some people hold to the theory that, since the athlete trains at higher speeds during interval training than during competition, there is an increase in speed as well as endurance. (There is no present conclusive evidence that this is so, however.) Interval training is used extensively throughout the world, especially by runners and swimmers.

When the athlete is first beginning her training program and effort is intense, most coaches prefer that the recovery lap be 2 or 3 times longer than the fast lap. Then, as the conditioning program progresses, the recovery lap is shortened. The athlete has to learn to adjust to this shorter recovery period while maintaining her speed on the next fast lap. The coach must keep the length of the rest interval adequate to meet the demands of the effort phase. For hard, maximal work, the recovery phase (slow jogging, walking, etc.) should be 2 to 3 times as long as the effort phase, while light work might have a time ratio of one to one. To determine whether the rest interval is adequate, the coach can measure the athlete's pulse.

When the coach has planned the program well, the athlete is able to develop her endurance gradually, until she can run a race at full speed. To allow sufficient time for progressive conditioning, the coach must start interval training well in advance of the competitive program. The importance of this training during the off-season and pre-season is stressed in Chapter 5.

To prevent staleness during endurance work, the coach can use *fartlek* training for 3 or 4 weeks and follow it up by interval training. Track coaches, when they use interval training to prepare athletes for middle-distance runs, follow one of two theories: (1) *Over-distance*, in which the athlete runs farther than he is going to run during com-

---

* Used successfully by Franz Stamptfl.

petition (for instance, running 550 yards in practice to prepare to run 440 in competition), or (2) *under-distance*, in which the athlete runs a shorter distance at full speed during practice (for instance, running 330 yards in practice, as fast as possible, to prepare to run 440 in competition).

For an athlete who is training for an event that requires running endurance, here are some suggestions for workouts (although of course all workouts depend on the condition of the player).

| *Monday* | *Tuesday* |
|---|---|
| 1. Warm up using stretching exercises. | 1. Warm up using stretching exercises. |
| 2. Jog around track once, then alternate jogging and sprinting while going around track again. | 2. Jog around track once, then alternate jogging and sprinting while going around track again. |
| 3. Run four 220's at full speed; try to increase time each week. | 3. Run 550 yards, using pace for first 440 yards. |
| 4. Rest four minutes between each 220 (by jogging or walking). | 4. Rest 4 minutes (jogging or walking). |
| 5. Jog and walk 2 to 3 laps. | 5. Run 660 yards, using pace for first 440 yards. |
| 6. Go in for shower. | 6. Rest 4 minutes (jogging or walking). |
| | 7. Jog and walk 2 to 3 laps. |
| | 8. Go in for shower. |

CIRCUIT TRAINING*

*Circuit training* increases muscular strength and endurance. In circuit training an athlete goes from one exercise station to another in a planned sequence and in the shortest possible time.

In planning a circuit training program, one chooses exercises to fit the needs of the individual. Each of these exercises is then numbered and assigned to a certain area (called a station). The athlete progresses from one station to another, performing a specific number of repetitions at each station. The circuit is usually repeated three times, although the number of times the athlete does the exercises depends on the individual and the training program. When the athlete has completed the circuit, her time should be recorded.

In circuit training, the athlete can increase her strength and endurance by (1) doing a greater number of exercises at each station, (2) doing the exercises in a shorter length of time, or (3) combining (1) and (2).

If the work load (number of exercises to be performed) is to be kept consistent, the athlete can develop strength and endurance by gradually decreasing the time it takes her to go around the circuit.

---

* Program developed by R. E. Morgan and G. T. Adamson.

This method of training emphasizes time rather than resistance, and is based on the theory that the athlete can increase her strength and endurance by working harder in a given length of time or by exerting the same amount of energy in less time. The circuit usually consists of 9 to 12 exercises, each requiring about half the athlete's maximum ability. At the beginning of the training program, the girl, while being timed, completes three rounds of the circuit without a rest period. To improve her level of conditioning, she tries to complete the circuit in one-third less time than her previous recorded time; when she reaches *this* level, the work load is increased, she is retested to see how long it takes her to complete this circuit three times, and then a new goal is set up, with a shorter time [34].

Circuit training is usually used to develop general all-round physical fitness, rather than specialized performance in a specific activity. However, if the specialist makes a wise choice of exercises, circuit training can hold many benefits for her if she combines it with practicing the fine points of the given sport.

Circuit training can be set up for one person or for groups, can be planned for any time period, does not require a lot of equipment, and gives motivation to the individual to compete against her own record. An additional benefit is that the athlete can follow her progress as she tries to beat her own time. Having the athlete pair up with another person of approximately the same skill level can also increase motivation.

Here are two examples of circuit programs.

*Station 1.* Jog in place slowly for 2 minutes.

*Station 2.* Do 15 modified push-ups.

*Station 3.* Do 25 sit-ups.

*Station 4.* Jump rope for 1 minute.

*Station 5.* Work with weights: 8 overhead presses; 8 two-arm curls; 8 half-squats with weight on shoulder; 8 heel raises; 8 supine pullovers.

*Station 6.* Basketball chest pass against wall from 5 feet away, 15 times.

*Station 7.* Stretching and flexibility exercises: Touch toes 20 times from standing position; 20 bear hugs; from sitting position bob three times and touch toes, repeating 8 times.

*Station 8.* Do 25 jumping jacks.

*Station 9.* Isometric exercises: Push one fist against the other; grasp fingers and pull in opposite directions; put hands behind head and pull forward; put hands on forehead and push backward (five times each for a count of 6 seconds).

*Station 10.* Run 4 laps around the gym.

*Station 1.* Jog 1 lap, then sprint one lap around gym.

*Station 2.* Jump into air as high as possible 8 times.

*Station 3.* Throw medicine ball for distance 3 times.

*Station 4.* Do 30 modified pull-ups.

*Station 5.* Flexibility and stretching exercises: Do the "inchworm" three times; kick right leg up and touch left hand 10 times; kick left leg up and touch right hand 10 times; do 30 big arm circles.

*Station 6.* Broad jump for distance 3 times.

*Station 7.* Make 10 free throws.

*Station 8.* Do 25 sit-ups.

*Station 9.* Walk on hands and feet for 15 yards.

*Station 10.* Run 440 yards.

## WEIGHT TRAINING

*Weight training* is the use of weight in exercising to develop muscle power and strength by the overload principle. Weight training should not be confused with weight lifting, which is the lifting of heavy weights with the goal of lifting more pounds than the opponent can. The confusion between weight lifting and weight training is probably the reason for the negative feelings about the use of weights in a woman's training program, since weight lifting is usually associated with powerful, muscled men, and has a masculine connotation. However, one can use weight training to improve a girl's general fitness and to raise her level of performance in a particular sport while at the same time adding to her femininity by improving her figure and muscle tone, since her muscles are strengthened by carefully selected weight training exercises.

In many events, strength is a prerequisite to success: the discus and javelin throw, gymnastics, swimming, and so forth. By increasing her strength with weight training, the girl also increases her chance to compete well.

A weight-training program usually involves repeating exercises a certain number of times, with workouts 2 or 3 times a week. The number of repetitions is gradually increased until a maximum number is reached. Then the work load is increased by adding additional weight, after which the girl goes back to the number of repetitions she started with. Increasing the work load increases strength. Girls who are able to handle only a small weight at the beginning of a weight-training program may need a preliminary program of calisthenics before training with weights. Specific exercises with weights are given on pages 62–63.

In order to start a girl off with the right amount of weight, the coach must test her at the beginning of the program to determine how much strength she has. The girl should start with a weight load that she can handle for 8 repetitions (of a specific exercise) without overstraining. (The number of repetitions in a set varies, but it has been suggested that the woman's program should use a set of 8 at the beginning [31].) The movements should be continuous; the weights should be lifted and lowered slowly. Unless the eighth repetition is fairly hard, then the load is too light for that person and there will not be an adequate gain in strength. When the athlete has increased her strength to the point at which she can do 12 repetitions of a given exercise, she should increase the weight load (usually an increase of 5 pounds is enough for girls) and then go back to 8 repetitions with the added weight load.

Others [45] have suggested that a girl start with a weight she can lift 4 to 5 times, and that she continue to exercise with this weight until she can perform the exercise 10 times. Then $2\frac{1}{2}$ to 10 pounds are added and the girl goes back to 5 repetitions. It was also suggested that some exercises could start with 8 to 10 repetitions with an increase of 2 until 20 repetitions are reached, at which time more weight is added and the girl goes back to 8 to 10 repetitions. This builds muscular endurance as well as strength.

ISOMETRIC, ISOTONIC, AND ISOKINETIC EXERCISES

The use of isotonic and isometric exercises in training was discussed on pages 46–47. Basically, isotonic exercises involve movement through a range of motion in the presence of resistance, or a load. Isometric exercises involve work against an object that does not move.

*Isokinetic* exercise is a new principle of exercising that involves work against a resistance or a load while movement occurs at a mechanically regulated rate of speed. The mechanical device sets up a resistance that helps develop dynamic tension in a muscle or a muscle group during the shortening range and at a specific and optimal shortening speed. The beneficial effects of isokinetic exercising on overall physical fitness, however, has not yet been completely determined [50].

**EXERCISES TO INCREASE STRENGTH, ENDURANCE, FLEXIBILITY, AND SPEED**

In setting up an exercise program or a training schedule, the coach should keep several principles in mind:

1. Regular practice sessions should be held; the length of the sessions should be consistent with the level of skill and fitness of the girl or girls involved.

2. The program should be set up to meet the needs of each individual. Since individual needs vary, the coach may have to modify or adapt parts of the program to fit the needs of certain girls.

3. So that the girls will perform specific exercises properly and thereby obtain the best results, the coach should explain the exercises and conditioning program clearly.

4. The coach should vary exercises in order to prevent the girls from getting bored and to eliminate staleness.

5. The training program should be progressive, the work load being gradually increased to allow the body to make the needed adjustments.

6. In order to prevent pulled muscles, strains, etc., the coach should see to it that an adequate warm-up period precedes any strenuous exercise.

7. For best results, exercises to increase strength, endurance, flexibility, and speed must be combined with practice of the specific skills the performer will be using.

The coach must carefully select the exercises for each individual engaging in a specific sport. Some girls need development in certain areas, while others need general overall fitness. Here are a few exercises that help athletes develop their overall physical fitness by increasing strength, endurance, flexibility, and speed.

## EXERCISES FOR INCREASING STRENGTH

A.  ABDOMEN

1.  Back-lying position, hands grasped behind the head, knees bent with heels on the floor. Curl up to a sitting position and touch right knee with opposite elbow. Go back down, come up again and touch left knee with right elbow. Repeat.

2.  Back-lying position, arms extended at sides and legs stretched out on floor. Bend knees and slide heels up close to hips, then pull knees to chest. Lower feet to floor close to hips and extend legs out on floor again.

3.  Back-lying position, arms extended out at shoulder level. Bring heels along floor to hips. Pull knees to chest, lifting pelvis off floor. Lower knees slowly to the left while rotating pelvis in that direction. Bring knees back over chest. Lower hips and go back to the starting position. Go to right side and continue alternately.

B.  LEGS AND HIPS

1.  In a standing position, with arms extended in front of body, bend knees and go down to a half-squat position. Keep most of weight on toes and balls of feet. Go back to standing position and continue. Hold 5-pound weight on shoulders and do the same.

2.  Begin in a standing position with feet spaced comfortably. Bend knees and go down to a half-squat, keeping weight on toes and balls of feet, then jump upward, extending arms in the air while jumping as high as possible. May be varied by holding weights on shoulders.

3.  Side-lying position. Lift leg straight upward slowly as far as possible and then return leg slowly to starting position. Repeat several times. Turn onto other side and repeat with other leg.

4. From a standing position, start with left foot forward, knees slightly bent, then change positions of feet with an easy jump. The knees should bend and relax on the jump to absorb the shock of the lunge. Continue exercise while alternating feet.

C. CALVES, ANKLES, AND FEET

1. Place balls of feet on an object that is about 2 inches thick. Lift heels off floor by rising up onto toes and balls of feet as high as possible. Extend arms in front of body for balance. Hold this position for 6 seconds, return to starting position, and repeat.

2. Draw a small circle on the floor within reaching distance of a bench. Then, sitting on the bench, pick up marbles with the toes and place them in the circle.

3. Sitting on bench, curl up a towel with the toes.

4. Remain in a sitting position on a chair or bench and lift one leg, moving foot in a circle. Change direction of circle. Repeat with other foot.

5. Stand on board or mat, with toes over edge. Grip board or mat with toes, curling them and grasping tight with them. Relax and repeat.

D. SHOULDERS, NECK, AND CHEST

1. Face-lying position, head turned to left or right, hands grasped behind back. Pull shoulder blades together, using a smooth and even motion. Hold position for a count of 6, then slowly relax shoulder muscles. Repeat.

2. Lie in same position with arms at shoulder level, elbows bent at an approximately 90-degree angle. Bring shoulder blades together, then lift arms from mat. Hold position from 3 to 5 seconds. Return to starting position. Repeat.

3. Modified push-up position. Let chest down halfway to floor and then hold for a count of 3 seconds. Return to starting position. Repeat.

4. Face-lying position, arms stretched out over head. Raise arms off floor as far as possible, while keeping elbows straight. Hold for count of 6, then return to starting position. Repeat.

5. Same position as above. Lift up one arm at a time.

6. Stand about arm's length from a wall. With arms extended, place hands against wall. Then, bending elbows only, allow body to move toward wall. Push body away from wall and return to starting position. Repeat.

7. Hang from a bar with palms toward face. Pull up until chin is above bar, hold a few seconds, then lower body slowly to extended position.

E. ARMS, WRIST, AND FINGERS

1. Use a two-arm support on parallel bars, keeping body in a vertical position. Bend elbows and lower body slowly. Return to starting position.

2. Use a modified pull-up position (on chinning bar, parallel bars, etc.) with palms toward face. Bend elbows, pulling chest to bar, or until elbows form a 90-degree angle. Return to starting position and repeat.

3. Use modified push-ups, putting most of weight on fingers rather than on palms of hand.

4. Sitting on floor, push hips and body up by pressing fingers against floor.

F. UPPER BACK

1. Face-lying position. Clasp hands at small of back, extend arms toward feet while bringing shoulder blades together. Then raise head and shoulders off the floor. Hold about 6 seconds. Relax and return to starting position.

2. Face-lying position. Grasp fingers behind head, raise elbows off floor, pull shoulder blades together, and raise head and chest off floor. Hold 3 to 5 seconds. Return to starting position.

3. Kneel, sitting on heels with hands clasped in small of back. Bend forward from hips, placing forehead on mat. Extend arms backward and upward, holding position for about 6 seconds. Lift head as arms are extended backward.

**EXERCISES FOR INCREASING ENDURANCE**

1. Jump rope, using any movement with feet. Jump continuously for 3 to 5 minutes. Increase time each practice session.

2. In a standing position, interchange feet with a hopping motion. Movement may be sideward, backward, etc.

3. Run in place, lifting knees high. Alternate with sprints and distance runs if space is available. Spot run in bursts if space is limited.

4. Jump upward repeatedly, as high as possible, at a fast pace.

5. Step up onto a bench approximately 18 inches high, then step down. Continue for 2 to 3 minutes, then change legs for the step up onto the bench. Increase time as endurance improves.

6. Engage in vigorous activity in the chosen sport, such as making fast break in basketball, swimming lengths of pool as fast as possible, etc.

## EXERCISES FOR INCREASING FLEXIBILITY

### A. TRUNK, HIPS, AND PELVIC REGION

1. In standing position, swing one leg forward and backward as far as possible. After several repetitions, exchange legs.

2. Standing with feet 3 or 4 inches apart and parallel to each other, bend forward from waist while keeping knees straight. Touch hands to floor until you can feel the stretch and tension. Hold for count of 6 and return to starting position.

3. Sit on floor with legs extended in front of body. Reach with hands and bend forward from waist while trying to reach beyond toes. Hold for count of 6. Return to starting position.

4. Lie on back. Bring one knee to chest and grasp leg just below knee while pulling knee toward chest until you feel a definite stretch in the muscles. Hold for a count of 6. Return to starting position.

5. Following above directions, bring both knees to the chest.

### B. HEEL CORDS

1. Stand about arm's length from a wall, keeping feet 3 to 4 inches apart and flat on the floor. Lean forward, keeping head, shoulders, hips, chest, and ankles in align-

ment. Keep bending the elbows until you feel stretch behind the knees and in the calves of the legs. Hold for approximately 6 seconds. Return to starting position.

C. SHOULDERS AND BACK

1. Sit with knees crossed and arms folded across chest. Move chin down to chest and curl forward in an attempt to touch the forehead to the knees. Hold for count of 6. Return to starting position.

2. Hang from stall bar or other fixed bar. Turn palms outward and hang with back to wall and stall bars. Hang as long as possible. Repeat after rest.

D. ARMS, NECK, AND SHOULDERS

1. Sit with legs crossed. Hold arms at shoulder level, with elbows bent and hands in front of chest. Pull elbows back, hold 6 counts, and return to starting position.

2. Stand with feet approximately shoulder width apart. Extend arms out to the side at shoulder level. Have arms make circles, starting with small circles, and gradually going into larger ones. Reverse direction.

3. Move head around in a circle by dropping head forward, moving it to the side, backward, to opposite side and then forward again. Reverse direction.

4. Standing, grasp hands behind back. Extend arms and pull shoulder blades together. Relax and repeat.

**EXERCISES FOR INCREASING SPEED**

1. Run in place, lifting knees high. Speed up tempo and then slow it down, etc.

2. Get into sprinter's position and push off hard by extending ankles and knees.

3. Get into sprinter's position and interchange feet, reaching out and backward as far as possible with the legs. (This is also excellent for developing endurance.)

4. Sprint and jog, increasing sprinting distance or decreasing jogging distance each day.

5. Run up inclines or along the beach or on any surface that requires more effort than normal running.

6. Practice starts and stops, keeping body weight low. Start up as quickly as possible and then stop in one step. Vary by having someone blow whistle to indicate stops and starts.

7. Use arms in running, exaggerating pumping motion until using the arms becomes natural.

## EXERCISES WITH USE OF WEIGHTS

1. Hold weights at chest. Push weights upward over head until arms are extended. Lower to chest again.

2. Hold weight below waist with arms extended. Lift up to shoulder level, then lower to extended arm position again.

3. With weight on shoulder behind head, do half-squats.

4. With weight on shoulder behind head, raise body onto toes.

5. Back-lying position, knees bent and weight behind head. Curl forward and do a modified sit-up.

6. Back-lying position, legs extended. Hold weight directly above chest, keeping arms extended. Move weight toward legs, then back up above chest, then move toward head. Repeat.

7. Lie on bench or table face down, with arms hanging down on each side. Lift weights up and then lower.

8. Lie on back with weight resting on chest. Push weight straight up away from chest until arms are extended. Lower weight back to chest.

9. Sit with weight resting on shoulder behind head. Lift weight straight upward until arms are extended. Lower weight back to shoulders.

10. Sit on table with legs hanging over the side. Place weight on foot. Extend leg upward and then lower. Alternate weight to other leg.

11. Tie a 2–3 pound weight to a stick or a bar with a rope. With arms extended forward at shoulder level, wind weight to bar slowly. Reverse hand motions to lower weight to floor.

12. Holding weights in each hand, go into half-squat, then jump forcefully upward.

13. Stand with feet comfortably spread, a dumbbell in each hand, palms facing body. Raise arms sideways until weights are level with shoulders. Lower hands to side and repeat.

## ISOMETRIC EXERCISES *

1. Sitting or standing, hold arms at shoulder height with elbows bent. Press palm of one hand against fist of other hand, exerting equal tension to keep arms from moving.

2. Sitting or standing, hold arms at shoulder height with elbows bent. Hook fingers together. Pull outward as hard as possible while keeping same arm position.

3. Sitting or standing, grasp hands behind back. Pull outward with both arms. Have someone push arms outward while you try to resist and maintain your arm position.

4. Sitting, place hands under thighs and pull upward with arms, resisting pull with legs. Push down against floor in reverse arm action.

5. Stand in an open door with arms against wall. Push outward. Then, catching door jamb, pull inward.

6. Sit on floor. Place fingers on floor next to hips and push down. Lift hips up and hold, exerting pressure with fingers.

7. Go into modified push-up position. Lower body halfway to floor. Hold for 6 seconds.

8. Place legs inside legs of a partner so that ankles touch. Push outward with legs while other girl pulls inward with equal tension. Exchange positions.

## DIET AND NUTRITION

Since athletic competition requires great exertion, an athlete's muscles and other tissues must have an adequate supply of the right food components. The foods she eats must provide the carbohydrates, fats, proteins, minerals, water, and vitamins her body needs for normal development. At the same time these foods must enable her body

---

* Maximum tension should be exerted for 4–6 seconds.

to function at its best under competition, should contain variety, but not be of such quantity or kind that she becomes overweight.

Carbohydrates are the sugars and starches found in foods such as breads and cereals, fruits, potatoes, candy and other sweets, etc. Carbohydrates are broken down into *glycogen* and stored in the liver and muscles. When energy is needed, glucose is supplied quickly from these two reservoirs. However, the greater part of the excess is converted in the liver and stored as fat in the body.

Fats are compounds of *glycerol* and *fatty acids*. Glycerol, when it is oxidized, can be utilized as energy for muscular work; fatty acid is oxidized to form a coenzyme. Fats form a reserve for the production of heat and energy, and are used as body fuel just as carbohydrates are. However, fat that has been stored is used only when the intake of carbohydrates is not adequate to meet the body's demands.

In order for the body to grow, repair tissues, manufacture gland secretions and digestive juices, and fight disease, it needs adequate protein. Protein differs from fats and carbohydrates in that it is almost never stored as fat or used for energy unless excessive amounts are present. Meat, eggs, or milk should provide approximately a third of the protein consumed daily. Protein molecules are broken down during the digestive process into simple units called *amino acids*, and it is in this form that protein is absorbed from the intestinal tract and used by the tissues.

Vitamins are organic compounds that are essential to good health. They do not furnish energy or build tissue, but act as catalysts which are necessary in the utilization of energy and the regulation of metabolism. A diet that is well-balanced and varied supplies all the vitamins that are necessary.

Minerals help develop strong bones and teeth, and help regulate many essential body processes. Again, a well-balanced diet supplies all the minerals needed. In the case of some minerals, excessive amounts may do as much harm as insufficient amounts. Foods such as milk and milk products, green vegetables, and lean meat provide the minerals the body needs.

Water is necessary to life as it serves as a solvent and diluting factor, helps transport body fuels and waste products, regulates body temperature, and serves as a lubricant. If balance is not maintained between water loss and water intake, the person becomes dehydrated and body functions suffer.

DIET AND THE PERFORMANCE OF THE ATHLETE

The human body, as it tries to maintain good working order, acts as a homeostatic mechanism. Due to the strenuous demands of competition, an athlete's body may demand more food than a nonathlete's in order to supply the materials necessary for the working body. The nonathlete may be able to maintain homeostatic balance with less intake of calories. The girl who is in training and under competitive conditions must have the foods needed for growth, development, repair, and function, but at the same time must keep herself at the weight desired for competition. An oversupply of calories leads to unnecessary pounds, which will handicap the athlete in competition. Adequate nutrition must not be confused with overeating. The quality of food eaten is more important than the quantity.

Some interesting facts about nutrition and the athlete have been found. In an early study of marathon runners, it was found that at the end of a race there was a definite fall in the runners' blood-sugar level. The runner's fatigue and his blood-sugar level, at the end of the race, seemed to be closely related. The athlete's exhaustion was similar to that found in progressive insulin shock. The investigators of these early studies suggested giving sweets to the athletes during the race, but recent studies indicate that sugar during competition does not effect aerobic work capacity, although it may have some value in helping the athlete to recover from fatigue, and to get prepared for later work [34].

Another factor research has uncovered is that sugar, as it is being digested and absorbed, depletes the body of fluid, and therefore tends to lead to a state of dehydration. It has been suggested that heavily sweetened tea with lemon may provide the sugar needed, while keeping the body adequately supplied with needed fluids [34].

Other studies have indicated that the intake of fat tends to be high in people engaged in hard work under severe environmental conditions. Fatty tissue not only serves as a protection against bruises and as an insulation against cold, but as a reservoir of energy, since fat is stored as reserve fuel. The meal high in fat is digested more slowly, and because of this slow passage of the meal from the stomach, the athlete does not feel hunger as quickly. However, in the athlete's diet, fat elements should not be more than double the carbohydrates. One disadvantage of a high-fat diet is that this slow movement of the food through the digestive tract allows decomposition, and —since some athletes have sensitive membranes lining the stomach and intestines which can be irritated by some of the products of food decomposition—the result can be diarrhea [34].

Mathews *et al.* [26] suggest that the athlete should taper off activity 48 hours before competing to allow the liver to replete the glycogen stores. Mayer [27] feels that if the activity is especially demanding, the athlete might be better off eating 4 or 5 lighter meals each day rather than the usual 3.

The use of liquid foods, before practice or games, has been successful in some cases. Woods [48] reports that the 1961 University of Arizona football team had a liquid food supplement 30 to 40 minutes before each practice. The coaches of this team felt that endurance and stamina of the players increased 5 to 15% as a result. The team that year had the best record in the history of the school.

The University of Nebraska football team [23] used a liquid meal called Sustagen in place of the pregame meal with the following results:

1. There was no significant weight change.
2. Players had some feelings of hunger, but this was solved by giving them toast, honey, and peaches with syrup along with the liquid food.
3. Nausea and vomiting were eliminated.
4. Stamina seemed to improve.
5. Diarrhea as result of emotional tension continued.
6. No cramps resulted.
7. There was greater gastrointestinal motility.

There have been some studies of wheat germ [7, 8] and its effect on the performance of the athlete. However, it seems that at present athletes' performances cannot, by such dietary additives, be improved to a point that is better than the performances they turn in when they eat a regular balanced diet [10]. Other fads, such as vitamin supplements, have also been used in an effort to obtain better performances, but, again, these help only if the athlete is not getting the right foods in an all-round good diet.

The athlete's daily diet should include meat, cheese, fish, eggs, milk, vegetables, fruits, and whole-grain cereals. A well-balanced diet from the "fundamental four" [15] food groups (milk and milk products, meat and meat substitutes, vegetables and fruits, and bread and cereals) gives the athlete's body enough nutrition to meet the demands of competition.

A high-carbohydrate diet on the day of competition might consist of:

### Breakfast

1/2 grapefruit with sugar, or orange juice

Cereal with milk and sugar (corn flakes, oatmeal, etc.)

1 or 2 eggs (poached or boiled)

Ham or bacon

Toast with jelly

Glass of milk

### Lunch

Soup (vegetable, cream of mushroom, chicken noodle, etc.)

Meat (roast beef, fish, chicken, etc., baked or broiled)

Salad (tossed, potato, etc.)

Vegetable (creamed potatoes, creamed corn, green beans, etc.)

Bread

Milk or tea

### Dinner or Pregame Meal*

Broiled steak

Baked potato

Bouillon

Toast and honey

Cake

Tea

---

* If competition is at night; otherwise this meal would take the place of lunch.

Water is especially important to the athlete. If the body is to operate efficiently, water must be replenished when the athlete has perspired greatly. The athlete often sweats out large amounts of water during a workout. The loss of water is no problem as long as she takes in enough fluids before, during, and after intensive activity. However, when there is excessive perspiration there is also a loss of body salt. This lessens the body's ability to retain water, which may lead to dehydration. Dehydration keeps the athlete from performing up to standard, and may lead to weakness and muscle cramps. Thus an athlete who perspires heavily or must compete in a hot gymnasium or a warm climate should replace the lost water and salt. Some athletes prefer to add more salt to their food at the table; others take salt tablets. When drinking fluids during and after competition, the athlete should avoid those that are very hot or very cold, or stomach cramps may result.

## THE PREGAME MEAL

The person who plans the pregame meal must consider how digestion influences the athlete's performance, and what nutrients the food will supply to aid that performance.

No athlete should eat a meal just before competing; preferably she should eat 3 to 4 hours before competition. What is in her stomach may affect her performance, especially with respect to its speed of absorption. A high-fat diet takes longer to digest. The longer it stays in her stomach, the longer it requires oxygen for metabolism. On the other hand, a high-protein meal requires the presence of water, which might otherwise be utilized in perspiration and temperature regulation, and also demands oxygen for its metabolism. Again, this oxygen could otherwise be used by the muscles. A high-carbohydrate meal, however, gives fuel for quick energy, which is needed by the athlete.

Any foods that might irritate the stomach, such as salads, spices, beans, etc., should not be eaten before a game. The athlete who knows which foods are hard for her to digest should forgo these on the day of the game.

The pregame meal should be free from tension and noise, and should please the athlete, for she will probably already be thinking about the game to come and will be a little nervous. Many coaches have their own ideas about pregame meals for their athletes. Because of individual differences and food preferences, it is impossible to say that one specific diet should be followed by the athlete. Supplements over and above a sound diet will not affect an athlete's performance physically, but it's possible that they will affect her psychologically. Therefore, if an athlete feels she must have a particular food at the training table or the pregame meal, her morale might benefit from having it even though there is no physical gain.

There are no miracle supplements that can help the athlete perform better. Neither does one meal make a big difference in the body's efficiency. Diet must be dealt with wisely the year around, especially every day the athlete is in training. Nutrition is the same for athletes as for other people. The difference lies only in the quantity of food.

Here are some suggestions for pregame meals.

| Pregame Meal A | Pregame Meal B | Pregame Meal C |
|---|---|---|
| Bouillon | Consomme | Cream of chicken soup |
| Broiled beefsteak | Baked fish | Roast beef |
| Baked potato with butter | Creamed potatoes | Macaroni and cheese |
| English peas | Cooked carrots | Green beans |
| Toast and honey | Rolls with jelly | Rolls and honey |
| Peach in heavy syrup | Pudding or jello | Custard or ice cream |
| Milk, water, or tea | Milk, water, or tea | Milk, water, or tea |

Substitutions can be made when finances are limited, so long as the diet remains a balanced one (for instance, fish can be substituted for steak, jello for ice cream, etc.).

## DRUGS

### STIMULANTS

Stimulating drugs are sometimes used in an effort to improve athletic competition. The use of drugs, regardless of the amount or frequency, is a question that every coach must answer in the light of ethical and medical aspects. The use of drugs by athletes cannot be justified on ethical grounds because fair play and good sportsmanship is the essence of athletics. Nor can one justify the use of drugs as an artificial means of bettering performance when the whole objective of sports is to teach the person to meet stress well and to depend on her own resources in competitive situations. When drugs are used without medical supervision, they can be harmful both physiologically and psychologically. When used indiscriminately, they may lead to addiction.

One of the participants in the 1960 Olympic Games, the Danish cyclist Knud Jensen, collapsed during the 100-kilometer race and died later. An investigation showed that he had taken a drug called Ronicol, which stimulates circulation by dilating the blood vessels. His death resulted from the combination of exertion, high temperature, and the effects of the drug [46].

Some of the drugs most commonly used in athletics, and their effects, are the following [34].

1. *Ephedrine.* Elevates blood pressure, speeds up heart rate, constricts peripheral blood vessels, causes greater cardiac output, dilates the bronchioles, and stimulates the respiratory center. Has little effect on persons not suffering from asthma or emphysema.

2. *Amphetamine* (benzedrine, dexedrine). Greatly stimulates the central nervous system. Speeds up the respiratory center and increases cardiac work and output. Used to cover fatigue symptoms caused by physical exertion.

3. *Desoxyephedrine.* Stimulates heart and central nervous system. Hides effects of fatigue, but does not make recovery from fatigue faster. May become addictive.

4. *Nikethamide.* Has been taken by European athletes to compensate for the vaso-motor circulatory disturbances resulting from violent physical exertion. When too much is taken, convulsions and death may occur because of respiratory paralysis.

5. *Pentylenetetrazol.* Stimulates central nervous system and cardiovascular system; has been widely used by European athletes.

6. *Digitalis.* Increases the strength of cardiac contraction. Has been used in treatment of congestive heart failure, but should not be used by normal people.

7. *Nitroglycerin.* Relaxes smooth muscles. May have unpleasant side effects. When used in excessive doses, it converts hemoglobin to methemoglobin and anemia results.

A newer drug that has come on the scene in athletics is the *anabolic steroid* which is a male hormone. It is thought to aid in muscle-building. Consequently, some women athletes use this drug in an effort to increase their strength.

The use of drugs has become such a problem in men's athletics that the International Amateur Athletic Federation has taken a strong stand on it. The IAAF has the power to prevent any athlete from participating in amateur athletics if he is found to be using drugs to improve his athletic performance [46]. A stronger stand was also taken in the 1968 Olympics to prevent athletes from using drugs to improve their performance [51].

When we consider all the facts, the use of any type of drug—either stimulant or depressant—in athletics cannot be justified on any grounds. The coach must strictly prohibit the use of drugs. The chance that the athlete might experience harmful effects from using drugs is enough of a deterrent to outweigh any benefit that might accrue if she used them.

SMOKING AND DRINKING

Because of the widespread use of tobacco and alcohol by both athletes and non-athletes, the facts about them should be mentioned here. Even though the Surgeon General and many other authorities have recently published evidence as to the harmful effects of smoking, more people are smoking than ever before. Yet there is a significant relationship between lung cancer and smoking; heavy cigarette smokers run 20 times as great a risk of lung cancer as nonsmokers. Other health hazards that seem to be connected with smoking are cancer of the mouth, larynx, esophagus and bladder. Heart and circulatory diseases are found much more often among male smokers than nonsmokers, and respiratory diseases such as asthma and emphysema are greatly worsened by smoking [52].

Tuttle and Frey [42] found that smokers are at a disadvantage in physical efficiency in comparison with nonsmokers. Questionnaires tabulated by Cureton [7] showed that 93% of track and field athletes at the 1956 Olympics at Melbourne did not smoke while in training, and 83% had never smoked in their lives.

The athlete undoubtedly has more to lose by smoking than the average person because it is necessary for her body to operate at optimum conditions.

The American Medical Association has indicated that there is acute impairment of pulmonary function in young smokers, and that smoking brings about significant decreases in breathing capacity. Smoking also greatly hampers the ability of the body to utilize oxygen efficiently. Since the above functions are so important in the athlete's ability to perform well, the American Medical Association has stated that there is no doubt that athletes should not smoke [15].

The effects of alcohol depend on the intake and the individual's reaction to it. However, even small amounts can affect judgment, perception, reflexes, and inhibitions. Alcohol reduces the athlete's endurance because it slows down the removal of lactic acid, which results in fatigue. Alcohol is a depressant, both mentally and physically; this puts the athlete at a disadvantage, since she must operate at full speed.

Some European athletes do drink light wines or beer (sometimes even at the training table). Coaches in the U.S. vary in their training rules on alcoholic beverages: Some coaches permit them any time except the day of the game or meet, and some don't allow them at all.

Some argue that athletes who are mature should make their own decisions on this question. Others argue that drinking and training do not mix. I feel that anything detrimental to an athlete's training should be eliminated. Present knowledge seems to indicate that smoking or drinking hurt the athlete's performance. Therefore the coach should stand as firm on this issue as she or he does on proper sleep, diet, and so forth.

## REDUCTION OF INJURIES

Chances for a great team often vanish when good players are injured. Once a player has received an injury, it is too late to think about what could have been done to prevent it. Thus the coach must try to eliminate in advance any factors that might lead to injury.

First, the coach should try to prevent injuries. Second, after an athlete has been hurt, the coach must try to prevent further injury. Third, the coach must try to get the athlete back into playing condition as soon as possible.

### PREVENTION OF INJURIES

Adequate warm-up periods, good techniques in performing, and gradual conditioning can prevent many injuries. An athlete should never start strenuous activity without a warm-up period, which should be long enough to limber her up but not so long that she becomes tired before the game or practice session even begins. Warm-ups are especially needed when it is cool, or when the girl is sore or stiff from previous workouts or contests. The same thing works in reverse: Heavy practice sessions should taper off and end with light activity, to give the girl's system a chance to adjust to the letdown in demands on it.

Another aid to safety: The coach should be careful not to demand too much of the players. Forcing them to keep going when they are tired is asking for trouble, since tired muscles invite injuries.

TREATMENT OF INJURIES

Immediate treatment of such injuries as sprains, scrapes, and pulled muscles can reduce not only the pain but also the length of time the athlete will be out of action. However, the coach must never treat an injury if she is not sure of the extent of it; she should refer the girl to a doctor at once. In fact, a doctor or nurse should be on the scene during all competitive contests; naturally this is impossible during practice sessions, but the coach should know where to get professional help quickly.

The pain and swelling of sprains can be reduced by immediate application of ice packs; later on, alternating hot and cold packs can keep swelling and soreness to a minimum. Scrapes should be washed, treated with a mild antiseptic, and covered with a clean dressing. Blisters should also receive immediate care, lest they continue to be irritated.

Pulled muscles require rest. At the first sign of a strained or pulled muscle, the coach should take the girl out of the game and wrap a supporting bandage or tape around the weakened area. Here again ice is good for reducing the pain and swelling.

Always remember that *only* a qualified person should make a diagnosis or undertake treatment.

PREVENTING REINJURY

It is important to get the player back into playing condition as soon as possible. When a girl is injured and out of action for a while, she is bound to have some weakness in the muscle or joint affected. The coach should have her do specific exercises to help strengthen that area before allowing her to participate in the regular training program. If the coach fails to do this, a reinjury may occur. Since a player naturally tends to favor an injured area, the coach must watch for a change in the girl's technique in performance. If the change in movement is extreme, another joint or muscle may be put under too much stress and the athlete may end up with an even worse injury.

RE-ENTERING COMPETITION

The longer the athlete is out of action, the less range of movement she will have in the joint that was injured. Because of this, the coach must start rehabilitation as soon as possible, with exercises that will rebuild the weak muscles, such as progressive resistance exercises. A well-planned exercise program, with stretching, bending, and other flexibility exercises, improves the range of movement in stiff joints.

One of the big problems of an athlete who has been injured is the psychological factor. The pain resulting from the injury can cause the athlete to favor the hurt area out of fear of reinjury, even though the injury may have healed. If the athlete is pushed too hard before the injury has completely healed, and a reinjury does occur, this fear may become so deeply instilled that it will take the girl a long time to get over it. The coach can help her by making sure that she has regained the use of the injured joint or muscle and is in top condition before allowing her to compete again, and by trying to reinforce her confidence in her ability to play the game at her usual pace.

In summary: To reduce injuries, the coach must see that her girls are conditioned and trained well, have proper warm-up periods, use their muscles correctly to prevent strains from incorrect techniques, are treated immediately after injury, and have a sound and a wise reconditioning program.

It goes without saying that every athlete should be covered by an insurance policy and that parents of the athletes recognize the fact that the school or organization bears no financial responsibility for athletes' injuries.

## BIBLIOGRAPHY

1. Armbruster, David A., Robert H. Allen, and Bruce Harlan, "Conditioning," in *Swimming and Diving*. St. Louis: C. V. Mosby, 1958, Chapter 13

2. Bannister, R. G., "Muscular Effort," *British Medical Bulletin,* **12**, 3222, 1956

3. Barney, Vernon, Cynthia Hirst, and Clayne Jensen, *Conditioning Exercises.* St. Louis: C. V. Mosby, 1965

4. Broer, Marion, *Efficiency of Human Movement.* Philadelphia: W. B. Saunders, 1960

5. Brouha, Lucien, "Physiology of Training, Including Age and Sex Differences," *Journal of Sports Medicine and Physical Fitness,* **2**, 3–11, March 1962

6. Brouha, Lucien, "Training," in *Science and Medicine of Exercise and Sports,* edited by Warren R. Johnson. New York: Harper, 1960, Chapter 21

7. Cureton, Thomas K., "New Training Methods and Dietary Supplements are Responsible for Many of the New Records," *Athletic Journal,* **45**, 12–14, January 1962

8. Cureton, Thomas K., "What About Wheat Germ?" *Scholastic Coach,* **29**, 24, November 1959

9. DeLorme, T. L., and A. L. Watkins, *Progressive Resistance Exercise.* New York: Appleton-Century-Crofts, 1951

10. DeVries, H. A., *Physiology of Exercise for Physical Education and Athletics.* Dubuque, Iowa: Wm. C. Brown, 1966

11. Durnin, J. V. G. A., "The Influence of Nutrition," in Proceedings of the International Symposium on Physical Activity and Cardiovascular Health, *Canadian Medical Association Journal,* **96**, 12, March 25, 1967

12. Epskamp, R., "Rx for Distance Runners," *Athletic Journal,* **43**, 16, March 1963

13. Fait, Hollis, *et al., A Manual of Physical Education Activities.* Philadelphia: W. B. Saunders, 1961

14. Guild, W., "Pre-Event Nutrition," in *Exercise and Fitness.* New York: Athletic Institute, 1960

15. Hein, Fred V., and Dana L. Farnsworth, *Living.* Chicago: Scott, Foresman, 1965

16. Hemmingway, A., "Physiological Bases of Training," *Ergonomics,* **2**, 133, February 1959

17. Henry, F. M., and W. E. Berg, "Physical and Performance Changes in Athletic Conditioning," *Journal of Applied Physiology,* **3**, 103, 1950

18. Hettinger, T., *The Physiology of Strength.* Springfield, Ill.: Charles C. Thomas, 1961

19. Humphrey, James H., *et al., Readings in Health Education.* Dubuque, Iowa: Wm. C. Brown, 1964

20. Jensen, Clayne R., "The Controversy of Warm-Up," *Athletic Journal,* **47**, 24, December 1966

21. Jokl, E., *Sports in the Cultural Pattern of the World.* Helsinki: Institute of Occupational Health, 1956

22. Kiputh, R. J. H., *Swimming.* New York: A. S. Barnes, 1942

23. "Liquid Pre-Game Meal," *Scholastic Coach,* **31**, 56–58, January 1962

24. Logan, G., and Egstrom, G. H., "The Effects of Slow and Fast Stretching on the Sacrofemoral Angle," *Journal of the Association for Physical and Mental Rehabilitation,* **15**, 85, 1961

25. Luke, G. Brother, *Coaching High School Track and Field.* Englewood Cliffs, N.J.: Prentice-Hall, 1958

26. Mathews, D. K., R. W. Stacy, and G. N. Hoover, *Physiology of Muscular Activity.* New York: The Ronald Press, 1964

27. Mayer, J., "Nutrition and Athletic Performance," *Physiological Reviews,* **40**, 369, 1960

28. McCue, Betty F., "Flexibility Measurement of College Women," *Research Quarterly,* **24**, 316, 1953

29. Metheny, E. L., *et al.,* "Some Physiologic Responses of Women and Men to Moderate and Strenuous Exercise," *American Journal of Physiology,* **137**, 318, 1942

30. Meyer, Margaret H., and Germaine Pella, "The Effect of Hard Laboratory Exercise on the Total and Differential Leucocyte Count of Young Women," *Research Quarterly,* **18**, 271, December 1947

31. Miller, Kenneth D., *Track and Field for Girls.* New York: The Ronald Press, 1964

32. Morehouse, L. E., "Physiological Bases of Strength Development," *Exercise and Fitness.* New York: Athletic Institute, 1960

33. Morehouse, L. E., *Physiology of Exercise,* fifth edition. St. Louis: C. V. Mosby, 1967

34. Morehouse, L. E., and Philip Rasch, *Sports Medicine for Trainers.* Philadelphia: W. B. Saunders, 1963

35. Muller, E. A., "The Physiological Bases of Rest Pauses in Heavy Work," *Quarterly Journal of Experimental Physiology,* **38**, 205, 1953

36. Osius, Theodore G., "Food for the Training Table," *Scholastic Coach,* **30**, 64–67, October 1960

37. Rasch, Philip, and Roger Burke, *Kinesiology and Applied Anatomy.* Philadelphia: Lea and Febiger, 1963

38. Scott, Phebe, and Virginia Crafts, *Track and Field for Girls and Women.* New York: Appleton-Century-Crofts, 1964

39. Sorani, Robert, *Circuit Training.* Dubuque, Iowa: Wm. C. Brown, 1966

40. Steinhaus, A. H., *Toward an Understanding of Health and Physical Education.* Dubuque, Iowa: Wm. C. Brown, 1963

41. Taylor, Henry Longstreet, "Exercise and Metabolism," in *Science and Medicine of Exercise and Sports,* edited by Warren R. Johnson. New York: Harper, 1960, Chapter 8

42. Tuttle, W. W., and H. Frey, "A Study of the Physical Efficiency of College Women as Shown by the Pulse-Ratio Test," *Research Quarterly,* **1**, 17–25, December 1930

43. Van Itallie, Theodore, Leonardo Sinisterra, and Fredrick J. Stare, "Nutrition and Athletic Performance," in *Science and Medicine of Exercise and Sports,* edited by Warren R. Johnson. New York: Harper, 1960, Chapter 15

44. Vannier, Maryhelen, and Hally Beth Poindexter, *Physical Activities for College Women.* Philadelphia: W. B. Saunders, 1964

45. *Weight Training in Sports and Physical Education.* Editorial committee: Frank D. Sills, Laurence E. Morehouse, and Thomas DeLorme. Washington, D.C.: AAHPER, 1962

46. Wilt, Fred, "From the Desk of Fred Wilt," *Track Technique,* **25**, 770, September 1966

47. Wilt, Fred, "Training Trends in Distance Running," *Scholastic Coach,* **6**, 10, February 1964

48. Woods, Richard R., "Liquid Food—An Aid to Athletes," *Athletic Journal,* **43**, 50, September 1962

49. Youngen, Lois, "A Comparison of Reaction and Movement Times of Women Athletes and Non-Athletes," *Research Quarterly,* **30**, 349, October 1959

50. Perrine, James J., "Isokinetic Exercise," *Journal of Health, Physical Education, and Recreation,* **39**, 40, May 1968

51. Underwood, John, "Games in Trouble," *Sports Illustrated,* **29**, 45, September 30, 1968

52. *Smoking and Health,* Report of the Advisory Committee to the Surgeon General of the Public Health Service. Princeton, New Jersey: D. Van Nostrand, 1964

53. Mortensen, Jesse P., and John M. Cooper, *Track and Field for Coach and Athlete.* Englewood Cliffs, N.J.: Prentice-Hall, 1959

# chapter five planning the season

Planning the season can be fun and exciting. A coach must start with a basic idea and mould her team in a desired direction. If she does a good job of coaching, by the season's end she will reach the goal she set out to reach.

## OBJECTIVES FOR THE SEASON

[One often thinks of "the season" as the time during which competitive meets are held. However, taking into account the specialization and year-round training programs of highly skilled athletes, the coach should include the off season, the pre-season, and the season itself in her planning. If the coach is working with a person who is of Olympic caliber, or is an outstanding competitor on a national level, she will probably want to work out a program of year-round practice of the skill involved, tapering off during the off season just enough to prevent staleness. However, most athletes prefer to devote the off months to an activity that has no connection with their chosen competitive field. This change in activity eliminates staleness and boredom and brings the athlete back to her sport with a refreshed mental attitude.]

[ Whether the coach considers the season as being year-round, several months, or only a month or so, there are some objectives she should keep in mind as she plans the program: (1) conditioning the athlete, (2) helping her perfect her skills, and (3) seeing to it that the athlete is mentally prepared.]

Conditioning should be a gradual process, beginning at a level that will not produce excessive fatigue and working progressively until the athlete is at peak condition for competition. The coach and the player must be aware that development of the cardiovascular, muscular, and respiratory systems can be accomplished only by taking the athlete beyond what she normally does. This means simply that discomfort is going to be necessary. An athlete who is unaware of the fact that conditioning means keeping on when the lungs burn and the muscles ache and the heart feels as though it is pounding a hundred times a minute will probably feel it is the end of the world for her. But this pain is necessary if the athlete is to reach a new level of conditioning.

The coach's second objective is to help the athlete improve her skills and perfect her coordination so that during the competitive event she can move naturally and without conscious thought. The adage "Practice makes perfect" is misleading, for practice makes perfect only if the person has practiced correctly, with the right techniques.

During practice sessions the coach should try to polish the rough spots and smooth out errors of performance. Once the athlete gets into competition, she must feel confident that she can perform her task without worrying about *how* she should do it.

The good coach should be aware of current material in her field and should pass this information on to her players. She should not be afraid of changing her coaching methods if someone proves that a new method is better, and she should seek up-to-date aids in getting the most out of the athlete. Many coaches use film to catch the athlete in motion in order to study her movements at a pace that can be regulated by the projector. Others plot the movements of their athletes. Some analyze each movement step by step to determine whether the athlete is getting the most out of her talents. Regardless of the method the coach uses to help the athlete perfect her skills, the coach must be tactful and remember that there is more to the individual than physical skills. Suggestions made at the right moment and in the right tone of voice are an important factor in coaching the skilled athlete.

The coach's third objective in planning the season is to see that her players are mentally prepared. With the stress on perfection in the sports world, and with the tendency of the top athlete to put in four to six hours a day practicing, an athlete's ability to enter competition mentally refreshed is one of the biggest factors in efficient performance. The stale athlete feels no joy in competition, and consequently does not have that extra spark of energy that is so important. Athletes who train the year around, or train steadily for months on end, generally do experience staleness. It is a natural reaction to stress, and simply means that the athlete needs a different outlook on her competition. In most cases, she only needs to get away from her sport for a few days and relax completely by engaging in an activity that is altogether different. A coach can help ward off staleness by varying the means for practicing: A change in drills, a change in environment for workout sessions, even a change in equipment might bring about the desired result. The coach should use her imagination to make practice a challenge and fun, and should be aware of the player's temperament and emotions, which usually give warning of approaching staleness.

Another factor in mental preparedness is understanding the strategy of the competitive event. Thinking while playing is an important part of competition. The athlete's ability to adjust plays a large role here, for strategy often involves a change to counteract the plans of the opponent. Strategy is connected with the ability to analyze, and after analysis, to come up with a plan of action that is effective. Naturally, because of the limit on time-outs, the coach can't stop game action and give suggestions at any point where new strategy should be employed. Therefore the coach should help her players to react in an intelligent, thinking way under game conditions.

Taking into account these three objectives—conditioning, perfection of skills, and mental alertness—the coach can usually break the season down into three parts: (1) off season, (2) pre-season, and (3) competitive season.

*The off season.* Unless an athlete is in training for international competition there are usually several months during which she is not involved in her sport. These months should be used to maintain a high plateau of physical conditioning and to regain a fresh mental attitude.

During the off season, the athlete should participate in activities that demand a lot of her physically, especially in endurance and strength. If she has been competing in track and field during the season, then gymnastics, hockey, speedball, tennis, swimming, basketball, etc., would be a good change. Any sport that demands good cardiovascular, muscular, and respiratory development and that keeps her in sound physical condition should be encouraged. A sport that has some carry-over value—as far as similarity of movement is concerned—for the sport that is her specialty during the competitive season, is excellent for a change, since it gives the athlete added practice while giving her a chance to get rid of any possible mental staleness. For instance, the tennis serve is very similar to the overhand softball throw, while the forehand in tennis is similar to batting and involves hand–eye coordination.

A change to weight training would be beneficial to the athlete whose sport demands strength, such as gymnastics, for example, provided that a program was worked out to develop the muscles needed for this training.

The coach should suggest off-season activities to her players which will give them a chance to remain in top physical condition while relaxing mentally.

*The pre-season.* The pre-season is the time to perfect skills, work on fundamentals, ponder strategy, and to strive for a high level of conditioning for a specific sport. Pre-season training should aim at improving coordination, putting together a team that runs smoothly, encouraging good mental and physical habits that will carry over during the season, and teaching athletes how to analyze and improve their performances in gamelike situations.

The program should be geared to the specific sport, with other activities put in the background except as relaxation measures. There should be a stepped-up program of conditioning, with emphasis on strengthening the muscles involved in the sport and improving the player's endurance. This program should lead to a gradual improvement in physical fitness, with the peak being reached during the season, preferably at the latter part if there is any danger that she'll reach her top efficiency too early and then slack off in her ability to perform.

Basic skills should be practiced faithfully. The coach should make it a point to take time to check the athlete often to make sure she has not developed bad habits or is working on a technique incorrectly. Discussion should be encouraged, so that if something is bothering an athlete or if there is anything she doesn't understand she will feel free to bring it up and have it clarified before the season starts.

A knowledge of strategy is important. New plays and methods should be worked in and practiced until they are second nature to players. The coach should set up gamelike situations and watch the way her players react under pressure. She should simulate close-game situations and teach her players to react with poise and confidence. When a game is lost because of players' indecision or lack of understanding of strategy, the fault lies with the coach, for knowledge that is not handed down to the players for use in on-the-spot situations is knowledge lost. A coach can't always get a time-out in crucial situations, since she can't stop a competitive meet during a crisis and send in instructions from the bench, nor should she depend on this even if she could. Part of competition is making split-second decisions and keeping a cool head under pressure. These things should be taught before the season begins.

If a coach is working with a team, she should evaluate her personnel before the season, and set up a pattern of play to fit the skill level of her players. The team should be organized into a workable unit that should improve and become even more unified as the season progresses. If the coach is working with a person who must compete as an individual rather than with a team, she must make sure the player has a feeling of loyalty to a cause. A person who competes for something other than herself has something worth while to compete for, and can usually call on a reserve store of energy when the going gets rough.

Also during the pre-season, the coach must be sure her athletes understand specific techniques they may be working on. To tell an athlete to jump higher to get over the bar is not much use to the girl. But if the coach explains the effects of the body's center of gravity and how to get the hips over the bar, this explanation will help her performance. Knowing how to analyze movement and how to apply scientific principles is an invaluable aid to both coach and player.

Many players make the same mistake over and over simply because they do not know what they are doing wrong. The coach does not want to make major adjustments in the habits of a skilled athlete, but helping her understand movement and strategy will undoubtedly benefit her.

## THE COMPETITIVE SEASON

The competitive season is the time when events, meets, and games are held, and includes the period between meets. The coach must plan three things during the competitive season: (1) scheduling of games, (2) the actual playing of the game, and (3) preparation between games.

*Scheduling.* The scheduling of games depends on the skill level of the athletes the coach is working with. Coaches of junior high, high school, or college girls should consult the current DGWS Guidelines for the length of period for competition, the number of practice sessions per week, etc. (see also Chapter 7 of this book).

Games should be played against other schools and organizations of approximately the same skill level. The schedule must not be too crowded or too long, since the girls have to have enough time to do justice to their studies and social life. In leagues outside the school system, sound judgment should be exercised in setting up a schedule that is beneficial for the participants, when the season is not regulated by guidelines and standards set up by a governing body.

Good officiating is a must, and the coach must know the type of officials being employed. For any highly competitive meet, officials who hold a DGWS National or comparable ratings should be obtained. If qualified women officials are available, good. If not, qualified men should be used in preference to unqualified women.

*Competing.* The game is the culmination of everything that has gone before, in off-season, pre-season, and seasonal training. This is the moment of truth for the coach as well as for the players.�

During the contest, if the strategy chosen is not working or if there are some unforeseen circumstances, the coach must be able to face facts and make changes accordingly. Of course, on-the-spot changes do not always work, often because players are unprepared, so the coach must not blame her players if the execution fails when there has been no practice beforehand. It is thus a good idea to set up *two* plans before a contest and to practice both. Then you are prepared for the possibility that plan A may not work, and you can change to plan B.

Depending on the type of meet, the coach may be able to offer suggestions as the competition is progressing. For instance, in track and field, there is enough time between events to enable the coach to talk to her athlete. In games as hockey, volleyball, tennis, etc., there is some time, but very little, and only at specified times. Be careful not to confuse or frustrate the athlete by suggesting changes that have not been tried or talked about before, unless it is a very simple thing that the athlete can do without a lot of thought. Learn how each person reacts in different situations and utilize this knowledge. Some athletes are great when they have a lead, then fold up under pressure. Others fight like mad when they are behind and then relax when they get ahead. Still others are indifferent about the results unless they are spurred by a strong emotion such as loyalty, personal pride, fear, or anger.

When the team or the player gets behind during the competition, the coach must draw on her full powers to keep morale high, for once the athlete has lost heart and is no longer willing to struggle, then the battle has truly been lost.

The means by which a coach gets a team up for a contest and keeps them up during the playing time is strictly up to the coach, for different individuals and teams require different methods. A coach's way of doing this should not be questioned except when the method is harmful to the athlete, either psychologically or physically.

Coaches who can time after time produce athletes who are psyched up for contests are usually the great coaches, for they are able to draw on the full resources of the players. Each coach should try to gain an understanding of her personnel that will enable her to use psychological methods to urge her team on to greater things, while at the same time realizing that some means are not worth the ends because of the negative effects on the athlete.

Some of the more common methods for getting a team or an individual up for a game are:

1. Appealing to their sense of pride as real competitors, even though the odds are against them.

2. Referring to past events which would increase their determination to win. ("Remember last year when we were inexperienced, and this team beat us 40 points by keeping their first team in the whole game?")

3. Reminding players of the importance of a particular contest. (*"If* we win tonight, we will get to compete in the regional tournament.")

4. Stressing belief in a team's ability to produce, and reinforcing their confidence by telling them they *can do it*.

5. Reminding them that even the top teams in the country are human. ("They wear the same brand of shoes we do.")

6. Pointing out the strengths of the team or the individual. ("We are in much better condition than this team, and we should still be going strong in the last minutes.")

7. Stressing the point that upsets happen every day, and naming some recent upsets that the players are familiar with.

8. Telling the team or player how a particular opponent can be beaten. ("If you keep the ball deep and to the backhand corner, she can't kill you with her forehand.")

Another important function of the coach during the game is to see that players who are injured get immediate medical attention. Some coaches allow injured players to keep on competing because they feel that the outcome of the contest depends on this particular individual. Needless to say, the coach is doing the player an injustice if she lets her go back in when there is a possibility of further injury or increased pain, even though the athlete may beg to continue playing. Follow the advice of a doctor or a person trained in first aid.

If a manager is not part of the team, the coach must see that necessary equipment and supplies are available for the competitive event. This includes any equipment utilized in the meet, as well as towels and sweat suits if each player does not bring her own. In endurance events, cool water or sliced oranges are good for replenishing water that has been lost through perspiration.

*Preparation between meets.* The period between games or meets is the time for ironing out any rough spots and for making any adjustments in the team's performance. It usually helps to review the preceding game, to discuss what was done wrong, and to point out the good things that were accomplished. If a team is fortunate enough to have films to review, this is the time for checking individual performance and to review the contest play by play. Chalk board, audiovisual aids, etc., can be used to advantage. Once the previous game has been discussed, it should be put out of mind, and all effort should be concentrated on the coming event. If new plays or strategy are necessary for the upcoming opponent, these should be practiced diligently.

Between contests the coach should be sensitive to the team's morale. A defeat in a previous contest can lead to a negative attitude that can influence the next contest; in the same way a previous victory can lead to overconfidence. For this reason, the coach must stress the importance of the way a team competes, rather than stressing victory alone. A team trained to give its best at all times is conscious only of doing its best, and the fear of defeat is not nearly as great as the fear of playing poorly. This type of team is oriented to playing the game with pride; the joy of accomplishment and self-giving becomes a pleasure of competing. This is not to say that a team shouldn't play to win, for the object of competition is to determine a winner, but winning shouldn't overshadow the methods used. By the same token, a coach should not ask her team to play poorly to keep from running up the score against an inferior opponent. To train a team to compete well and then to ask it to play poorly is an insult to talent. Instead, take care to schedule games against teams of equal skill; in cases of mismatched opponents, substitute bench-warmers in order to keep the score down.

Emphasize things in the order of their importance: *one*, to compete with honor and pride, and *two*, to channel effort constructively so that victory is a natural outcome, but not the only desired outcome.

Between games, the rehabilitation of injured athletes should be undertaken. A hurt athlete should do exercises to strengthen the injured joint or muscle, and should try to prevent strain or further injury. If whirlpools, heat treatments, etc., are available, they should be utilized. If trainers are not available to the girls, perhaps they can get help and advice from the men's trainer.

Another objective between games is to see that athletes maintain their conditioning, but do not overwork and become stale. A change in workout procedure and even a day off may be necessary.

## PRACTICE SCHEDULE

The way the time is spent during a workout or practice session is an important consideration. Depending on the nature of the sport, there will be some minor differences in the schedule given here. Basically, however, the practice period should consist of: (1) instruction, (2) warm-ups, (3) drills, and (4) practice under game conditions.

*Instruction.* Instruction is a very important part of the practice period, for it is at this time that errors in performance, strategy, etc., should be corrected and worked on. Instruction can take place during any phase of the session; it precedes any change in practice routine. The highly skilled athlete needs individual help less often than the novice, but still needs it in a more specialized way.

In instructing the less-skilled person, be specific in explaining the movement to be performed, why it should be done in a certain way, and what results can be expected when it is done correctly. However, the skilled athlete should concentrate more on the overall movement than on movement of a given muscle; she can be confused by a suggestion that she contract a specific muscle in a specific sequence to accomplish a skill. More general suggestions give the skilled girl freedom to concentrate on the total job to be done rather than the step-by-step movement of her body. At the same time, don't be too general in your suggestions. Telling the volleyball player to jump higher to spike the ball, if she doesn't know how to jump higher, is like telling her to create a miracle. But telling her to bend her knees, push hard with her feet and toes, and reach upward with her arms will help her do what you want her to do.

For both the novice and the skilled player, a new movement or a new skill requires understanding. When the athlete is learning a new motor skill, she must be given a clear picture of what she is to do and how to go about doing it. To mention to a diver a new skill such as a one-and-a-half-gainer can confuse her if she does not know just what it is and how it is to be executed.

In describing a new motor skill, use terms that are familiar to the athlete. In some cases you may be able to relate the new skill to one she has already perfected: for instance, relating the movements for the overhead smash in tennis to the movement made in serving the tennis ball.

The coach who knows something about kinesiology and mechanical analysis is way ahead of the coach who does not. If you know when and how to apply leverage, force, spin, and other physical factors, you can help an athlete to perform better. Even though you may not have had a lot of experience in different sports, if you have a basic knowledge of mechanics, you'll be able to relate this knowledge to areas that are less familiar.

The body build of an athlete should be taken into consideration because it can limit her potential in a particular sport. If she wants to compete in an activity in which her physical makeup is bound to limit her, she should be aware of the fact. The coach who realizes her athletes' limitations due to body build should build her system of play according to the personnel she has. A volleyball team composed of short, speedy players might be more successful playing defense and forcing errors from the opponents, while the volleyball team with plenty of height would be more apt to compile their points from spikes and offensive rather than defensive play.

Another responsibility of the coach during instruction is to see that injuries do not go unnoticed. *All* injuries, regardless of how minor they may seem to the player, should be reported to the coach. Even a small injury can be exaggerated if the activity is too strenuous for the weakened area. The coach should see to it that injuries are diagnosed and cared for by a doctor or a nurse, since there is always the possibility that she may be held liable if improper care and treatment are given.

Instruction—whether it deals with strategy, safety, motor skills and movement, morale, teamwork, or is simply a result of the coach's interest in the player—gives the athlete a sounder basis for performing well.

*Warm-ups.* The effects of warming up are controversial; however, it seems that specific warm-ups done for a specific reason are almost always beneficial. Any activity that involves coordination and timing seems to be helped by a warm-up period that gives the athlete the chance to make minor changes. The girl who shoots free-throws before a game, for example, has a chance to improve her timing. Also, an activity that demands extensive stretching and bending, such as dancing and gymnastics, can be improved by a warm-up period.

If an athlete is competing outdoors on a cold day, or in a cold gym, a warm-up period is especially needed. Activity before competition increases circulation, helps warm up the muscles, and aids kinesthetic awareness. When a sense of touch is involved, such as there is in handling a ball, a warm-up before the game is almost a necessity if a girl is to play her best. If her performance depends on her ability to move quickly, or if excessive strain or tension is placed on the muscles and joints during competition, warm-ups tend to reduce injury and improve performance.

Research studies [5] indicate that warm-ups are beneficial to performance of motor skills, but the effect seems to be influenced by many factors:

1. Type of skill to be performed.
2. Method of warm-up used.
3. Physical condition, age, sex, and psychological condition of the performer.
4. Intensity of the warm-up.
5. Length of rest period between warm-up and performance.

The main reason a person should warm up is to increase the internal temperature of the body, which enables the muscles to function better. When a girl has warmed up, she is capable of a greater range of movement, has better timing and coordination, and is not as likely to suffer an injury [2].

In warm-up, since there is an increase in body temperature, the tonus of the muscles improves; as a result they are more ready to respond to activity. As circulation and respiration also improve, a uniformity of temperature results; therefore the muscles' ability to respond is equalized [1]. There is also evidence that warming up improves the athlete's endurance because it leads to an increase of maximum oxygen intake of approximately 5% [4].

Opinions on the amount of warm-up needed varies from several minutes to an hour or more. The time spent in warm-up exercises varies with the event, as do the exercises used. Basketball players may spend only 15 or 20 minutes warming up; gymnasts, dancers, and track and field participants may take much longer. The amount of time an athlete takes to warm up also depends largely on her conditioning. A warm-up could lose all its advantages if the girl warmed up for so long that she was tired before she actually engaged in competition.

Some athletes have used hot baths, massages, and other means of heating the body, although there is no proof that these means are better than exercise. The exercises used to warm up vary, from bending and stretching exercises to intense practice on the specific skills to be used during the game.

Although most coaches and athletes feel that warm-ups are a very important part of preparing for a contest, the fact remains that many players go into a game or a meet without any warm-up whatsoever, and play exceptionally well without it. At the same time, many who have a sufficient warm-up period perform poorly.

The important thing in warming up is that the athlete should feel sufficiently loose and relaxed. After she has warmed up by running, bending, stretching, and other light exercises, she should do movements similar to those she will be using as she competes, slowly building up her ability to go full speed.

*Drills.* There are three main reasons for using drills: (1) as a warm-up, (2) for conditioning, and (3) for improvement of skills.

Select drills that will produce the results you want. If conditioning is the main objective, choose drills that will improve conditioning, with warm-up and improvement of skills a secondary objective. Some drills fulfill all three objectives at the same time.

Drills are a good way to improve the skill of an athlete by repeated movement. Be sure that players understand how the drill should be executed, for a drill done incorrectly is a hindrance rather than a help. Keep drills as simple as possible to give the players a chance to concentrate on their execution of it. To prevent boredom, change drills every 5 or 10 minutes.

*Practice Under Game or Meet Conditions.* Practicing skills under game or meet conditions is necessary to good performance. You can achieve this by setting up an actual practice game, or by using drills that contain elements of the competition to be engaged in. Situations that require strategy are especially valuable during practice sessions.

A team or an individual athlete should be trained to react well under pressure. Coaches should not expect their players to play with poise and confidence in a tight game if they have never been trained to react in this manner. Practice sessions that require the athlete to press hard and to give everything she's got will pay dividends during competition.

Every coach can come up with situations that simulate game conditions, in which the team must be on their toes to win. The volleyball coach might tell team A that they have a one-point lead and need one more point to win the game, but team B is serving. Team A has to get the serve and make the point or else lose the game. The hockey coach might give the red team the ball and tell the blue team they are behind one goal with three and a half minutes left in the game. The track coach might give her number 2 runner a foot lead in the 100-yard dash and tell her number 1 girl she has to make up the difference to win the event, etc.

Another way of simulating game conditions is to set up a team with characteristics similar to those of the opponent to be faced. If a tennis player must compete against a left-handed player who serves well and rushes the net, bring in someone who is left-handed and can rush the net. If the basketball team is to play an opponent that uses a double post on offense and a man-to-man full-court press, set up this type of situation and get the team to practice against it. Some situations cannot be simulated, but the mental attitude can be: Explain the characteristics of the opponent to be faced, and what the players should expect; have an athlete scout her opponent when possible.

In setting up these tight situations, be careful that you give the underdog a chance for a possible victory, provided they keep their heads and react well under the pressure. To set up a situation in which the team knows it doesn't have a chance is to defeat the purpose, and won't result in hustle or determination. Afterward, discuss the reasons why the team managed to win, or why they failed to.

Another advantage of practicing under gamelike conditions is to give the team an idea of how it should pace itself. Many coaches work their players harder during practice than they would have to work during competition, which makes the game seem like play because of the previous conditioning. However, some events require that the athlete pace herself for the best results. The long-distance run, free exercise in gymnastics, and softball pitching are examples of cases in which the athlete must conserve energy or work within a limited framework which should be learned under gamelike conditions.

When an athlete knows that so-and-so-much time is left, or that there must still be a toss of so many feet, or that there are so many yards left to run, psychological factors play a part. Knowing what bounds she must work in gives an athlete added confidence. If the contest is not so different from things she has experienced during practice sessions, things will be much easier for her.

Most butterflies in the stomach result from fear of the unknown or from being afraid one cannot measure up to the competition. Practice sessions that enable a person to recognize her attributes and weaknesses permit her to look at herself under pressure and to know what she can expect of herself and her teammates. Knowing that the world does not fall apart when the bowler doesn't hit a 250 or when the hockey player misses a tackle in a crucial moment helps a girl accept the fact that she can only do her best and hope that it's enough. But when an athlete is thrown into a situation without any previous experience to draw from, she doesn't know what she is capable of doing, and is hampered by fear of the worst unknown area there is: the self.

Therefore, during practice sessions, try to develop leadership in each individual. Especially in team sports, work with the captain to see that she can keep a level head while making quick decisions. This can be done through question-and-answer periods, stress on strategy, and practicing under tight game conditions. Audiovisual aids—such as films, blackboards, posters, etc.—can be used to help the athlete's thinking. The ability to analyze situations and to make decisions based on an understanding of strategy and personnel are good weapons for coach as well as athlete.

## BIBLIOGRAPHY

1. Allen, George H., *Complete Book of Winning Football Drills.* Englewood Cliffs, N.J.: Prentice-Hall, 1959

2. Capen, Edward K., *et al., Physical Fitness.* Dubuque, Iowa: Wm. C. Brown, 1966

3. Morehouse, Laurence E., and Philip J. Rasch, *Sports Medicine for Trainers.* Philadelphia: W. B. Saunders, 1963

4. Taylor, Henry Longstreet, "Exercise and Metabolism," in *Science and Medicine of Exercise and Sports*, edited by Warren R. Johnson. New York: Harper, 1960, Chapter 8

5. Van Grundy, William, "More About Warm-Up," *Scholastic Coach,* **34**, 44–45, May 1965

# chapter six prerequisites for champions

What makes the difference between the champion and the nonchampion? There is no ready-made formula, no pat answer. There are three factors in athletics—the physical, mental, and emotional attributes of the performer—and the perfection of all three seems to make the difference between excellence and near-excellence. Some athletes are gifted in one or two of these areas, but the real champion, the outstanding athlete, is one who has developed her resources to a high degree in all three areas.

## PHYSICAL SKILLS

We all admire the grace and poise of the athlete who has worked until she has perfected her physical skills. The smooth stroke of a tennis player, the spinning action of the diver, the gliding run of a distance runner, the coordinated rhythm of a gymnast, and the powerful strokes of the swimmer are works of art. And like all works of art, they are the result of hard work. Such skills are learned through repetition over a long period of time.

True, some people are gifted with bodies more readily adaptable to sports than others. The sprinter with long legs, the tennis player with height and a long reach, the golfer with long arms and good leverage, and the high jumper with small hips undoubtedly have advantages over people with different body types, provided they have equally developed coordination and strength. However, even athletes with body builds that give them an advantage in a specific sport can be beaten by athletes with less height and less strength when the opponents have practiced more and worked harder on perfecting what potential they have.

Then, too, background and previous experience in the physical world may limit the point some people can reach within a given time. The absolute beginner in bowling will probably be unable to reach winning form in a year; but the bowler who had experience over a period of years and stopped bowling for some reason can probably get back into peak form within a year or less.

Another aspect of a person's physical development is her capacity or potential, or the limits beyond which she cannot go. Some athletes are so physically gifted that

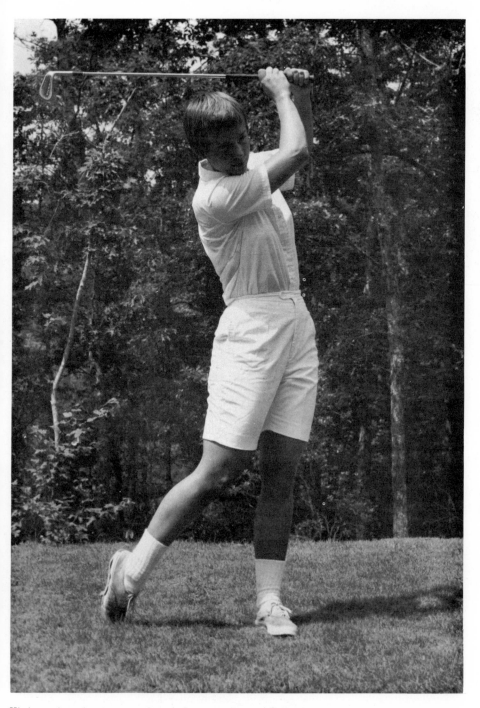

Hitting an iron shot (courtesy Joseph C. Bowles, Brevard College).

there seems to be no limit to what they can do by dedication and hard work. Others reach a point at which further improvement is impossible, regardless of the time and effort they put in. The broad jumper who lacks speed will reach a point beyond which her jump cannot be improved without improving her speed before takeoff. But if she has reached the limit of her speed, will power alone cannot make her move faster. The high jumper who has short legs is limited in the distance she can jump, even after she has reached her full potential in timing, push-off, and lift. The basketball player who is short may make an excellent guard, but there are limits to her rebounding power because she can jump only so high into the air.

The girl who starts young is more likely to reach her full potential physically than the girl who engages in sports at a later age. This fact is being brought closer to home by the many young athletes who are breaking world records. Examples: Karen Muir, who held the world swimming record at 13. Randy Matson, the shot putter. Jim Ryun, who was the fastest miler in the world while he was still in high school, and who is still breaking records today. Youth has the advantage of speed and endurance, and in events that do not require strength over and above everything else, the young person who develops her talents to the $n$th degree definitely has the advantage.

Coaching is another important aspect of developing physical skills. The person who has learned to perform correctly and with efficient techniques can accomplish much more than the person who is limited by bad techniques.

So the development of physical skills is determined by several factors. Some of the more important are: (1) age at which the person begins training, (2) body build and physical characteristics, (3) good or poor coaching, (4) time put in on practicing or developing skills, and (5) previous experience which is similar or has carry-over value in the sport.

Champions must have more than physical skills, as we know from the cases of Glenn Cunningham, Ben Hogan, and others who overcame tremendous physical handicaps to become champions in their chosen sports. They combined determination and desire with talent; or one might say that they cultivated their mental and emotional skills along with their physical skills.

## MENTAL SKILLS

In sports, the development of mental skills is just as important as the development of physical skills. Yet many coaches neglect this area because it is less tangible.

The athlete who has learned to *think* during practice is a much better player than the one who, during competition, thinks about everything except what she is doing. The subject of mental skill is sometimes covered under the heading of strategy, but the thought process in sports is much more complicated than strategy. To know what one should do and to understand why one should do it are two different things. An athlete can memorize the best angles for shots and the correct way to do a spike, but if she fails to understand why she should perform in a certain way, she does not have one of the most powerful weapons: the ability to analyze movements and make corrections when needed that improves an athlete's game on the spot.

Many athletes make the same mistake over and over. It's nòt necessarily that they aren't thinking about what they are doing; in most cases it is that they don't really know what they are doing wrong. Therefore the athlete should be taught to be a thinker in the fullest sense of the word, and the younger she learns, the better. She should be kinesthetically aware of her movements. She should be able to break each movement down into parts and analyze them if things aren't going right. If she is able to note an opponent's weaknesses and incorrect movements, this power of observation gives her an advantage. She should be able to make split-second decisions on the spot. She can do this if she has been taught to react with confidence and poise, and if she knows that if she makes a mistake she can figure out what it was and go on from there, applying good principles the next time the same thing happens.

Another mental skill is determination and will power. If an athlete isn't willing to sacrifice and to work daily on perfecting her skills, she doesn't have much chance of competing against topnotch performers. Many athletes work four or five hours a day, 12 months a year. The girl who can't stick to a schedule and who doesn't have the mental discipline to eliminate anything that might be harmful to her training seldom rises above the level of the average.

The champion athlete must also have self-confidence. Self-confidence comes through self-evaluation. If she has looked at herself objectively and faced her limitations and strengths, she is more apt to believe in herself because she won't attempt the impossible and then weaken her self-confidence by failing to achieve it. Another thing that adds to self-confidence in one's ability to perform correctly in a game situation is to practice a skill over and over so that one is able to perform it correctly in a practice situation.

Another trait well worth cultivating in the athlete is a positive attitude. People are often awed by the tremendous performances of athletes under pressure. Some athletes never seem to perform better than they do when they are backed into a corner. Then they seem to draw on some undeveloped resources. This is usually called "guts," or having an attitude of "I can do it and I will do it." The athlete must feel that she *can* do it and *will* do it.

The athlete must develop the ability to face what seem to be insurmountable odds and refuse to quit until the contest is over. People always admire the scrappy underdog who has heart, for she is the one who can pull off an upset. People support a certain team or athlete even when they know the odds are against them, simply because everyone knows they are going to battle right down to the wire, and with a few breaks might be able to win, mainly because they are fighters. This ability to stick out a contest even when one is behind, and to put out completely all the way is often the difference between being good or great. How else do underrated teams pull off upsets? In many cases, it is simply that they refuse to lie down and die. Even with the odds against them, they go into competition determined to do their best, to give every ounce of effort they have every second of the game. This ability to never give up, even when the chances for victory seems nonexistent, is pure pride.

The athlete must, in addition, have the mental trait of being able to work with teammates. Teamwork is vital. Most of our great athletes are team players. They are outstanding because of their ability to make the great pass or to set up the perfect play, or to help their teammates out of trouble. This trait of unselfishness is not easily learned. It is a natural impulse for a player to want to make the winning goal, to hit the final spike, to make the outstanding play of the game. But the athlete who is willing to sacrifice this moment in preference to getting the ball to a player who has a better chance for the play is the athlete who should be congratulated. There is as much self-satisfaction—sometimes more—in assisting a player on a goal as there is in scoring. Teamwork is a relative thing. It consists of being aware of the situation when someone else on the team has a better opportunity than you do for making the play. It means being thoughtful of another player on the team who may not be as outstanding nor as good as you are, but who needs help to build up her self-confidence. It involves caring enough for others to work hard for their success as well as for your own.

"Caring for others" suggests another mental trait: empathy. Empathy means putting yourself in someone else's place and being able to understand how he or she feels. There is a great need for empathy on the part of the athlete. To beat a lesser team into the ground just for the sake of a large score shows a lack of empathy. To humiliate an opponent to make yourself look good shows a lack of empathy. To rub in the fact that your opponent is inferior shows a lack of empathy.

All athletes lose at one time or another. Therefore the athlete should understand the hurt of the person who is the loser. Athletes should be aware of the pain of going beyond a certain point of fatigue because they too have gone beyond that point. Athletes should know what it is like to face a stronger opponent without a chance of being able to win because of lack of experience, because they too were once beginners. Competition is a wonderful thing when people can compete in a humanistic manner.

Another mental trait the athlete needs is the ability to endure pain. Pain and success in athletics are almost inseparable, especially in endurance events. The great athlete can make the fast break down the court that one more time, can run with a "kick" at the end of the distance run in spite of the pain, can swim the length of the pool one more time when her lungs are aching for air. When she can keep going that extra minute or that extra 100 yards, she suddenly comes into her own. Her body readjusts to the demands and she hits that wonderful plateau known as the "second wind." Then, the next time, the same amount of effort is easier, but she must strive for a still higher plateau, which means more pain, more burning lungs, more fatigue. However, when she has reached the point she has aimed at, she can compete at top efficiency, and she will know that it was worth it.

Finally, an athlete should develop the mental skill of giving. All athletes receive benefits from their participation in sports, but many fail to give anything back to the game. An athlete owes something to the sport that has been good to her. The good athlete can settle her debt by the teaching and coaching of others, and should feel the responsibility of accepting these opportunities whenever possible.

## EMOTIONAL SKILLS

Emotions can cause many changes in the body. Fear, for example, can make the heart beat faster, the hands perspire, and the glands shoot adrenaline into the system to prepare it to meet a threatening situation. These physiological changes during stress are the body's way of preparing for a flight-or-fight reaction.

Stress in competition is a result of both internal and external pressures. It forces the athlete to improve her skills and enables her to perform well under highly competitive situations. In fact, the commonest pressure on the skilled athlete is the pressure to perform at top efficiency during a competitive event. To do this, she must develop emotional skills that will help her control her feelings, especially the ones that will make her too tense, fearful, or angry to be at her best.

The two emotions the athlete must control are fear and anger. Fear is an instinct that works to protect the individual, from either a real or an imagined danger. In the days of the cavemen, it served to prepare a person to run from danger or to stand and fight for his survival. Fear today is usually not fear of physical harm, but fear of something that threatens us emotionally. Threats to our ego or our self-esteem can lead to a feeling of tension, resulting in anxiety and sometimes panic. Some of the commonest fears of athletes are connected with the pain that results from extreme fatigue, the possibility of failure during a competitive situation, and the reputation of the opponent.

When an athlete is competing, fear that is not controlled can cause her to expend energy that could better be used in the execution of skills. When she can't play well because of fear, she puts herself at a disadvantage before she begins. By utilizing sound emotional skills, however, she can learn to control her fear and make it work for rather than against her. The excess energy brought about by fear or anger can be used constructively instead of destructively.

Here is an example of positive versus negative reaction. When an athlete is frustrated in her effort to win, her fear of failure may change into feelings of anger: anger at herself because she isn't competing well, or anger at the opponent because she is the one standing in the way of victory. Now anger can be useful to the athlete, since it can delay fatigue and may motivate her to an all-or-nothing effort. But temper during competition is usually a result of an inability to accept defeat. Temper causes the athlete to display anger and aggression, which uses up needed energy in a negative way.

If the person can harness this excess energy and concentrate on getting even by running harder or jumping higher, the energy aroused by her emotions will make her a better athlete and competitor. When she develops these emotional skills, she can *use* her emotions to combat the frustrations and anxieties she is faced with. The key is to realize that one is afraid or mad, and then to react positively rather than negatively.

Another example of a positive or negative emotional reaction is one's feelings of self-worth or self-confidence. When an athlete meets someone in competition, she may feel confident she can win, or she may feel incapable of holding her own. A basketball player may evaluate her opponent's height, speed, agility, and past performances, judging all these things in relation to what she feels *she* can do. If she thinks she is less skilled than her opponent, she gets a feeling of inferiority. If she feels she can do as well as her opponent, or if she thinks she holds certain advantages, then she may feel superior. Lack of confidence leads to poor performance because the athlete can't concentrate all her energy toward victory; she expends some on thoughts of self-doubt and self-reproach. The unknown athlete has these emotions when she must compete against a well-known one, and even a well-known athlete may have them when she must compete against another well-known athlete.

Regardless of how an athlete feels toward her opponent, she must control her tendency to worry, or to fear the results of a contest. She should reinforce her confidence by concentrating on her strengths and by working on her weak points *before* a competitive situation. She should try to maintain an appearance of confidence and poise, reminding herself that the sport after all is a game and should be enjoyed as such. She should not let the outer appearance of another athlete fool her. Everyone is human. Probably the opponent who looks so self-confident and calm is also experiencing moments of self-doubt and fear of failure. When an athlete thinks of her opponent in this light, it makes the opponent appear a little more vulnerable, and thus subject to defeat like anyone else.

The point is that the athlete can benefit by her emotions, or she can be defeated by them, if she can't channel them constructively. Fear and anger and self-doubt can lead to a better performance or to tightness and lack of poise, and therefore a poor performance. By the same token, over-confidence can hinder her efforts because she is not "up" for the game.

Acquiring emotional skill is hard, and takes practice, but it is necessary if one is to become a great athlete. The athlete must continually remind herself that fear, anger, and self-doubt are common to everyone, while at the same time she must be willing to face up to her emotions and use them to improve her game. Just as she practices a physical skill until she can handle it without conscious thought, so must she practice the emotional skills until she can react to stress without panic.

Habits are learned, and therefore they can be relearned. If the athlete can't handle certain situations well because of her emotions, she must study her reactions, clarify what she feels and why, and then seek reasons for reacting otherwise. If she wishes to excel, doing her best should be reason enough to want more control over her emotions. After she has seen the need for change and has adopted a more positive approach, she must continually picture the type of athlete she *wants* to be. If she is in the habit of falling apart at the seams whenever she is losing and is unable to function well under pressure, she must think of herself as being poised and calm in stressful situations. If she carries a thousand worries and self-doubts into a contest and cannot function well because of tension and fear of failure, she must cultivate the habit of taking things as they come and be content with doing the best she can regardless of the outcome. If she gets mad when an opponent blocks every move or makes a good play, she must try to learn to put her anger to good use by becoming more determined to get by her opponent, or at least to out-think her.

The sky is the limit for the athlete who can exercise self-discipline when others around her are experiencing panic and anxiety, and are reacting accordingly. If she can win the battle with herself, there is no such thing as defeat.

**BIBLIOGRAPHY**

1. Corbitt, Ted, "The Emotions in Athletics," *Track Techniques,* **21**, 662–663, September 1965

# chapter seven  standards and guidelines for athletic programs for women

Today we are seeing increased interest in athletic programs for skilled women athletes. Since 1963, in an effort to train educators to work with the skilled as well as the average girl, the United States Olympic Development Board and the American Association for Health, Physical Education, and Recreation (AAHPER) have been co-sponsoring National Institutes for Girls' and Women's Sports. The Amateur Athletic Union (AAU) has also stepped up its program, with junior Olympics, physical fitness programs, and more foreign competitions.

A great factor in the growth of athletic programs for girls and women has been the new interpretation given by AAHPER's Division for Girls' and Women's Sports (DGWS) concerning competition for girls and women. Educators used to feel that DGWS discouraged programs of this type. But DGWS has published new statements, guidelines, and standards to clarify their attitude toward competition for the highly skilled.

In May of 1963, the DGWS approved a statement of policies for competition in girls' and women's sports which suggested interscholastic programs as one means of supplementing school intramural and instructional programs that might not be sufficient for the highly skilled individual. At that time, they suggested that an interscholastic program have the following prerequisites: (1) leaders who are qualified, (2) funds which are budgeted, and (3) specific objectives and standards (proper travel conditions, insurance, adequate facilities, sound equipment, etc.) [2, 3, 4].

As the public became more interested in the possibilities of developing interscholastic programs for girls and women, the DGWS felt it was time to establish guidelines in this area. Therefore, for this purpose, in February of 1965 they held a study conference on competition for girls and women. The result of this conference was a set of statements giving standards for interscholastic competition at the secondary and college level. These policy statements, "Guidelines for Interscholastic Athletic Programs for High School Girls" and "Guidelines for Intercollegiate Athletic Programs for Women," were published in the September 1965 *Journal of Health, Physical Education, and Recreation*. Pamphlet forms of these statements were also made available to interested persons [4].

It was felt that an additional statement was needed for junior high school competition for girls. After approval by the DGWS executive council and the AAHPER board

of directors at the 1966 convention in Chicago, the official policy on sports participation and competition for junior high school girls was published in the September
1966 issue of the *Journal of Health, Physical Education, and Recreation,* entitled
"Guidelines for Interscholastic Athletic Programs for Junior High School Girls." This
too can be obtained in pamphlet form [4].

These guidelines were intended to establish *minimum* standards, and to act as aids
in setting up an extended program in cases in which a school's intramural and extramural programs were not sufficient to meet the needs of the highly skilled girl. They
were not set up as directives from DGWS and should not be interpreted as such.

Interscholastic and intercollegiate programs should be organized *only* after a sound
instructional and intramural program has been developed and is running smoothly.
They should be an extension of any existing extramural program that is not challenging enough for the girl who is very talented in sports. No school should begin a program of this type if it lacks adequate facilities, qualified people for coaching, and/or
money to operate on over and above the money allotted to the basic program in the
classroom and in intramurals.

The leadership of DGWS in setting up guidelines for junior high, high school, and
college programs has led to great gains in athletics for women. If skilled athletes are
to receive the full benefits from interscholastic and intercollegiate programs, these programs must be guided, and this is made possible only by the instruction, interest, and
actions of qualified people.

This chapter is based on the DGWS suggestions, as found in the DGWS Statement
of Beliefs [5], Guidelines for Interscholastic Athletic Programs for Junior High School
Girls [4], Guidelines for Interscholastic Athletic Programs for High School Girls [3],
and Guidelines for Intercollegiate Athletic Programs for Women [2].*

## ORGANIZATION OF ATHLETIC PROGRAMS

Before a school tries to organize an interscholastic or intercollegiate program, those
people who are doing the organizing must understand the objectives of athletic competition for women. One of the best statements of such objectives is the pamphlet
prepared by DGWS, called "We Believe" [5]. This revised statement of their beliefs
should be read by everyone who works with skilled girl athletes.

This pamphlet says that educational experiences should give each girl a chance for
instruction in sports as well as the chance to use athletic skills by participating in
sports. It says further that today emphasis is placed on competing well, and that sports
have become a very important part of our culture. As the woman takes part in society,
she wishes to contribute to those around her; athletic skills and participation in sports
will be valuable to her as "social and recreational tools."

However, sports opportunities should not be limited to one level of skill, but
should be offered at all levels—for the beginner, the intermediate, and the advanced

---

* Used by permission of the American Association of Health, Physical Education, and Recreation.

player—and be available to any girl who is interested in competition and who wants to take part in a sports program that offers experience at her skill level. How intense and broad the competitive program should be depends on the skill of the girls taking part in the program. Since "competition and cooperation" are basic ingredients of our society, these two factors should be utilized in our sports programs and are results to be desired of the programs.

The DGWS Statement of Beliefs also points out that physical activity and sports play an important role in keeping up the all-round health of the girl who participates. Sports also give her the chance to develop self-confidence and to learn how to get along with others. For these reasons, DGWS believes that "comprehensive school and community programs of sports and recreation" should be provided for women at all age levels, and that the girls should be encouraged to take advantage of them [5].

A sports program for women should be extensive, should involve many different types of activities, and should be set up for people with different degrees of skill. The people who organize the program should understand the differences in individuals, so that the program will provide for all "types, ages, and skill levels" [5].

Sound, up-to-date knowledge should guide those who administer the sports program for women: (1) knowledge of growth rates and factors involved in development, (2) an understanding of "motor learning," (3) an awareness of interpersonal relationships and the role they play as individuals mature, (4) a belief in the positive aspects and values resulting from participation in sports[5].

As outlined in "We Believe," a balanced, comprehensive program in physical education should be planned for girls in Grades 1 through 6. This program should enable girls to have experience in fundamental movements like "skipping, simple dance steps, bending, reaching, climbing," etc., and should also provide different types of play activities involving "basic sport skills such as catching, throwing, batting, and kicking."

In Grades 4, 5, and 6, the instructional program should be supplemented by intramural sports experiences in activities that have been modified to meet the needs of the participants. If a broader program is needed for the highly skilled girl, extramural sports activities in the upper elementary grades should be limited to occasional "play days" (involving teams made up of people from several schools or groups), "sports days" (in which girls from a school or group play as a unified team), and "invitational events" (in which a host school or group asks other schools or groups to participate).

In the secondary schools (Grades 7 through 12), a good overall program of instruction in physical education should be supplemented by chances to participate in intramurals and extramurals. However, extramural programs should be set up only if the school already has a sound instructional program and a broad intramural program, and only if there is sufficient space, time, and personnel for handling new programs [5].

At the college level, the instructional program should include activities beyond those offered at the high school level. The college student should have the opportunity to expand her ability to utilize skills in many types of activities and to acquire different skills; the emphasis should be on individual sports. The extramural program, because it offers experiences beyond the intramural program for the skilled woman who wishes to compete, is desirable at the college level.

The DGWS Statement of Beliefs gives four basic classifications of competition: (1) intramural, (2) extramural, (3) international, and (4) co-recreational.

Intramural competition involves participants who are connected with the "same school, community center, club, organization, institution, or industry," or living within a small designated area or community.

Extramural competition takes place when "participants from two or more schools, community centers, clubs, organizations, institutions, industries, or neighborhoods compete." Extramural competition includes "sports days," "telegraphic meets" (in which individuals or schools run competitive events on their own campus and then send in the results by mail or wire for comparison with other individuals or schools), "invitational events," and "interscholastic, intercollegiate, or interagency programs" (in which coached individuals or groups compete on a regular scheduled basis and/or in tournaments against other coached individuals or groups) [5].

In international competition, the best athletes from different countries compete. Women taking part in international competition should be selected for their maturity and emotional control as well as for their skill. Sometimes girls of secondary school age are selected for international competition, but in most cases such competitions should involve people with more maturity.

Co-recreational activities give boys and girls a chance to combine their talents as a team in order to compete, in noncontact sports, against teams composed of other girls and boys. Teams of this type should be organized to help develop teamwork. The DGWS says that girls should not be allowed to play "on a boys' intercollegiate or interscholastic team, against a boys' intercollegiate or interscholastic team, or against a boy in a scheduled intercollegiate or interscholastic contest" [5].

## ADMINISTRATION OF ATHLETIC PROGRAMS

The administration of a girls' athletic program involves planning for the budget, facilities, leadership, and standards.

*Budget.* The money for the women's athletic program should be set aside for that purpose in the overall budget for the school. If this is done, many problems can be avoided, because the program will not depend on income from gate receipts, student fees, etc., which might fluctuate each season. If money is collected as a result of the program through gate receipts, state monies, and other means, it should go into the general school fund. Money spent for the women's athletic program should be handled by the women's physical education department as a part of their total responsibilities in administration of the program [2].

Needless to say, one of the problems of the budget is determining what amount will be spent on each sport. If the budget designated for women's athletics includes funds for intramurals as well as extramurals, it should be itemized carefully, with adequate funds allotted to intramurals first. Funds that are left over should be used wisely to run the best interscholastic program possible. The leaders should see to it that a variety of activities are included in the budget. Each school has a unique situation, in that only its own administration knows what type program will best benefit its students.

Some items any school must consider when planning the budget are: (1) equipment, (2) insurance (if provided by the school rather than by the participating individual), (3) travel, (4) uniforms, pennies, or other means of team identification, and (5) officials.

*Facilities.* Facilities are a major problem in the planning of athletic programs for women. In most schools, the academic programs and the men's athletic program utilizes most of the facilities. When this problem exists, it takes a broad-minded, progressive administration to revise schedules to allow the women adequate use of the facilities. A meeting of all the men and women coaches and administrators involved should provide a basis for working out a schedule that is satisfying to all concerned. In some cases, the women may feel that they are getting what is left over, but if they can back up their arguments for having the facilities at a specific time by showing that they have a good women's program organized, scheduling should not create conflicts that can't be solved.

Any school that does not have adequate facilities for expansion beyond the instructional and intramural program should not consider an interscholastic program for women until funds are available for the construction of facilities that are safe, sound, and adequate for the student body and the proposed program.

*Leadership.* Of all the factors connected with women's athletics, leadership is probably the most important. The leader of the women's interscholastic or intercollegiate program should come from the women's physical education department. If the women physical educators are imaginative, enthusiastic, and knowledgeable, the women's athletic program should provide challenging opportunities for skilled athletes.

The role of administration differs slightly for the junior high school, high school, and college. Competition for junior high school girls should be planned as a separate program, different from that of senior high school girls, regardless of whether or not the junior high program is controlled by the state high school athletic organization. Emphasis should be placed on the program's values for each girl taking part, rather than on the activity as a means of entertaining spectators or as a means of developing future talent for the teams in senior high schools [4].

When the interscholastic program is expanded in high schools, the state high school athletic association should be the body responsible for the regulation of its member schools. In some states all schools are not members. In such a case, a regulatory body from the state department of education may need to be formed to govern the schools not belonging to the state high school athletic association. In those states that have a legislative and administrative body for controlling interscholastic athletic programs, these bodies should keep final control of the competitive program for girls, with guidance from a women's advisory board composed of women physical education teachers from the state's high school system. This board should suggest policies to these administrative and legislative groups, as well as re-examine policies already set up and approved by them [3]. The women's physical education field should naturally be represented in any group that controls the women's athletic program.

In college programs, the members of the women's physical education faculty should formulate the policy for the expansion of women's competitive programs. Their recommendations should then be submitted to those who decide on the college's policies.

As of September of 1967, all DGWS sanctioning for "closed intercollegiate events, meets, or tournaments which are state or regional in scope and/or involve five or more participating institutions" must be obtained from the Commission on Intercollegiate Sports for Women. This commission is also responsible for increasing the number of sports offered in DGWS national championships for college women [1].

In the junior high school, high school, and college programs, the local school administration should have "total responsibility for the administration and supervision" of the interscholastic program. Since the interscholastic athletic program is designed to meet women's needs, the leadership should come from the women's physical education staff. Therefore the school administration should see that the responsibility for running a sound athletic program for the women belongs to the faculty of the women's physical education department. Their responsibilities should include the "planning, organizing, coaching," and supervision of the sports program for the girls and women, although the "ultimate authority" lies with the school administration [2, 3, 4].

*Standards.* In interscholastic or intercollegiate competition, standards should be set in five areas: (1) for participants, (2) for officiating, (3) for coaching and overall leadership, (4) for medical supervision, and (5) for administration of the program.

These guidelines by DGWS are suggested as the minimum standards necessary. Additional restrictions may be necessary when the situation requires higher standards to protect the welfare of the participants.

STANDARDS FOR PARTICIPANTS

In the junior high and the high school, a participant on an athletic team must be a student of the school that she is representing. If a student has been temporarily suspended or is on probation for disciplinary reasons, she should not be allowed to participate. In high school, a student should not be eligible for the athletic team if she has spent more than eight semesters in high school after starting the ninth grade. She must also be successfully carrying a full academic load [3, 4].

On the junior college, college, or university level, the participant must be a full-time student of the school she represents, and she must keep up the grade average her school requires students to have in order to be eligible to take part in any "major activities." Eligibility should be restricted to undergraduate students; graduate students should not be eligible to participate in the intercollegiate program. (The undergraduate student is "one who has not received the B.A. degree or its equivalent.") A student who transfers from one institution to another should be eligible for participation in the intercollegiate program as soon as she has officially enrolled in the institution

[2]. For summer competition, a woman is eligible if she is enrolled as a full-time undergraduate student, maintains the necessary academic average, and has been registered the preceding quarter, semester, or trimester before the summer she wishes to compete.* A woman is ineligible to compete in the "same annual event more than four times."*

A participant on the junior high, high school, and college level must be an amateur and hold this amateur standing during her participation [2, 3, 4]. An amateur is defined as a person who has never received money for participating in sports (with the exception of travel and housing expenses while competing). If a girl, because of varying rules concerning officiating, teaching, etc., is unsure of what constitutes amateur status, she should refer her questions to the organization responsible for the competitive event.†

If a student in a junior high or high school wants to participate in an interscholastic program, she must get written permission from a parent or guardian and file it with the appropriate school personnel. She must also file a doctor's certificate stating that she is physically fit to participate in the interscholastic athletic program. This certificate must be turned in before the first practice session of the sport she wants to participate in, and the examination by the doctor must have taken place within the "time period specified by local regulations" governing her school [3, 4].

If a girl wants to participate in an intercollegiate program, she must be examined by a doctor within six months of the beginning of the sports season each year. If a family doctor does the examining, "a covering letter" should state which activities the student is going to be involved in, and explain what information is needed from the physician [2].

In both interscholastic and intercollegiate sports, the student who has had a serious illness, injury, or surgery should present written permission from her doctor before she can participate in the athletic program again [2, 3, 4].

If the school does not have an insurance policy to cover students during athletic competition, each girl should be required to have some type of accident insurance that will cover her in the event of injury or illness.

Other standards apply to intercollegiate competition but not to junior high or high school competition. The Guidelines for Intercollegiate Athletic Programs for Women state that "no scholarships or financial assistance" should be set aside specifically for women participating in athletics. This does not mean, of course, that a girl who participates in the intercollegiate athletic program cannot hold a scholarship or a grant-in-aid in another area that has been awarded through the normal scholarship program of the school. Women should not be allowed to take part "on a men's intercollegiate team, against a men's intercollegiate team, or against a man in a scheduled intercollegiate contest" [2].

---

* Changes approved by DGWS executive council, March 1967, for College Guidelines.

† Also see article by Dr. Mildred Barnes, "Officiating and Amateur Status in Girls' and Women's Sports," Journal of Health, Physical Education, and Recreation, 39, 24, October 1968.

## STANDARDS FOR OFFICIATING

Officiating can make or break an athletic program. In a program geared especially to skilled athletes, the officiating should be equal to the playing ability of the participants. It goes without saying that qualified officials will stay abreast of rule changes and be aware of proper officiating techniques. On the junior high and high school levels, officials should hold an intramural or higher DGWS rating that is current, or should have an "equivalent rating in the specific sport," and should be properly certified by the appropriate organization controlling officials' ratings [3, 4].

At the college or university level, all intercollegiate events should be officiated by persons who have received the DGWS National rating. If the sport is one in which DGWS does not give ratings, the officials should hold an "equivalent rating" [2].

## STANDARDS FOR COACHING AND OVERALL LEADERSHIP

If a sports program is to yield all the benefits possible from competition, it must have good leadership. The qualified leader is one who: (1) understands the role of sports in the educational system, (2) has a knowledge of the human body, which includes understanding how young people develop, (3) knows the changes that take place in the body as a result of exercise, (4) is aware of the need for accident prevention and training in first-aid techniques, (5) has the ability to analyze and understand specific athletic skills, and (6) knows good teaching methods and has the ability to instruct and coach through application of these methods [2].

"Personal experience in organized extramural competition" is valuable to leaders of women's sports, and women interested in going into the physical education field or into coaching should take advantage of any chances to participate in extramural competition. They should, in addition, have a strong "personal integrity" and a deep "concern for the welfare of the participant" in the sports program [2].

As pointed out in the Guidelines, women who are qualified should be selected to "teach, coach, and officiate" women's sports whenever possible. The women in charge of the athletic program should be careful that it does not expand beyond their ability to handle it.

Junior high or high school coaches should hold teacher certificates, and should be hired through the local board of education. If a trained woman physical educator is not available to coach, the teacher selected to do the job should work closely with the women's physical education department [3, 4]. On the college or intercollegiate level, it is "strongly recommended that an official's rating be considered a prerequisite for coaching," since this enhances the coach's awareness of the official's role [2].

On the junior high and high school level, the principal should appoint a woman faculty member to act in a supervisory capacity and to go with the members of the girls' team to all competitive events or meets [3, 4]. At the college level, if the team is being coached by someone who is not a member of the teaching staff, then a woman from the physical education faculty should go with the team to all competitive events, to act as a supervisor and a chaperone for the participants. Institutions should cooperate in providing for clinics and "pre-service and in-service programs" for the teachers, coaches, and leaders [2].

The leaders should see that DGWS-approved standards are used for competition in all sports, and that DGWS rules are used in conducting the sports engaged in [2, 3, 4].

If there is a question as to whether a girl is fit to play or not, the official has the right to make the final decision, and, to protect the girl from further injury, may annul the coach's decision [3, 4].

## STANDARDS FOR MEDICAL SUPERVISION

It is the responsibility of the administration to provide a "healthful, safe, and sanitary environment" for everyone taking part in the sports program. There should be a doctor on call for all competitive games and meets, and a person trained in first aid should be present. No girl should be allowed to participate in the sports program without certification from a physician stating that she is physically fit to do so. After any serious illness, injury, or surgery, the girl should have written permission from a doctor before she is allowed to engage in athletics again [2, 3, 4].

## STANDARDS FOR ADMINISTRATION OF THE PROGRAM

On the junior high and high school level, all competitive contests must be under the "direct sponsorship and supervision of the schools involved." Post-season games involving individuals or teams should not be allowed. To avoid conflicts, a girl may not play for more than one interscholastic team during the season; until that school season is over, she may not engage in a game or meet for any team outside her school. When a girl participates in her first game or meet, she is considered to be a member of a team [3, 4].

Administration of the athletic program should include setting up interscholastic competition that is limited to the sports that are covered by rules and standards published by DGWS, and in seeing that these rules and standards are followed [2, 3, 4].

On the junior high level, "one or two sports days" at the end of the intramural season will give sufficient opportunity for competition in sports for this age group. However, if the school administration feels that more activity should be offered, individual participation should not go beyond one competitive meet per week and three competitive meets per season [4].

On the high school level, the sports season should not run more than twelve weeks. The first three weeks should be used for "training and conditioning" the participants. A girl should not be involved in more than five activity periods a week, including meets and games. There should not be more than two games in one week. These games should be spaced out during the week, and not be played on consecutive days [3].

Because of the differences in growth and development during the junior high school years, competition should give the girls a chance to compete against others of the same "skill level, age, and/or size." Travel for competition in junior high school should be limited as much as possible by scheduling events only with schools close by. All trips should be made in "school buses or with bonded carriers" [4]. On the high school level, all competitive meets should be held close enough to the competing school to allow the teams to get home at a reasonable time. Again, all trips should be made via carriers that provide safe transportation [3].

If awards are given for junior high, high school, and college competition, they should consist of keepsakes that are not expensive, "such as ribbons, letters, and small pins." Any other "expensive or elaborate awards," or the raising of money for them, would constitute a violation of the guidelines set up by DGWS, since they feel that awards should be "symbolic only" [3, 4].*

The standards for intercollegiate competition state that participation in sports should not prevent a girl from pursuing her primary objective: getting an education. A student who plays on an intercollegiate team cannot play on another team outside her college or university at the same time in the same sport. However, groups that have the authority to set up local policies may wish to change this policy to fit the needs of exceptional cases involving certain students. The college athletic schedule should not be so crowded that it will interfere with classwork and study. Where specific sports are involved, the administrator should follow the standards given in the DGWS guide concerning the number of practice sessions and/or games or meets each week. The colleges taking part in the athletic program should set up a policy for the "length of the season and the number of games" to be scheduled. The time a season covers varies in different areas and according to the sport, but it should not go beyond twelve weeks. The first three weeks should be spent mainly in conditioning and training the participants. Women should not, of course, be allowed to compete with or against men in a scheduled intercollegiate match [2].

## BIBLIOGRAPHY

1. "Commission on Intercollegiate Sports for Women," *Journal of Health, Physical Education, and Recreation,* **37**, 8, October 1966, pages 10, 76

2. "Guidelines for Intercollegiate Athletic Programs for Women," published by the American Association for Health, Physical Education, and Recreation. Originally published in September 1965 issue of *Journal of Health, Physical Education, and Recreation*

3. "Guidelines for Interscholastic Athletic Programs for High School Girls," published by the American Association for Health, Physical Education, and Recreation. Originally published in September 1965 issue of *Journal of Health, Physical Education, and Recreation*

4. "Guidelines for Interscholastic Athletic Programs for Junior High School Girls," *Journal of Health, Physical Education, and Recreation,* **37**, 7, September 1966, pages 36–37

5. "We Believe," DGWS Statement of Beliefs, published by American Association for Health, Physical Education, and Recreation, 1201 Sixteenth St., N.W., Washington, D.C. 20036

* Changes approved by DGWS executive council, March 1967, for College Guidelines.

# chapter eight problems of competition

Because the trend toward programs of athletic competition for women is relatively so new, there are no ready-made solutions to most of the problems that may arise. This chapter, therefore, will raise some questions that need to be looked at carefully.

Everyone involved in programs for skilled women athletes should try to make decisions on the basis of the chosen objectives of the competitive program. Coaches and administrators ought to keep in mind that some procedures are applicable only in certain situations; a solution that might work well for one area or one program might create chaos in another area or program.

The following material is a reflection of my own thinking and does not necessarily coincide with DGWS policy.

There are three main areas in which there are problems connected with athletic programs for women: (1) player image, (2) organization and administration, and (3) state–national control.

## PLAYER IMAGE

### DRESS

The dress habits of teams, and of individual players, constitute a problem in that they unfailingly make an impression on the general public. The problem is intensified because of the conflict between the athletes' desire to dress for comfort and their wish to create a positive image.

On long trips, many athletes prefer to wear shorts or slacks because traveling is more comfortable in clothes of this type. The problem is usually not so much the wearing of shorts or slacks while traveling as the way they are worn, and whether they should be changed before the athletes reach the place where the competition is to be held.

Some associations have solved the problem by setting forth rules that all teams and individual players must arrive at the scene of competition in skirts (or dresses) and shoes with heels. This gives the women the option of wearing whatever they want while they are traveling and yet being groomed so that they will make a good impression on the public at the place of competition.

When the team is playing away from home and must stay in a motel or a hotel and travel back and forth from the gym or playing field, other problems arise. Often coaches allow their teams to wear their playing uniforms while they are in transit. Sometimes, in fact, it's necessary. But most of the time there are perfectly adequate on-the-spot facilities for showering and changing clothes before and after the athletic event. Personal hygiene, as well as the desire to look attractive, should lead players to take advantage of such facilities whenever they exist. When girls have to wear their playing uniforms while they are en route to the competition, neat, clean warm-ups over the uniforms are a good idea, from the standpoint of both appearance and comfort. The wearing of hair curlers in public should, of course, be prohibited.

Often the coach must make the final decision about dress. She must consider several things: (1) the general appearance of the girls she is working with, (2) whether her players look feminine in anything other than skirts and blouses or dresses, and (3) means of travel and dressing facilities.

## MANNERISMS

One of the commonest complaints concerning women athletes is that they tend to copy men, or that they appear masculine in their play. One often hears comments such as "she shoots just like a boy," or "she plays just like a man." However, in most cases, it is not that women are trying to copy men's movements; they are simply performing in the most effective way they can, which means that they have to use the same techniques men use.

To shoot a jump shot in basketball means that a person has to be able to jump high into the air, bring the ball above his or her head, and release it with a flip of the wrist and an extension of the arm at the height of the jump. If a woman were to try to do it any other way, it would make the shot even harder than it already is.

This is why good women athletes perform in a way that is basically similar to that of men. At the same time, it is why good men athletes perform in a way basically similar to that of women. Women, like men, wish to execute movements in the most efficient way, to get the most out of the ability they have, and to use scientific techniques. Because of the human body's limitations, anatomy, and physiological workings, certain movements must be made in a specific pattern, whether they are done by a man or a woman.

So actually, to say of a woman that "she plays like a boy"—when her movements are such that they produce the greatest efficiency—is to compliment her intelligence and motor coordination.

It is true that *some* women athletes do appear masculine because of their mannerisms on and off the court; but then, so do some nonathletes. Some women could not look feminine even if they wanted to. A few sportswomen appear extremely masculine, partly because of their body build and partly because of their behavior patterns. Sports has not necessarily led to this masculinity; in many cases the girl has chosen sports because her body build enables her to adapt easily to the movements required in athletics. But the great majority of the women competing in sports are very feminine.

Coaches should put a damper on masculine mannerisms that are not necessary to a girl's performance or that create an undesirable impression. Personal habits that go unnoticed off the playing field are often intensified in competitive situations. Mannerisms such as chewing gum, profanity, poor posture, loudness of voice, etc., are frequently given as reasons for the public's negativism toward athletics for women.

Profanity has become common everywhere, and is becoming more and more prevalent among athletes. Because of the restrictions imposed by our society, people can't display feelings of anger or aggression in a physical way. An athlete who is frustrated can't use physical force to release these pent-up emotions; if she does, she will encounter even greater feelings of frustration because of the intense social disapproval of physical displays of anger. Therefore most people use a more subtle means. They turn to profanity, a nonphysical outlet that society accepts more readily than physical aggression.

Profanity may be a means of letting off steam, but for the athlete it has no place if one of the values of competition is self-control. Admittedly, even the best intentions at times are not enough; sometimes the frustrations brought on by competition would cause even an angel to lose control. But both coach and players should always work toward self-control in all situations.

Chewing gum is another mannerism that should be eliminated. Gum-chewing not only creates a negative impression and makes a woman look tough, but in many cases, gum can be dangerous if swallowed or inhaled during competition. Many athletes use gum because they claim that it keeps their mouths moist during competition. However, oranges or water can be just as effective in combating dryness in the mouth. If an athlete chews gum out of nervousness or habit, reminders by the coach can help her stop.

Many coaches feel that it's not their job to change their athletes' habits and mannerisms. Yet one of the greatest things about athletics is that it is a training ground, not only for physical achievement, but for personality and character development. If a girl is crude in her talk, obnoxious in her behavior, or discourteous toward others— whether off the field or on—it *is* the responsibility of the coach to try to change her. The coach should sieze every opportunity to improve the girl's behavior. It may not make the woman a better athlete, but it will eventually make the athlete a better woman.

### SPORTSMANSHIP

Sportsmanship used to be a way of life for athletes. It was accepted that the athlete would try to play by the rules, and would conform to a code of conduct that included fairness, courtesy, and kindness. Today—and perhaps it is a reflection of our whole way of life—a lack of sportsmanship is permeating sports. Spectators boo officials and razz the players. Bookies fix games and bribe the athletes. Pressures are numerous and come from many directions, and caught up in the middle of them all is the athlete.

On one side the athlete is cheered, on the other he is jeered. Sometimes he is encouraged to compete well, other times he is pressured to slack off. One coach demands self-control, while another sits on the bench and throws temper tantrums. Winning depends on teamwork, but stardom demands individualism. The public continually asks, "Did you win" and hardly ever "How did you play?"

Sportsmanship, in fact, is now at the point at which it must be reinforced or we must admit that our values are no longer applicable to sports. Sportsmanship is the responsibility of four factions: (1) the spectator, (2) the official, (3) the player and (4) the coach.

Spectators' conduct, like players' and coaches' conduct, can become a problem in women's competitive programs. The temper of a crowd usually (though not always) depends on the conduct of the players and the coaches. When the competition is on a school-versus-school basis, school authorities are responsible for the actions of spectators. When people pay admission to watch an athletic contest, they have paid only for the right to watch the athletes perform, not for the right to abuse players or officials, unless the school authorities, by failing to speak out when spectators display poor sportsmanship, give them this right. When people attend an event for which there is no admission charge, they go as invited guests of the sponsoring school, and should behave as just that. Otherwise, the invitation to future competitions should be withdrawn.

The officials should be responsible for sportsmanship on the floor or the field; this includes the sportsmanship of coaches as well as players. If a player or a coach is abusive, displays temper, or is guilty of unfair play, the officials should exercise their authority to dismiss her from the game on grounds of poor sportsmanship.

It takes courage for an official to make such a decision. But if the official makes the decision objectively and impartially, and in a manner consistent with the code of conduct for athletics, he or she should never regret or withhold it. An athlete who wants to remain in the game will learn to react accordingly.

The player herself is of course chiefly responsible for her reactions, both on and off the playing field. An athlete's sportsmanship, especially under pressure, should be one of the prime objectives of competition. The ideal player is one who keeps her temper, ignores comments by spectators or other players, and who can concentrate on playing the game regardless of the provocations of others. She is neither at the mercy of the spectators, the officials, the coach, or the opponent. She obeys only her own conscience and her own concept of right and wrong, and the external pressures on her do not nearly match the internal ones.

The person who can influence sportsmanship the most is undoubtedly the coach. Although the interactions of spectators, officials, players, and coaches influence sportsmanship, only the coach has complete authority over players' actions. The coach, more than anyone else, guides the women's competitive programs in the direction they should go, first because her actions under pressure set an example, second because her attitude toward winning affects the athletes' objectives, and third because, by demanding good sportsmanship of her players, she has a chance to teach them an invaluable lesson.

It is hard to sit on the sidelines and coach a team. The coach can't release her mental tension through physical action. And though she can see things from the bench that the players can't, and can set up plans of action, she can't execute the plans; somehow she has to get the players to do that. If the coach fails to transfer her knowledge to her players, she has to endure the frustration of sitting and watching at a distance as her team fails. This is why many coaches express anger at officials' calls or athletes' poor play. Blowing up at least gives a coach an outlet for her frustration, although at the same time it is an admission that she needs a scapegoat to soothe her ego and to cover up her own failure to communicate with her athletes. The coach who must shift the blame to others by shouting or ridicule or disagreement from the bench is not only a poor sport, but a poor coach.

Another factor that affects players' sportsmanship during a contest is the objectives set up by the coach. If the coach feels that winning is the chief objective, the means become secondary in the players' minds; this can lead to unsportsmanlike behavior. If the coach puts the emphasis on competing well, the players feel that the final score is secondary; this can lead to a good clean performance. Winning-at-all-costs is not usually synonymous with good sportsmanship.

Teachers must often use pressure as a means of enforcement. The coach puts pressure on her athletes when she demands of them a specific code of conduct. If she makes it clear that she will not tolerate poor sportsmanship any more than she will tolerate poor physical achievement, athletes will learn to develop their emotional along with their physical control. A coach is inconsistent if she pulls one player for poor physical performance and allows another to stay in the game even though she is giving a poor emotional performance. As Chapter 6 emphasized, athletics is not all physical activity. It demands mental, social, and emotional activity as well, and for the coach to ignore the emotional phase is as bad as ignoring a fundamental physical skill.

## ORGANIZATION AND ADMINISTRATION

### CHEERLEADERS

There is much to be said for and against cheerleaders. By organized yells, cheerleaders can set the pace. They can encourage sportsmanship and spectators' support, and they can become participants in athletic events from which their physical skill might otherwise have excluded them. At the same time, cheerleaders can give an exaggerated impression of spectators' loyalty. The fact that the yells are organized and that instant enthusiasm appears on cue can, if there is a poor choice of yells and unthinking leadership, lead to poor sportsmanship and lend athletic contests the air of circuses.

Two questions must be faced: (1) Are cheerleaders an integral part of athletics? (2) Are *your* cheerleaders a contribution to your program?

### GATE RECEIPTS

What part does an admission fee play in the sports program? In some cases, it is the only means of support. Gate receipts pay for athletes' traveling expenses, uniforms, equipment, and for officials. However, when gate receipts are the only means of support, winning becomes desperately important, since most spectators do not like to support a loser. Some athletic programs suffer greatly during a losing season because the gate receipts fall off so.

Athletic programs demand money; the problem is the *source*, and what effect it has on the objectives of the program.

As the DGWS quite reasonably suggests, money for school programs should be set aside in the overall budget and should not depend on the income at the gate. If a fee is charged, it should go into the general budget. However, if there are programs that can't be run on this basis, and if gate receipts are the only possible source of money, then using gate receipts to pay for the program is better than not running a program at all.

COMPETITION AT AN EARLY AGE

How old should girls be in order to compete on an athletic team, and how intensive should their training be?

Girls today are not only maturing at a younger age than ever before, but they are, on the average, taller and heavier than girls used to be. Champions are becoming younger and younger, and in many cases are participating in sports at an earlier age.

However, people don't really know what effects competition has on the very young: what psychological effects it has on them, or how much physical stress they can take without harmful effects. There has not been enough research on the subject to justify a stand for or against very early participation in sports. This area should be thoroughly investigated, not just to determine the physiological effects of competition at an early age, but to determine the sociological and psychological effects.

The Joint Committee of AAHPER and the Society of State Directors of Health, Physical Education, and Recreation on Desirable Athletic Competition for Children of Elementary Age, in their 1962 report, "definitely disapproved" of varsity-type interschool competition for young people below the level of ninth grade. A later report indicates that the two main arguments against varsity-type competition in elementary school are probably that the young athletes tend to specialize (thereby neglecting other basic skills), and the possibility that this type of program might lead to a "distorted sense of values" [1].

Meanwhile, until we have more research on the subject, youngsters should not be pushed into competition; even when very young girls want competitive activities, leaders should investigate current findings carefully before initiating strenuous competitive programs for them.

COMPETING ON TWO TEAMS SIMULTANEOUSLY

Should a girl be allowed to compete on two teams during a season? At present, this is a real problem because of the danger of scheduling conflicts. If there are two games at the same time, a girl has to make a choice of which team to play for. This means that she has to let one team down.

Australia-New Zealand game at Fort Collins, Colorado (courtesy Keichi Nakamoto, Colorado State University Photo Service).

The underlying problem is the fact that in most cases the girls' athletic programs set up by schools and organizations are not extensive enough to challenge the really skilled athlete. Another problem is: What will happen to the less-developed programs when the good athletes must make a choice?

If a girl has to choose between a college team that plays three or four games per season and an AAU team that has a schedule of 15 games, it's not hard to guess what her choice will be. Naturally she'll want to compete as often as she can. On the other hand, if a school is running a competitive program that involves a good schedule, and another organization such as AAU is running a comparable program, she is more likely to choose the school program. But how many high schools or colleges today are running programs that are extensive enough to satisfy the talented girl athlete's need for competitive experiences?

And what about the girl whose school program offers just enough to make her want more? Or the student who can compete for a school during the day and for a recreational or an AAU team at night without conflicts? Or the skilled athlete who is continually seeking more competition than one team can offer her in her area?

In fields in which competition on an interscholastic and intercollegiate basis is just beginning, should we force the better student athletes to choose a more developed program outside the school until the schools can offer satisfying competitive experiences? If the best student athletes play elsewhere, what will this do to the skill level of the interscholastic programs?

When the school program is limited—due to facilities, finances, or leadership—should the coaches try to work out conflicts, to enable the talented woman athlete to pick up valuable playing experience elsewhere?

All these are problems which need to be considered when one is planning girls' interscholastic or intercollegiate programs.

## PRACTICE AGAINST MEN

In many areas, there are only a few schools—and in some cases only a few persons—who want competitive activities. These people find that due to a lack of competition at their level they are unable to progress beyond a certain point. Thus there are many fine women athletes who can't achieve their potential or even rise anywhere near it because they do not have worthy female opponents in their area. Should these girls be encouraged to practice against men in noncontact sports?

Although the DGWS rightfully stipulates that women should not be allowed to compete on a men's team or against a man or a men's team in a *scheduled* contest or match, there is nothing wrong in a good girl tennis player perfecting her strokes by practicing against an equally good man, nor is there harm in a golfer, a badminton player, a bowler, or a diver practicing with or against a man in order to improve her skill. If the girls' athletic program is not sufficiently developed to challenge the skilled girl, and if there is a lack of competitive experiences for women, this justifies practice against men in noncontact sports. In fact, such practice should be encouraged.

## COACHING BY MEN

Should women's teams always be coached by women? Not necessarily. Many excellent men coaches have volunteered their time to work with women's sports and have done a tremendous job. When one is choosing a coach for a woman's team, the primary consideration should be the coach's qualifications for coaching. If we want to upgrade the caliber of women's sports programs, we must not hire a less-qualified person to coach our girls simply because the applicant happens to be a woman.

On the international scene, the AAU has already experienced a setback in one of its programs because it selected a coach on the basis of sex rather than coaching experience. The same thing has happened in a number of school situations recently. It's all very well to put emphasis on women handling women's sports programs, but big changes in coaching personnel cannot effectively be made until qualified women are available to do the coaching. Indeed, as far as actual coaching is concerned, women still have a lot to learn from men. Women should in fact take every opportunity to learn from them. They can do this by serving as assistant coaches under men or by watching men's coaching techniques while they are traveling with teams as chaperones.

## AWARDS

Does the athlete compete for the award or for the fun of the game? Would it make any difference in the way she performed if the athlete were given an impressive trophy, or just an inexpensive award? When an athlete is competing, what does she think about: Winning? The thrill of playing? The possibility of getting a trophy?

A handsome trophy certainly doesn't mean any money for the athlete, since she can't sell it or pawn it without losing her amateur status. A trophy is simply a bonus for a job well done, a symbol of the fact that by work and self-discipline she has reached the top. A good feature of trophies, however, is that they are permanent. Over the years they remind the athlete that she did achieve a goal and that she did excel. But this sort of recollection would stay with her without reminders.

Pins or ribbons are also good, simply because they are symbolic. Athletes do not compete just for an award, as witness the fact that thousands compete in school programs in which only inexpensive awards are given. The competition itself is its own reward. The athlete doesn't care what she gets after the contest. Yet regardless of the motive of the achiever, achievement does deserve to be recognized. Whether this recognition comes in the form of an expensive trophy or an inexpensive pin or ribbon is not important. Some organizations that have the money give splendid trophies, a practice which certainly does not ruin the competition for the good athlete nor corrupt the average one. However, sometimes the money could be better spent to provide competition for a larger number, or to make necessary expansions in athletic programs; in such cases expensive awards should not be given.

SCHOLARSHIPS

Scholarships today are commonplace. A person skilled in mathematics, music, art, and other activities can get a scholarship on the basis of this skill. Should a woman be given a scholarship on the basis of physical skill? Some schools are already giving them to outstanding women athletes, although these are few at present.

The chief problem of granting athletic scholarships to women is that of recruiting the better athletes for the program. Men coaches, of course, are familiar with this same headache. The pressure to produce winning teams and to show results when financial aid is given are justifiably called "the evils of athletics."

Another problem in giving scholarships is the process of elimination and selection. This in some cases involves tryouts, in others scouting, and in all cases paperwork and decisions, based not only on athletic skill but on academic ability as well.

Still another problem is the money for the scholarships. Where does this money come from and what demands are made as a result of the giving? Do scholarships fluctuate according to the season's record, or do they remain the same whether the school's athletes win or lose? If money for the scholarships comes in as a contribution, who is to control the giving of the scholarships: the coach, the administration, or the donor? What are the criteria—other than athletic ability—for receiving the scholarships? What grade-point average has to be maintained?

If scholarships are limited, which sports receive them?

What happens to the athletic program in areas in which some schools have money for athletic scholarships while others do not? Who controls schools to see that scholarships and financial aid do not exceed the amount allowable under the amateur athletic code?

Is the girls sports program extensive enough to warrant the giving of scholarships? Are the administrators of women's competitive programs mature enough to handle the problems involved? Do the benefits overshadow the problems?

Should skilled girl athletes be denied educational opportunities because educators are afraid of the problems involved?

Is the field of women's sports an area of achievement that deserves recognition in the form of a scholarship?

## LENGTH OF SEASONS

The length of an athletic season should depend on the skill level of the participant and the objectives of her training program. For the average woman athlete and the average competitive program, the twelve weeks suggested in the DGWS guidelines is sufficient (with three weeks for conditioning). But for the athlete who wants perfection and top-flight competition, twelve weeks is hardly enough.

Schools and colleges with a highly competitive schedule may need 6 to 8 weeks just for conditioning and training purposes. In the case of schools that supply teams for international competition—such as Wayland Baptist College in Plainview, Texas, and Nashville Business College (basketball) and Tennessee State University (track and field)—the sports season may even have to be extended into the summer.

When schools compete in an organized league, the number of games and the length of the season should be determined by the governing body, which should base its decision on the skill level and interest of the participants. When 12 weeks is not considered enough, the conditioning program should be extended to meet the demands of the competitive program, with a minimum of three weeks, as suggested by DGWS.

## GOVERNING BODIES

The people responsible for governing women's athletic programs must have authority to enforce standards and regulations on two levels: high school and college.

The state high school athletic association usually organizes competition on the high school level. It handles interschool competition not only in sports but in speech, music, etc. However, the inclusion of women's athletics under this body varies with different states. The amount and type of sports activity allowed for girls also varies from state to state. Some states allow extensive competition, including state tournaments; others allow only limited participation, such as play days or occasional sports days. Educators have recently been trying to achieve three goals in all the states:

1. Inclusion of the girls' interscholastic sports program under the state high school athletic association (DGWS state chairmen have been working toward this by appointing qualified high school teachers to work with the state executive secretary in an effort to gain the approval of the board of control).

2. The appointment of a women's committee responsible for setting up standards and rules for schools in the state with the help of the executive secretary of the state high school athletic association.

3. A re-examination of existing programs set up under the state high school athletic association.

In some states the big problem has been not only acceptance of the responsibility for the girls' interscholastic sports program by the state high school athletic association, but adequate representation of the women physical educators on policy-making committees. In states in which progress in women's sports is slow due to tradition and cultural taboos, each teacher and coach should use her influence to make the needs of a girls' competitive program known by the school administration as well as by the state high school athletic association.

The college level presents another problem, since there is no state body comparable to the state high school athletic association which can handle women's athletics. Some colleges, recognizing the need for a governing body, have formed athletic associations. A number of these involve member colleges from neighboring states, and some are connected with the Athletic and Recreation Federation of College Women. These athletic associations have set up policies governing competition and have the power to enforce the rules. Whenever there are intercollegiate competitive programs, women physical educators should organize governing bodies to control the sports activities in their area, giving each participating school adequate representation and a vote in the policymaking. Since problems differ with locale and degree of interest of the participants, the organization should be a working one that can handle changes and expansion in the program as they become necessary.

## STATE-NATIONAL CONTROL

### REGIONAL AND STATE TOURNAMENTS

Some schools provide tournaments for girls on a regional and state basis; some do not allow even city tournaments.

When programs have been organized for a long time, and the skill level is high because of good coaching over the years, tournaments on a regional and a state basis can be a valuable experience to talented girl athletes.

However, in newly organized programs, emphasis should be placed first on developing skill. Competition should be limited to nearby schools whose students have equal skill and experience in competition. As the girls become more skilled and learn to handle competitive experiences on a limited basis, the governing body may expand the program, so that it offers more challenge.

All tournaments and competitive programs should be cleared by the state high school athletic association or the equivalent governing body for the girls' athletic program.

## NATIONAL AND INTERNATIONAL COMPETITION

What role our school and college women athletes will play on the national and international scene in the next few years is a question that demands a lot of thought. We must first consider whether this is the direction we want our sports program for girls to take. How strong is our desire to turn out skilled competitors? And how will it affect our overall program of physical training?

The object of the competitive programs in schools and colleges should *not* be to produce Olympic-caliber performers. However, if a good all-round program is carried out, the natural result *will* be better athletes for national and international competition. As more and more girls become active in competition in the schools, as coaches become more experienced, and as more scientific principles are used as a result of research, the skill level will improve. There will be a greater number of girls participating in sports, and thus we shall have a wider selection for Olympic teams.

But the big question is the direction the schools' women's programs should take. Should they be geared to fundamental instruction, with relatively moderate competitive experiences? Or should the better athletes be thoroughly coached for intensely competitive experiences, with the schools giving the skilled athlete a chance to compete on a nationwide and possibly an international basis?

If so, what organization will control the competition? Should a college team be allowed to compete internationally? Who will sanction and control competition when a college team competes against a foreign team? How should these teams be chosen? How should the coaches be chosen? Who will finance them?

Steps have already been taken to control closed intercollegiate competition on a state and regional basis. When five or more schools are involved, and wish to be sanctioned, permission must be channeled through the Commission on Intercollegiate Sports for Women. This organization is also working to offer more sports for college women on a nationally competitive basis.

At present, some teams composed of college students are participating in the World Games under the auspices of the United States Collegiate Sports Council. Extensive national and international competition as an outgrowth of intercollegiate programs for women may seem distant and unlikely, but the time to plan for it is now. Responsible leaders must make many difficult decisions in the next few years.

## ELIGIBILITY FOR COMPETITION

For several years, men athletes have been debating who is to control competition and what determines eligibility of athletes who compete in the United States and against foreign competitors. The issues are too involved to detail here, but a few items will suffice to show the sort of things that women, too, may eventually have to come to grips with.

The basic issue is whether the AAU (Amateur Athletic Union) has the sole jurisdiction over amateur athletics in national and international competition in track and field, basketball, baton twirling, bobsledding, boxing, gymnastics, handball, horseshoe pitching, judo, luge, swimming, water polo, weight-lifting, and wrestling. The NCAA, the

NAIA, the U.S. Track and Field Federation, and other organizations that furnish athletes for some of these sports are at odds with the AAU's claim to sole jurisdiction. These bodies are bargaining for more power and representation on competitive teams representing the United States.

Therefore women competing in track and field, basketball, gymnastics, and swimming may eventually also have to decide which organization they recognize as the official one.

At present there is no NAIA or NCAA organization for college women as there is for college men, but finances for the women's intercollegiate programs are often controlled by the men and come from the director of athletics' funds. This could conceivably lead to pressure on women to form a unified front in the dispute with the AAU. If top college women competitors were forced to withdraw from college competition in order to remain eligible for AAU competition in the Olympics, Pan-American games, etc., this could also result in pressure.

When the women's program becomes so extensive that many women athletes reach Olympic caliber at high school or college age, women may be caught up in the middle of the power struggle and may be subject to pressure from both sides. College teams are already beginning to participate in AAU tournaments, some on a national level. What is going to happen when and if they are forced to choose between college tournaments and AAU competition?

The problem is intensified because women do not have representatives in the top sports organizations who can exert influence when policies for competition are formed. The expansion of sports for women in the states, however, may eventually prove that women should be represented on these top-level bodies.

THE FUTURE

The possibilities of sports for women are unlimited—but so are the problems. Competition can be negative or positive; it can make women athletes better citizens or it can give them a false set of values. What effect do mental and physical stress have on women? What untapped reservoirs in women are waiting to be developed?

Where do we want our women to go, and how far can we take them without counteracting the beneficial results of competition? What role should competition play? Do we have enough mature people to handle competitive programs?

These are some of the many questions that must be answered. Some can't be answered; some can be, but not on the basis of our present knowledge. Some can be answered only when the problem concerns a specific program.

We are at the threshold of a challenging experience. What we do with it will depend completely on our leadership.

BIBLIOGRAPHY

1. *Desirable Athletic Competition For Children of Elementary School Age*, published by American Association for Health, Physical Education, and Recreation (1201 Sixteenth St., N.W., Washington, D.C.), 1968

# chapter nine analyses of sports and strategy

To be able to analyze her athletes' strengths and weaknesses is one of the greatest assets a coach can have. Every situation demands that the coach be able to do this, and that she then be able to work out a plan of action so that she can obtain better results from her athletes. And she has to be able to make these decisions on the spot —for example, during a crisis in a game—when a wrong decision can lose the contest.

The coach who is good at *analysis* can, so to speak, take a movement apart and study it, and understand the separate parts that make it up. The coach who is good at *strategy* can put this knowledge into practice to get desired results. Basically, analysis concerns physical characteristics and movement, while strategy concerns mental readiness. The two factors are complementary.

Better equipment, increased knowledge of movement, new techniques in performance, weight training, better diet, and many other things have brought about an improvement in sports performances. However, as opportunities become equalized, and as all individuals gain the chance to engage in athletic programs, the factor that is going to make the difference in performance is the coaching. Good coaching must combine an accurate inventory of potential (analysis) with a plan of attack compatible to the personnel (strategy).

## STUDYING AND ANALYZING MOVEMENT

In studying movement to determine potential, a coach may use many methods. It is up to the coach to select the method most appropriate to her needs. Films, photographs, charts, and plotting are some of the more modern ones. The money and time available are major considerations for those wishing to utilize these methods. Simple observation is one of the easiest and most often used methods, although naturally it is subjective, and therefore not always valid.

In analyzing the player in action, the coach should: (1) watch the performer's overall movement, (2) follow one specific part of the body (for example, the hand) as the girl performs the movement, (3) take film or photographs when possible (so that she can study action by means of stills or slow-motion film), (4) record action through plotting when possible, (5) discuss her findings with the athlete, and (6) suggest the movements that the athlete should practice. When specific measurements such as plotting are used, the coach should: (1) find the center of body movement (center of mass is slowest-moving part, and easiest to see), (2) know the distance from this center to the base, (3) know the extent and direction of hip movement during the action, (4) determine where the body weight is at start and finish of action (weight shift is usually at climax of action), (5) look at position of head, (6) check to see how wide the base of support is (wide stance usually means stability), (7) determine direction of feet during the action, (8) look for sway, dip, and unusual twist during the performance, (9) note the extent, direction, and pattern of the follow-through of the arm, hand, and leg, (10) try to see a picture of the total range of movement, (11) follow the movement of the hand or foot, paying special attention to the hand, wrist, and fingers, and (12) write down her impression of the performer.*

The coach who is dealing with skilled athletes will find analysis much easier if she knows the components and movements that make up the sport. For instance, basketball is composed of running, jumping, throwing, catching, etc. The coach can get hints for improvement in the overall game by looking at some of the other fields of motion, and then transferring this knowledge to her specific sport. Hints on how to achieve speed on the fast break, for example, can come from observation of sprinters in track; aids in teaching catching and throwing can be transferred from softball.

CHANGING AND IMPROVING PERFORMANCE

The coach should not try to change the overall performance of the skilled athlete (for often this would throw off all her movements and reactions), but should try to bring about minor changes which could improve the athlete's performance without ruining the confidence, pattern of movement, and coordination that has been built up through the years. For instance, in analyzing the movements of a broad jumper, the coach might suggest a longer approach to help build up speed rather than insisting that the athlete go back to the basics of running. Or in the case of the tennis player, it might be a wrist snap late in the serve that needs comment, rather than a complete overhaul of the swing.

Any major changes necessary should be made in the off-season to allow the girl time to master the skill before the competitive season. Regardless of the extent of needed changes, once an analysis has been made, the next step is improving the athlete's performance. What works with one individual may not work with another. The psychological factors involved in sports are immeasurable and in many instances uncontrollable. The coach must always exercise tact and not go beyond a point that will cause the athlete to lose self-confidence. Some people respond physically when the coach explains what should be done and why. Others find it easier to verbalize what the coach has tried to get across. Others may respond more readily to written notes that the coach has made during observation. Some react best if they can see the film or photographs, so that they can follow their own movements step by step. Others need to be encouraged every step of the way, humored, or prodded by other psycho-

---

* From notes taken in class on Analysis of Sports, conducted by Dr. John Cooper at the University of Utah; used by permission.

logical means. At any rate, the coach must work within the limitations of the athlete, using the athlete's weaknesses to her advantage when possible.)

(People at different skill levels react to changes in movement in different ways. In coaching the beginning player, the coach must give the athlete a chance to see *how* a movement is performed. But once she is past the beginning stage, the girl must know *why* a movement is performed in a certain way. At first, visualizing an action makes learning and change easier, but when athletes are skilled, it is insight that makes performance more effective. So it is with the coach: She must be able to see the movement in its entirety, understand how it is accomplished, and as a result have an insight as to what changes are necessary for more efficient performance.)

Sometimes a coach can improve performance just by changing some of the implements used in competition. Balls in most instances are standardized, but uniforms can be varied to help a team's vision and peripheral perception. If a girl is afraid of hustling after a ball on the floor, knee pads or knee socks can eliminate the fear of floor burns. Examples of changing the implement used in competition and thereby changing performances are the fiberglass pole in high jumping and the steel racket in tennis.

(For a skilled athlete, one of the best means of improving performance is to compare her movements with those of a champion. Top athletes have perfected minute details, and the athlete wishing to improve can learn from the champion. Reading about outstanding athletes, watching movies of top teams and individuals, and observing performances first-hand can certainly aid the aspiring athlete, provided she will take her own limitations and unique movements into consideration.)

Once a motion has been started, it is hard to stop it. Getting an opponent to commit her body weight in the wrong direction is the key to faking in basketball, and can be utilized in other ways when competition depends on balance and timing. In order to counteract an opponent's move, a defensive player must move quickly, and through a greater arch. Because of this, the offense has the advantage; this advantage can be equalized only by anticipation and speed in reaction time on the part of the defense. If the defense uses correct positioning, and keeps plenty of space between herself and the opponent, this can prevent the opponent's having an advantage in speed before the defense can counteract the offensive moves. On the other hand, this gives the offense a different advantage in that it allows her greater choice of movements in the added space.

Another thing to remember is that an athlete cannot make a movement in one plane without first moving in another. Flexion cannot be accomplished without extension first, nor can you extend without flexing. To extend the legs on a jump, a person must first flex the knees. To get wrist action in shooting or throwing, a person must first cock the wrist.

## UTILIZATION OF STRATEGY

(Strategy involves a plan of action, and demands that a player be mentally ready to move in a prearranged direction to extract a desired reaction from the opponent. With strategy, an athlete can out-think the opponent and counteract her plans. Every plan of strategy must take into consideration the weaknesses and strengths of one's own players, as well as the opponents'. If the athlete is simply competing against her own time or record, coaching strategy will involve getting the most from her psychologically as well as physically.

## UNANSWERED QUESTIONS IN COACHING

Coaching cannot be summed up in exact statements. There is no set formula for coaching because there are too many variables connected with it. Each coach brings unique contributions to the coaching field. The coach has to work with individual players, each of whom has unique mental, physical, and emotional skills, and then pit these players against opponents, each of whom also has a unique combination of skills.

We do not yet know—in fact, we'll probably never know—the *best* way to coach an individual or a team. There are so many untried methods that the field is relatively wide open for the coach who is willing to try new methods of getting the most from the athlete.

There are so many questions the coach and teacher must answer in order to tap the full potential of athletes. Some answers to the questions below can be revealed through research and experience. Others we may never know the complete answers to.

1. Why do some people perform better under pressure, while others perform worse?
2. How do you teach poise under stressful situations?
3. How do you teach self-confidence while at the same time giving the person a true picture of her strengths and weaknesses?
4. How can you detect staleness, and what is the best way to prevent it?
5. Should coaching for sports in which implements such as rackets, bats, etc., are used be different from coaching for sports which do not require implements?
6. Should coaching for sports such as golf, bowling, archery, etc., be different from coaching for sports which involve body contact, such as hockey and basketball?
7. How does coaching individual sports differ from coaching team sports?
8. How do you teach aggression?
9. What personality traits are best suited for particular sports?
10. How do you teach a person to react faster in a competitive situation?
11. At what age should competitive programs be started?
12. How do you get an athlete "up" for a contest?
13. How do you motivate a person to practice on her own?
14. How can you improvise equipment for better teaching and coaching results?
15. Why is it that when a player is in the best frame of mind, she sometimes gives the poorest physical performance (and vice versa)?
16. How can the athlete control tension to achieve the best results?

17. What is the best means of teaching a person to: (1) jump higher, (2) throw farther, (3) catch better, (4) swing harder, (5) run faster, (6) endure longer?

18. What is the best progression for teaching physical education, and why isn't this progression reasonably uniform in our school systems?

19. How do you teach people to compete in a humanistic way?

20. What are the *real* values of sports?

21. Are the same values inherent in sports for girls as in sports for boys? If so, why is the girls' competitive program so limited?

22. Are athletes less prone to crime and other antisocial behavior than nonathletes?

23. What psychological traits do top athletes have that average athletes do not have?

24. What is the pain threshold for the athlete training for an endurance event?

These are only a few of the questions that need to be answered. We very much need research on the subject of competition, as it concerns the athlete and the coach.

To be useful, analysis and strategy must be specific. Therefore this chapter will discuss some intermediate and advanced techniques and strategy needed by the skilled player, rather than the basic fundamentals, which the advanced player should already have mastered, and which are fully described in many other textbooks. It is impossible to cover all the refinements of technique in this book. Thus I have tried to select ones that ought to be useful to most coaches working with girls who have progressed beyond the beginning level.

## ARCHERY

### COACHING EMPHASIS

1. Use same anchor point each time.

2. Draw arrow back same distance each time.

3. Check aim for accuracy each time before releasing the arrow.

4. Practice consistency in moves; for best results, archer should operate like a machine.

### MECHANICS

1. Corner-of-the mouth anchor (high anchor); see Fig. 9–1. Often used in field archery.

   a) Any one of three fingers (usually forefinger) drawing arrow may be anchored at corner of mouth. Same finger should be used each time.

   b) To give firmness, anchor finger should be braced against tooth. Mouth should remain closed.

   c) Thumb should be turned down and hooked under jaw when arrow is at full draw.

**Fig. 9-1.** High anchor. Finger braced in corner of mouth to keep draw and aim consistent.

2. Under-the-chin anchor (low anchor); see Fig. 9-2. Usually used in target shooting.

   a) Arrow is drawn back directly under chin.

   b) String cuts across the center of chin, lips, and nose.

   c) Thumb is relaxed and close against neck.

   d) Use button or ball of serving on the string at a point above the arrow nock so contact with the lips will result. To ensure consistent movements, button or serving should contact lips at same spot each time. See Fig. 9-3.

3. Methods of aiming (sight, point-of-aim, and instinctive).

   a) *Sight:* most accurate. Sights can be made or bought. To make one, take cork or sponge, adhesive tape, and large-headed pin. Use tongue depressor or popsicle

Fig. 9-2. Low anchor. Some hold string slightly to side of center of face; others bring string back to touch center of nose and chin.

Fig. 9-3. Use of button to increase accuracy.

stick for marking the point of aim. (See Fig. 9–4.) Attach cork to bow with adhesive tape; stick pin in cork to left of bow. Experiment at different distances, moving pin until distance can be accurately marked in yardage on the stick. In adjusting a bought sight, move the sight bar in the same direction as the error: If arrow hits high, push the sight up; if arrow is to the right of the target, push the sight in, etc. Either keep both eyes open, or close left eye and use right one to line up the target.

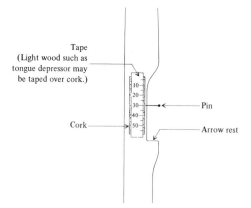

**Fig. 9–4.** Homemade sight for back of bow.

b) *Point-of-aim:* indirect method. Sight with the use of some object, such as golf ball or stick, placed in position on the ground according to the range you are shooting from. In adjusting the marker or the point-of-aim, move it in the direction opposite to that of the error. If the arrow goes high, the point-of-aim should be placed lower or closer to the archer; if the arrow goes to the left of the target, the point-of-aim should be moved to the right, etc. In this method, you are looking at the point-of-aim but seeing the point of the arrow as a secondary object.

c) *Instinctive:* Look at the target and shoot according to visual reckoning rather than lining the target up with something else.

4. Shooting aids. A full-length mirror is useful during practice to check form. A nocking point attachment on the bowstring will help establish consistency and increase accuracy (some attachments eliminate the need for shooting glove or tab). Foot markers may be used to ensure the same stance each time. Fiberglass and aluminum arrows should be considered by the advanced archer.

OTHER FACTORS

People have won national tournaments and meets by using both the under-the-chin anchor and the corner-of-the-mouth anchor, so you can take your choice. Many think that the under-the-chin anchor is best for long-range shooting and that the corner-of-the-mouth anchor is best for short-range shooting, because of the angle of the arrow at the draw.

Since the arrow leaves the bow on a curved path, the farther the target is away from the archer, the higher she must aim the arrow. It is easier to aim high when you are using the under-the-chin method.

Shooting from a short distance requires that the archer point the arrow straight ahead or even toward the ground. The corner-of-the-mouth position makes this easier and also places the arrow closer to the sighting eye.

Archers who are consistent in their point-of-aim, their draw, and their anchor point often still miss the target because they do not hold their aim steady before the release. For steadiness, keep the left shoulder firm, eliminate creeping, relax the fingertips, use the shoulder and back muscles to keep the tension in the right arm, and hold the aim just long enough to get set. Exercises to build up strength in the arms and shoulders should be used.

| *Problems* | *Corrections and Coaching Hints* |
|---|---|
| *Arrow goes too high.* Possible causes: arrow nocked too low, anchor point too low, archer's mouth open. | Place serving on string so arrow may be nocked at right angle to string; adjust anchor point by placing first finger under chin if using low anchor, or index finger to mouth if using high anchor; keep teeth together. |
| *Arrow falls short.* Possible causes: underdrawing, creeping, holding aim too long, dropping bow arm, wind blowing toward archer. | Draw arrow completely before release; hold hand steady on anchor point; hold aim just long enough to get set; don't allow bow arm to drop, but keep arm parallel to ground; allow for wind by lifting point-of-aim. |
| *Arrow goes left.* Possible causes: anchor hand moving away from face, string hitting clothing or arm, tightening grip on bow too much, hyperextension of bow arm, failure to judge wind, sighting with left eye. | Keep finger on anchor point; keep hand holding bow relaxed; rotate bow arm so elbow is turned outward; allow for wind blowing from right side by aiming more to right of target; aim with right eye. |
| *Arrow goes right.* Possible causes: relaxing grip on bow too much, lifting of elbow on drawing arm, turning head more than usual, failure to judge wind, bow tilted to right. | Tighten grip on bow slightly; drawing elbow should not be higher than arrow and drawing arm should be parallel to ground; allow for wind blowing from left by aiming more to left of target; keep bow level. |
| *Arrow goes over target.* Possible causes: overdrawing, only two fingers of drawing hand on string, leaning away from target, wind coming from behind archer. | Draw arrow back to pile; keep three fingers on string; keep body in alignment, with shoulders level; lower point-of-aim when wind comes from behind. |

*Hand or forearm is hit by string.* Possible causes: hyperextension of wrist of bow arm, allowing upper limb of bow to tilt to left, putting too much pressure on string with first and second fingers.

Keep wrist in straight line with bow arm; keep bow upright; distribute pressure equally among three fingers on string; keep arm on straight line from elbow to nock.

*Arrow slides off arrow rest.* Possible causes: squeezing the nock, flexion of wrist of drawing arm.

Relax fingers while holding nock and pulling string for draw; hold wrist in straight line with elbow.

*Arrow flies in erratic line.* Possible causes: unsteady hand at anchor point, not opening fingers simultaneously to release arrow, too much strain from pull, holding aim too long (which causes drawing arm to shake).

Keep drawing hand steady at anchor point; relax all three fingers simultaneously; release arrow as soon as aim is found.

*String hits wrist.* Possible cause: string not tight enough.

Check distance between string and braced bow (*fistmele*); this distance should be approximately 6–7 inches.

*Inconsistency of results even when all movements up to release of arrow have been correct.* Possible causes: poor follow-through; body or bow moves before arrow hits target.

Hold shooting position, with anchor point and stance steady, until arrow hits target.

## STRATEGY

Strategy in archery is not as complicated as it is in most sports. Mental readiness is important. One must also allow for environmental elements such as wind, sun, and rain. The archer naturally does not have to counteract opponents' moves, but must concentrate only on what *she* must do to get the arrow into the target. She must not worry about her opponent's score or let the opponent's accuracy upset her. The archer who can close out everything from her mind except her own movements and her own score has the battle half won. Concentration is necessary; so is consistency, which depends on concentration.

The archer should remember exactly where she aimed on the previous shot in order to make any needed adjustments for error. Once she decides on her point-of-aim, she must be determined and confident as she shoots. To hesitate is to ask for trouble, because strain in muscles builds up.

Wind is one of the most frustrating factors to an archer, especially at long ranges; if the wind comes in gusts, it is hard to determine how much to allow for it. The degree of adjustment depends on the strength of the wind. The archer should make it a point to practice on windy days in order to learn how much to allow for the wind.

Some archers prefer to use plastic vanes instead of feather ones when the wind is blowing hard or it is raining. The plastic gives more accuracy, since wind drift is reduced to a minimum and rain does not affect the plastic as much as it does feathers. Because plastic vanes are all identical, the archer does not run the risk of the arrow going off course, which can happen when the feather fletching has become damaged. However, the archer, before using arrows with plastic vanes in competition, should practice with them, since the flight of plastic-vaned arrows differs slightly from that of feather-fletched ones.

## BADMINTON

### COACHING EMPHASIS

1. Wrist snap (important for power, speed, and deception).
2. Deepness of forehand and backhand clears as defensive strokes.
3. Accuracy of forehand and backhand drives down the sidelines as offensive strokes.
4. Placement of shuttle for the serve.
5. Power and deception on overheads.
6. Pinpoint accuracy on drop shots.
7. Development of the round-the-head stroke.
8. Strategy.

### MECHANICS

1. Wrist snap: Cock wrist prior to the hit and then rapidly flex the wrist as the racket contacts the shuttle.
2. Clear: Snap wrist vigorously and shift body weight forward. High, deep clear should be used to allow player time to get back into position, to force opponent back from net, and to allow player to slow the pace when she is tired. As an offensive stroke, the clear follows a path just high enough to go over the opponent's head without allowing her time to drop back into position for the return shot.
3. Drive: Most effective when shuttle is hit at shoulder height, since path of flight should be nearly parallel to floor and as close to top of net as possible. Excellent for quick placement when opponent is out of position, or to draw opponent from side to side. Take care that the shuttle does not rise upward after it passes net; otherwise opponent may have chance to smash it back.
4. Serve

   a) Hold shuttle in same position in relation to the body each time. (The higher the point of contact, the flatter the arc as the shuttle goes over the net. Must be contacted below waist to be legal.)

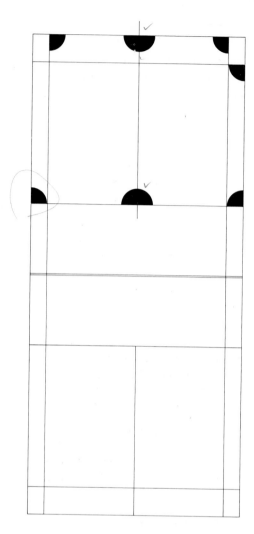

**Fig. 9-5.** Marked-off areas of court for practice in serving for singles and doubles.

b) Cock wrist to same degree each time, allowing for soft touch on short serve and enough power to execute long serve by a powerful flexing of the wrist.

c) Degree of flexing determines the distance the shuttle will travel; angle of racket head determines trajectory of shuttle flight.

d) Slight rotation of the wrist immediately before contact of racket with shuttle can, with practice, send shuttle to any desired spot on court.

e) Mark off specific areas on the court for player to aim for during practice. Example: Draw a semicircle about a foot in radius in the deep corner of the singles service court on the opponent's backhand side, or a circle with a 6-inch radius for the short serve in the corner of the doubles service box on the opponent's forehand side, etc. (See Fig. 9-5.)

| *Problems with Serve* | *Corrections and Coaching Hints* |
|---|---|
| *Short serve: hitting shuttle too high.* Possible causes: too much wrist flexion; racket face angled up too much on contact with shuttle. | There is little wrist action on the short serve. When contact is made racket face should be angled to send shuttle just over top of net. Tie a string about 6 inches above the net and practice hitting between net and string. |
| *Short serve: serve goes into net.* Possible causes: shuttle drops too low before contact; wrist is extended too much when shuttle is hit. | Racket should contact shuttle just below waistline; *guide* shuttle over net with a gentle flexing of the wrist. |
| *Lack of accuracy.* Possible causes: shuttle held at a different position for each serve; racket head angled differently. Increasing or decreasing arm swing. | Use same service position on all serves; racket head should be angled in direction of desired flight. Only difference between one serve and another should be in amount of force applied on contact with shuttle. |
| *Long serve: shuttle doesn't go deep enough.* Possible causes: too little power; too little wrist action; failure to follow through; shuttle held too close to body. | Hold shuttle away from body by extending arm; cock wrist and snap it through rapidly on contact; allow natural follow-through by continuing upward swing. |
| *Illegal serve.* Possible causes: racket head is above wrist on contact; both feet do not remain on the floor; racket is higher than waist when shuttle is hit. | Swing underhanded rather than sidearm; be sure both feet are in service box; let shuttle drop lower to keep racket head below hand and waist before contact with the shuttle. |

5. Smash or overhead (see Fig. 9-6).

   a) Use motion similar to the smash in tennis (except that in badminton the wrist does more work).

   b) Bring racket to a position behind head, with wrist cocked.

   c) Allow shuttle to drop slightly in front of body.

   d) Reach up and contact it at its highest possible point, snapping wrist as contact with the shuttle is made and following through.

   e) Make follow-through motion down and across left side of body.

   f) Just before racket contacts shuttle, shift weight from rear to forward foot.

   g) Ordinarily, keep feet in contact with floor, even though you rise up on toes to get most height and best body weight shift. However, at times, you may leave the floor just before hit in order to gain more height on the reach, allowing better angle from which to hit shuttle down into opposite court.

(a)  (b)  (c)

**Fig. 9-6.** Overhead stroke.

| Problems on Smash | Corrections and Coaching Hints |
|---|---|
| *Lack of power and speed.* Possible causes: body facing net; improper weight shift; feet leaving floor when not necessary; too little wrist action. | Body should be at about a 45-degree angle to net; begin with weight on rear foot and then shift to forward foot, with feet remaining on floor to help in transfer of weight; cock wrist when racket is brought behind head; snap it through as contact is made. |
| *Smash is too flat rather than angled down.* Possible causes: shuttle allowed to drop too low; not enough wrist snap; elbow bent when racket contacts shuttle. | Extend arm upward for shuttle; snap wrist to get downward angle; make contact as high as possible. |
| *Smash is hit too deep or flight is too high.* Possible causes: shuttle allowed to drop too far behind head; poor positioning of body; late wrist snap. | Get under clear quickly; allow shuttle to drop slightly in front of body. Snap wrist immediately upon contact. |
| *Smash goes into net.* Possible causes: shuttle dropping too far in front of the body; hitting at too much of an angle when overhead is taken from deep in the court. | Bring body more directly under the shuttle; when smashing from deep in the court, do not use as much angle; reduce acuteness of wrist snap. |
| *Inaccurate placement.* Possible causes: incorrect follow-through; lack of practice. | Allow racket and arm to follow through on left side of body; during practice, concentrate on placing shuttle. Place baskets on court and try to hit into them. |

6. Drop shot

   a) After a smash or deep clear, use a drop shot for change of pace or to get opponent off-balance.

   b) You can take a drop shot on forehand or backhand side, with either underhand motion or overhead swing.

   c) Try to make shuttle cross as close as possible to net and then drop vertically on opponent's side.

   d) Generally speaking, use same movement for a drop shot as for a more powerful stroke such as the smash; same backswing, transfer of weight, etc. However, at moment of impact, use little wrist action, so that you hit shuttle softly and it barely goes over the net.

   e) Use delicate touch, with little follow-through.

f) Use deception: a powerful smash or a deep clear one moment, the next moment a drop shot starting with the same motion.

g) When you have an advantage on an angle for placement of a stronger stroke such as the smash, always take the stronger in preference to the slower stroke or drop shot, since a slight inaccuracy can allow opponent time to make the return.

h) Aim drop shot to force opponent to hit up.

i) Use hairpin shot to return drop shot. Effective because opponent has usually taken a couple of steps backward to regain her position in middle of court, and can be caught with her weight moving away from net.

j) When opponent is playing deep, use cross-court drop shots, with shuttle angled from one side of court to the other.

k) Expect drop shot when opponent must run fast to play a short shot that has dropped below the top of the net. Opponent must hit up, forcing her to hit a return drop shot or a deep clear.

| *Problems with Drop Shot* | *Corrections and Coaching Hints* |
|---|---|
| *Lack of deception.* Possible cause: player does not go through preliminary motions of a more powerful shot. | Use same backswing, shift of weight, etc., as for a more powerful stroke, differing only in follow-through and in force applied by wrist action. |
| *Shuttle goes into net.* Possible causes: shuttle has dropped below top of net before player contacts it; racket not angled up enough to clear net on return; incorrect wrist action and lack of "touch." | Racket face must be angled according to position of shuttle in relation to net; wrist must guide shuttle and stroke must be firm but soft. Touch is developed only through practice. |
| *Shuttle goes too high when crossing net.* Possible causes: too much force from wrist; angle of racket face improper with respect to relation of shuttle to net. | Use gentle wrist action and "tap" shuttle over; adjust angle of racket face on contact to send shuttle just over net; very little follow-through. At times, the racket face will "recoil" on contact to take force from hard hit by opponent. Tie string 4–6 inches above net and practice hitting drop shots between string and net. |

7. Round-the-head stroke (see Fig. 9–7).

a) Use this stroke to hit a shuttle on left side of head.

b) Bring racket back behind head with elbow bent and wrist turned to allow contact on forehand face of racket.

c) Stroke forward, with forearm brushing top of head.

**Fig. 9-7.** Round-the-head stroke.

d) As contact is made with shuttle, extend arm and snap through with wrist.

e) Make slight follow-through, coming down on right side of body.

f) Remember that this stroke is possible only in badminton, because the light-weight racket and shuttle put little strain on arm and body during execution.

g) Use this stroke in place of backhand at times; it allows more power and speed.

h) You should limit your use of this stroke because of weight shift to left, which can leave right side of court open to fast return by opponent.

i) The greater the distance the shuttle is from your left side, the more you must lean to left, keeping weight on left foot.

j) If shuttle is close to left side, you can obtain greater speed and power from the round-the-head stroke than from the backhand stroke. However, if there is time, move under shuttle and hit the smash, since this is an even more forceful shot.

| *Problems with Round-the-Head Stroke* | *Corrections and Coaching Hints* |
| --- | --- |
| *Lack of power.* Possible causes: player keeping elbow bent during stroke; too little wrist action. | Reach up and out, extending arm on stroke; wrist should be cocked and snapped quickly as contact is made. |
| *Shuttle goes into net.* Possible causes: letting shuttle drop too low before contact is made; shuttle too far in front of body. | Start stroke sooner; reach for shuttle; position body in line that will allow shuttle to drop to left of head. |
| *Lack of deception.* Possible cause: player uses same placement shots, allowing opponent to anticipate stroke. | Cross-court shots should be varied with shots down the sideline and with drop shots. |

STRATEGY

Strategy in badminton is similar to strategy in tennis in the sense that the object is to hit the shuttle where the opponent can't reach it, and to get her moving and off-balance before attempting the put-away shot. Especially in playing singles, it takes a lot of patience to keep the shuttle in play until the opponent makes a weak return.

However, too much aggressiveness can pull the player out of position and leave part of the court open. Hitting the shuttle away from the opponent or to a place where there is a large unprotected area can be effective, since the opponent must move to get to the shuttle. Most players can't hit as well on the move as they can from a stationary position, so placing the shuttle can force the opponent into errors.

Learn to use a variety of shots. A clear, followed by a drop shot or a smash—or a combination of drives, clears, smashes, drop shots, and sharply angled cross-court shots—can thoroughly confuse the opponent. In badminton, variety of shots and the ability to think while moving is as necessary as speed and quick reflexes.

## Strategy for Singles

### SERVING

In singles, the serve must either be short and low, or high and deep. To keep the opponent from gaining an advantage that would allow her to go on the attack, the deep serve is usually used. The deep serve forces the receiver back, and, if placed properly, is very hard for the opponent to smash. The receiver usually has to use a defensive stroke such as the clear to return the well-placed deep serve.

The short serve should be used as a change of pace to keep the receiver honest, and is effective against a player who is slow or who has shifted her weight backward in anticipation of the deep serve. A short serve that is too high or a deep serve that is too short is disastrous.

### SERVER'S POSITION AND PLACEMENT

When serving, stand approximately 4 feet from the short service line, and near the center line. This distance may be varied according to the height and speed of the server and her ability to cover the court. After serving, and after the return of shots, move to the approximate center of the court, since this puts you in the best place to cover all possible shots. (This position should be slightly closer to the net than the exact center, since clears must cover a greater distance than drop shots; this gives the player a little more time to move back than to go forward.) This center position may vary about a foot on each side of the center line, according to the possible angles of the opponent's return.

The best placement for the serve is to a deep corner of the service box; best of all is a serve that is high and deep and near the center line, because this cuts down the angle of the opponent's return. If, after serving, you return to your defensive position in the middle of the court, the only way the receiver can pass you on the return of a long serve at the center line is to try to get the shuttle down one of the sidelines. However, if you are alert, you can easily intercept any sideline passing shot. A serve to the sideline corner rather than to the center-line corner allows the receiver a greater angle for her return, since she may return it down the sideline or cross-court. (See Fig. 9-8.)

In any situation in which you have sent the shuttle to the sideline corner, wait about a foot to the side of the center line in the direction of the shuttle in order to reach the shortest-angled shot, which would be the return down the sideline. If she were to send it back with a cross-court shot, the shuttle would have to travel a greater distance, and this would give you more time to move across court to cut off the return.

### RECEIVER'S POSITION

If you are the receiver, wait for the serve about 5 feet behind the short service line. Your position in relation to the center line depends on which service court you are in. When possible, take a position that will enable you to take the shot on your forehand

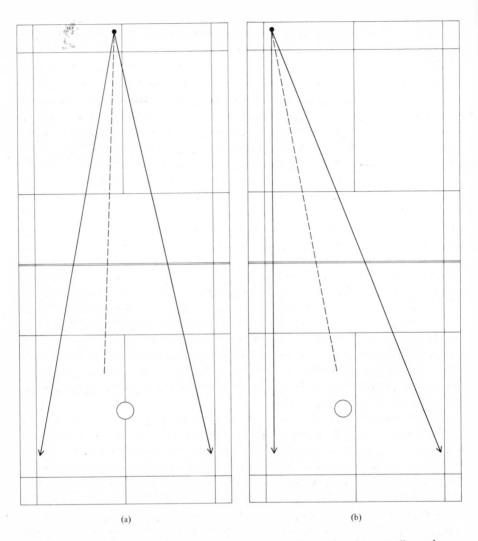

**Fig. 9-8.** Angles of return on the serve. (a) Placing the serve deep and to the center line makes possible the angle shot to either side. If server moves into position correctly in middle of court, she should be able to cut off either of these returns. (b) Placing the serve deep but to the sideline makes possible a cross-court or a sideline return. The server must move slightly toward the sideline to cut off the shortest return down the sideline.

side and which will allow you a slight advantage in being able to get into position for the deep serve to the center line corner. If you are receiving in the right-hand court, stand near the center line; if in the left-hand court, stand about 3 feet from the center line. However, be careful not to overplay.

When you are the receiver, you must be able to anticipate the direction of the serve, but not move before the shuttle has been hit, because the server may detect the shift in your weight and place the shuttle accordingly. Since the long, deep serve is most often used in singles, you must be prepared for this type of serve without putting yourself at a disadvantage if the serve goes short instead.

Keeping the body weight low, with one foot forward, and the weight evenly balanced will help you get a good push-off in either direction. Once you have determined the direction of the shuttle, you must get into position at once, arriving within hitting range before it can drop. If you can move quickly and get into position, you have a chance to smash the service return, although most returns are clears or drops. Learning to move backward, sideward, and forward at full speed and then coming to a controlled stop is a must for the skilled player. Once the serve has been hit, the receiver must move quickly back to the center of the court.

GENERAL STRATEGY

Some good returns of the high serve are: a drop shot just over the net but to the center of the court (to cut down the possible angle of return), a clear to the opponent's backhand, or a smash. One of the best returns on a short serve is a high clear, deep into the backcourt, preferably to the backhand of the opponent, or a drop shot if she has already started moving back and you see her shift her weight backward.

Strategy in badminton is a little like strategy in chess: you plan a couple of shots ahead and try to get your opponent to move and react to your advantage. Many players tire if the opponent runs them constantly, and begin to make errors as a result of fatigue. Others can't hit the shuttle as well moving backward as forward, or vice versa. Others have one definite weakness such as inability to handle a drop shot to the backhand. You must pick out these weaknesses and incorporate them into a plan of attack. For every shot that is sent across the net, there are specific angles of return open to the opponent, so you should overplay slightly in the direction of these hits in order to cut down the angle of return as much as possible. When the shuttle is close to the net and near the sideline, the opponent has the widest possible angle for her return, while shots in the center of the court allow the smallest angles for return. Ordinarily, when you must play a shot that has been hit down your sideline, your best return is back down the opponent's sideline on the same side of the court, because the shuttle takes less time to travel on this straight path than it would cross-court. When you must come in close to the net to play a shuttle, a high clear deep in the opponent's court is usually the safest, although a hairpin drop shot, well placed, can often catch the opponent asleep. Drop shots are always effective when the opponent has been forced back to her endline or is off-balanced. Cross-court shots are effective if the opponent has been pulled out of position toward the sideline, or has started her move toward the sideline to cut off a possible sideline shot.

If you can get your opponent moving from side to side, and then place a shot to the side she has just left, you can usually catch her moving in the wrong direction. Because of the speed of a smash, cross-court smashes are always effective. A drop shot as a return to a smash from deep in the court is also a good shot. Always try to get into good position before hitting the shuttle, rather than trying to reach back for a shuttle that has dropped behind your head, or that has fallen too far in front of your body.

*Strategy for Doubles*

SERVING

A good doubles team must have an accurate serving game because every shot that enables the opponents to hit downward gives them a definite advantage. In doubles, because of the shorter service courts, the deep serve is more dangerous to the serving side than the short one. The short serve to either corner is better than the long one. A serve that is short and near the center line is the best, because it allows less angle for the opponents' return. The player serving should stand about a foot back of the short service line and approximately 3 feet to the side of the center line.

Sometimes the server can gain an advantage by hitting the shuttle toward either shoulder of the receiver. The receiver will react by reflex; her most natural movement is to lift her racket at an angle that returns the shuttle cross-court, which server and partner should anticipate. As a result, the return will often go out-of-bounds or to one of the waiting players [3].

If the receivers are moving forward on each serve because they are expecting the short serve, use the long serve as a change of pace. In this case, if you are serving into the right service court, the long serve toward the center line is best. If you are serving into the left service court, the long serve toward the sideline will place the serve to the opponent's backhand. However, the return down the sideline should be anticipated.

RECEIVING

The receiving position in doubles depends on the speed and height of the receiver, although most women prefer to stand approximately 3 feet behind the short service line. The receiver has a definite advantage if she can rush the net on the short serve and make contact with the shuttle while it is still above net height, because this enables her to hit downward.

The whole objective in doubles is to gain an advantage so that the team can go on the attack. When a team can hit downward on the shuttle or when they have the opponents working defensively to keep the shuttle in play, they are the offensive or attacking team. A team that must hit the shuttle upward or return shuttles weakly as a result of poor positioning is considered to be on defense.

You gain an advantage by hitting the shuttle as soon as possible, both because you may hit it before it drops below the level of the net and because the sooner it is hit, the less time the opponents will have to get ready for the return. One of the best times for starting an attack is when the serve is received. The reason is that all serves must go slightly upward in order to clear the net, since the racket head must be kept below the waist and wrist until contact is made on the serve. Once a team goes on attack, they must keep their opponents under pressure and on defense until the point has been won. You can do this only by using speed, deceptive techniques, and accurate placement of shots through a variety of angles.

PLACEMENT

In doubles, the three important weapons are the smash, the clear, and the drop shot. Placement depends on the opponents' weaknesses and methods of play. Sometimes a shot placed directly between the opponents creates confusion as to who should hit it. Some teams have trouble with sideline shots or shots hit directly at them. Often a smash hit at the body of an opponent will result in a weak return because she can't move out of the way quickly enough and must hit with her arm and swing cramped. Any shot hit at the feet of the opponent is hard to return, especially if she is moving forward or backward at the time.

SYSTEMS OF PLAY

The best defensive formation for doubles is usually side-by-side. On offense, a team can usually attack better with one up and one back, but the system of play depends on the personnel. There are four different systems commonly used in doubles. Two of these—the parallel and the up and back—are fairly simple and are usually used by beginners, while the other two—the diagonal and the rotation—are more complicated and are usually only used by highly skilled players. (The players usually slide in and out of the side-by-side system as they go from defense to offense, while using the diagonal, the up and back, or the rotation systems.) The advantages and disadvantages of the four systems of play for doubles are as follows:

1. *Parallel.* Easy system to understand, but some confusion may result when shuttle is hit between the two players. Agree beforehand that all shots in the middle will be taken by the girl on the left, since she will be able to use her forehand. Both girls must cover full length of the court, which means that both girls must have a variety of shots and be capable of moving well. If one girl is weaker than the other, a team will "play" that one girl, creating a game of singles against two opponents.

2. *Up and Back.* Weak when used by players on the defensive, since it leaves much of the side area uncovered. Also poor system when the weaker player is forced to take the back position. Good system for cutting off weak returns at the net, and for getting sharply angled shots.

3. *Diagonal.* Allows for protection against clears to the deep backhand corner, especially if the team consists of one right-handed player and one left-handed player; however, leaves the left-hand corner near the net open for drop shots, and the right-hand deep corner fairly open for well-placed clears. At times the weaker player may end up playing the backhand clears.

4. *Rotation.* Difficult and complicated to execute properly, especially if a team is made up of one right-handed player and one left-handed player. The players are continually moving and thus can move into their shots, using their forehands to best advantage. Demands that both players do a great degree of running and react smoothly as a unit. Leaves some areas open and vulnerable.

In the parallel system, each girl covers one half of the court, the division line being the center line. The girl on the left takes all shots hit down the middle, since it is her forehand, and each girl must cover all deep and short shots on her half of the court.

In the up-and-back system, one player must cover approximately one-third of the court from the net back to the short service line (sideline to sideline) and the other player must cover the rear two-thirds of the court. The player at the net sets up in the middle of the court just inside the short service line (heels usually on this line), while the girl in the back of the court positions herself about 5 feet inside the back boundary line, also in the center of the court. Who plays the net position and who plays the deep position is determined in three ways: (1) The server becomes the front player while her partner becomes the back player. Then, when the team receives, the receiver becomes the front player and her partner plays the back. (2) When serving, the girl serving is the front player and her partner the back player. But when they receive, the type of serve sent over by the opponents determines who goes up and who goes back. On short serves, the receiver becomes the front player and her partner drops to the back; however, if the serve is long, the receiver becomes the back player and her partner must come up to the net. (3) If one player is stronger than the other, she takes the back position at the first possible moment, while her partner plays at the net. (See Fig. 9–9.)

In using the diagonal system, a team combines the parallel and the up-and-back methods. An imaginary diagonal line separates the court. This line runs from about six feet from the back boundary line (right-hand court) to a point at which the short service line and the left sideline meet. The girl playing the right-hand court must take all shots along the net and down most of the right sideline, while her partner playing on the left must handle shots along all of the back boundary line and down most of the left sideline. This system is much easier if the team happens to be made up of one girl who is right-handed and one who is left-handed. In the unlikely event that both players are left-handed, the imaginary diagonal line would run from right to left. When both players are equally skilled, whoever is in the right area covers that area, while the other one takes the left. However, if a team has one strong player, the better player should take the left diagonal whenever possible in order to return the backhand shots more effectively. (See Fig. 9–10.)

Probably the hardest system of doubles play to understand and execute is the rotation or revolving method. It is a modification of the diagonal system, and involves coverage of the two areas while players are moving in a counterclockwise direction. This rotation evolves from a side-by-side defensive position to a one-up-one-back position when advantageous on offense. The player on the right covers short shots, while the player on the left covers deep shots. The position of the player on the right-hand side of the court is usually about two feet closer to the net than that of the player on the left-hand side: this makes it easier for the right-hand player to take all drop shots. Ordinarily, the player on the right-hand side does not back up more than one step to hit an opponent's shot. Instead, the player on the left will come over to take the shot on her forehand side, while her partner moves over to the left-hand-side position. When the player on the right-hand side must move over to take a shot at the net in the

Fig. 9-9. Playing up and back in doubles.

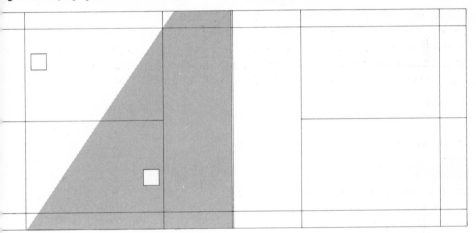

Fig. 9-10. Diagonal positioning in doubles.

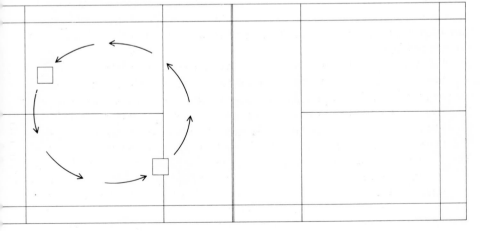

Fig. 9-11. Rotation method.

left corner, her partner moves over to the right side and replaces her in the right-hand net position. As soon as the first girl makes her return, she drops back to the left-hand corner. If both players were left-handed, the movements would be made in a clockwise direction, to allow them to use their forehands to the best advantage. If the team were to consist of one right-handed and one left-handed player, it would be very hard to use this system effectively. (See Fig. 9–11.)

**BOWLING**

COACHING EMPHASIS

1. Perfection of timing and balance.
2. Accuracy in picking up spares.
3. Consistency in scoring.
4. Working within established patterns of movement that bowler already has.

MECHANICS

1. Timing

   a) Remember that timing depends on coordination of arm swing and steps.

   b) Check a bowler's timing by standing to side and watching ball and feet of bowler.

   c) In four-step approach, if ball isn't back to left foot on second step, ball will go into backswing late. Bowler will have to cut backswing short or slow down approach during last two steps to allow ball to catch up. Correction: (1) start ball higher to gain momentum for swing, or (2) hold ball lower to give it a head start on the first step.

   d) If ball has gone past left foot on second step, ball will go into backswing too early, causing bowler to hesitate at top of backswing or to carry the ball back too high on backswing to allow feet to catch up. Correction: (1) lift ball slightly on first step so fall won't start until second step, or (2) hold ball closer to body so there will be less momentum on the downswing.

   e) Speed of approach can be controlled by pushaway. For a slower approach: (1) hold ball lower, (2) hold ball out farther from body, or (3) step before starting the pushaway. For a faster approach: (1) hold ball higher, (2) hold ball closer to body, or (3) start pushaway before first step.

   f) Let your sliding foot stop just before the lift.

2. Method of aim

   a) Avoid changing from pin bowling to spot bowling or line bowling indiscriminately; choose one method and stick to it.

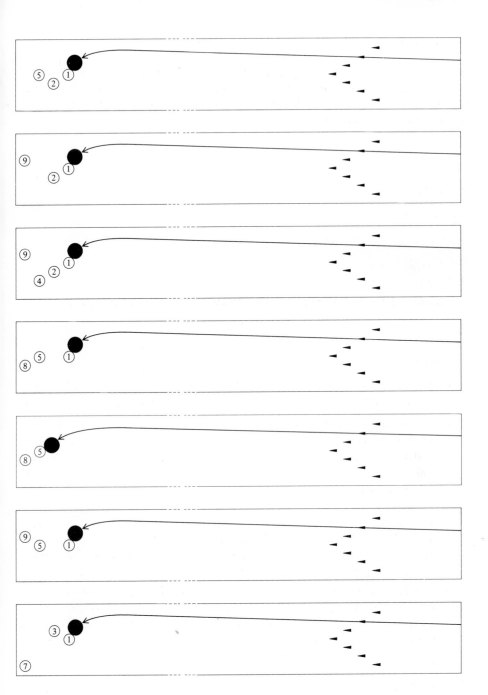

**Fig. 9-12.** Angles for picking up spares with hook ball. (a) Pins can be knocked down by hitting 1–3 pocket.

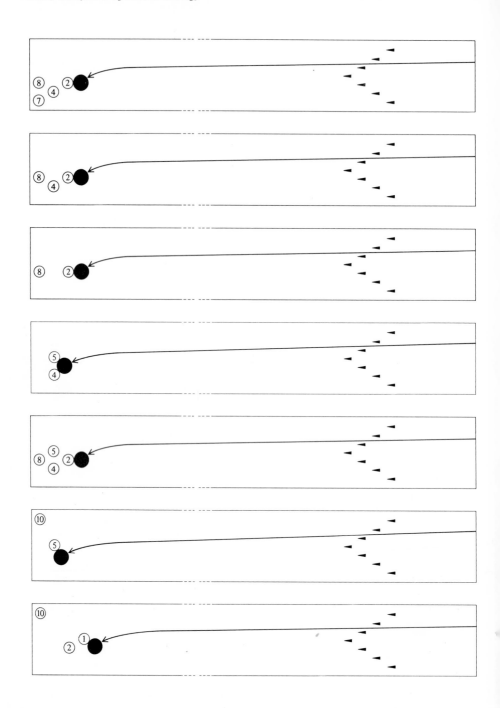

**Fig. 9-12(b).** Pins can be knocked down by hitting 1–2 pocket.

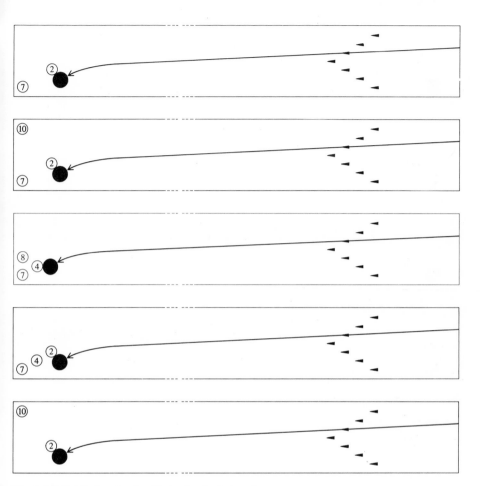

**Fig. 9-12(c).** The bowler should aim for the 2-4 pocket.

b) Spot bowling seems easier to most bowlers, because the spot they are aiming for is closer to them. Advanced bowlers usually select a specific board to roll their ball over (anywhere from 8-12 boards in from the gutter, depending on the type of ball thrown and the speed of the lane).

c) Regardless of the method of aim, concentration is necessary.

3. Picking up spares

a) Principles of angle and ball roll are important.

b) Pin movement is based on force and angle of ball when contact is made: (1) If you hit pin dead-center, it goes straight backward. (2) If you hit pin on side, it moves

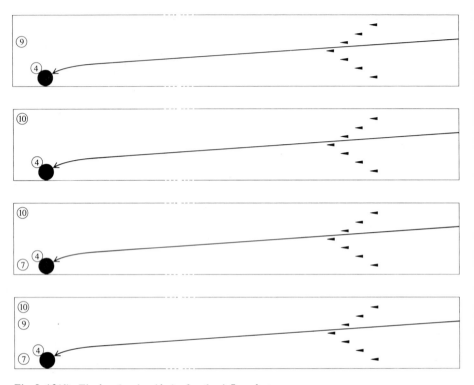

**Fig. 9–12(d).** The bowler should aim for the 4–7 pocket.

diagonally and backward. (3) If you barely touch pin on side, it moves to opposite side with very little backward movement.

c) Movement of ball depends on its weight and the speed it has been thrown: (1) The heavier the ball and the faster it has been thrown, the less it deviates from its path when it makes contact with pins. (2) Given equal force, the path of a heavy ball varies less than that of a light ball. (3) A fast ball is deflected less than a slow ball. Therefore a bowler should select a heavy ball that she can throw with a reasonable amount of speed.

d) To increase pin action, approach should allow ball to roll toward pins from as great an angle as possible.

e) When pins are left on a side, the ball should be rolled from opposite side to allow more alley for error and to increase angle at impact.

f) If only one pin is left, aim ball at center of pin to allow for slight error to either side.

g) To pick up sleeper (one pin directly behind another pin), aim ball at center of first pin to force it straight back into second pin.

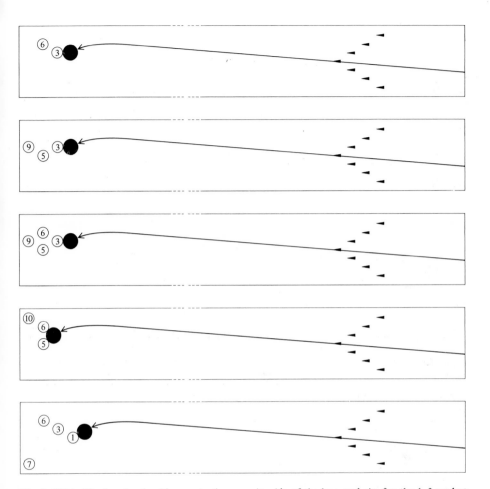

**Fig. 9–12(e).** The bowler should move to the opposite side of the lane and aim for the 1–3 pocket.

h) When several pins are left standing, use the principles of force and angle to deflect the first pin so that it will hit into the other pins.

i) See Fig. 9–12 for angle in picking up spares. Keep in mind that this angle will vary slightly depending on the type of ball being thrown.

j) If you are using the heaviest ball you are capable of controlling but can't get enough speed to knock pins down after hitting in pocket, you can increase speed of ball by: (1) holding ball higher to gain more momentum on swing, (2) using more pushaway, (3) taking ball higher on backswing (up to shoulder level), and (4) improving timing on footwork and swing.

4. Grips

   a) *Hook ball.* The V between thumb and first finger does not rotate. The thumb points toward 9 o'clock and fingers toward 2 o'clock position (some prefer to place thumb at the 10 o'clock position). Thumb comes out first; then, as fingers come out, the ball is lifted and a counterclockwise spin is created (when bowler is right-handed). Wrist should not be turned to get spin; spin will automatically result if bowler has correct grip on ball.

   b) *Curve ball.* Grip is the same as for hook ball, but a greater arc is obtained by rotating hand and wrist from right to left as ball is released. On the curve ball, the turn or lift should not be started until ball has passed left foot at foul line.

   c) See Fig. 9–13 for the stance, approach, and roll of the ball for the straight, hook, and curve ball. Note that this figure shows the straight approach and an approach with a "drift." The "drift" is not usually taught, although some prefer this type of approach because in some cases it allows an easier arm swing. Also, keep in mind that the stance, approach, and ball roll shown in Fig. 9–13 vary according to individual preference, spin on the ball, and the conditions of the lane.

| *Problems* | *Corrections and Coaching Hints* |
|---|---|
| *One shoulder ahead of the other.* Possible results: sidearm motion; ball being angled off to side. | Start approach with both shoulders parallel, facing pins. Check this position after delivery to see if parallel position has been maintained. |
| *Uneven approach.* Possible cause: first step taken out to side of approach line. | Concentrate on first step. Point toe toward approach line. Place piece of tape on floor where first step should be taken. |
| *Sidearm swing.* Possible cause: right shoulder behind left shoulder; ball held too far to left before approach is started; arm too far from body on the swing. | Keep head, shoulders, and body in straight line; hold ball more to right to allow swing to go straight backward; swing arm close to hip. |
| *Backswing too high.* Possible cause: incorrect pushaway. Results: too much speed, poor timing, and inaccuracy because of lack of control. | Don't force ball down alley in attempt to get more speed; hold ball closer to body; shorten pushaway. |
| *Not enough backswing.* Possible cause: incorrect pushaway. Results: lack of speed, little pin action, poor timing. | Hold ball higher; push ball out more on pushaway. |
| *Lack of smooth movements at foul line.* Possible causes: lack of balance or poor timing. Results: inaccuracy; too much spin. | Make slide smoothly, with weight balanced on left foot; don't apply turn until ball has passed left foot (curve ball); check grip before starting approach. |

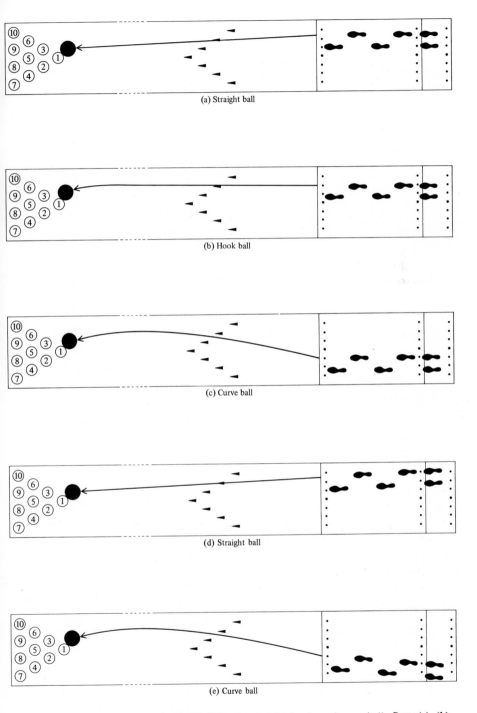

(a) Straight ball

(b) Hook ball

(c) Curve ball

(d) Straight ball

(e) Curve ball

**Fig. 9-13.** Stance, approach, and roll of ball for the straight, hook, and curve ball. Parts (a), (b), and (c) show a straight approach. Parts (d) and (e) show a slant approach.

*Wrong position during follow-through.* Possible causes: right foot may be too far to side; hand may not be pointing toward pins. Result: poor balance.

Balance weight on left foot; point left toe toward pins; keep shoulders squared to foul line; right leg should be back, right arm and hand extended toward pins.

*Releasing ball too soon.* Results: lack of speed, lack of control, hard bounce.

Take ball past left foot before release; pick out spot a few inches past foul line and "reach" out toward spot before release.

*Releasing ball too late.* Possible cause: weight staying on rear foot. Results: "lobbing" of ball and lack of control.

Balance body weight over sliding foot; bend from the waist; release ball when it is just past the left foot.

*Poor timing.* Possible causes: footwork too fast or too slow; backswing too low or too high; first step too long or too short; approach too fast; skip part of approach.

Take deliberate steps; build up speed slowly; if backswing is too low use more pushaway; if backswing is too high, keep ball in closer to body.

*Inconsistency in movements.* Possible causes: failure to start from same position each time; holding ball too far to left side of body; lack of pendulum swing; incorrect pushaway.

Line up the same each time for the first ball; hold ball at center of body or to right side before pushaway; take ball straight back and straight forward; push ball away before first step in three-step approach; push ball away on first step in four-step approach.

*Pins are left because of poor pin action.* Possible causes: ball rolled with too much speed or too slowly; too much skid or slide on the ball, pocket not hit correctly.

For more speed, increase pushaway to gain height on backswing and momentum on approach; if ball is too fast, keep pushaway close to body, and use a shorter approach or a heavier ball; try to get more lift and follow-through with hand toward pins.

STRATEGY

Strategy in bowling involves using a point of aim, understanding angle and force, consistency in picking up spares, ability to adjust to differences in lanes, and mental readiness, especially when pressure is present. Mental readiness consists of concentration and self-confidence, as well as the ability to adjust the point of aim until accuracy is obtained.

Pressure affects different people in different ways. If you are usually a relaxed bowler, you should be aware that you are feeling pressure when you begin to feel tense and your muscles tighten up. If you usually take your time and do everything deliberately, you are feeling the pressure when you begin to lose your concentration and vary your pattern of execution. Pressure especially affects the bowler who does not have self-confidence and determination. This type of person can cope with tension only by re-evaluating and accepting her own skills.

The most tension-prone person is the one who has had no competitive experience and who is not prepared for the pressures of competition. The only way she can cope with the pressure is to enter into competition every chance she gets, until she knows what to expect. The inconsistent bowler, because she must push herself to maintain a high score, also feels the pressure of competition.

Reasonable goals and concentration on the game, however, can lead to a relaxed competitor. The athlete prone to pressure should compete only against her own score and not that of an opponent. It goes without saying that there is no substitute for practice.

## GOLF

### COACHING EMPHASIS

1. Perfecting swing for accuracy and power.
2. Changing grip for deliberate slice or hook.
3. Hitting effectively out of poor lies.
4. Putting and reading greens accurately.

### MECHANICS

1. Swinging for accuracy

   a) Work to "groove" swing, so that movements are same each time.

   b) Check grip, stance, weight shift, swing, etc., to see that you do them consistently.

   c) Concentrate on hitting ball to a specific spot each time.

2. Swinging for power

   a) Remember that power depends on position of ball in relation to feet, leverage applied on swing, and timing on wrist snap.

   b) For woods and long irons, play ball opposite left heel; for medium irons, center it between feet; for height and less roll (usually short-iron shots), play ball farther back toward right heel.

   c) The more power you want, the more you should move ball toward forward foot and the wider the base of support should be (feet should seldom be farther apart than shoulder width).

   d) In the complete motion of the swing ("waggle," forward press, backswing, downswing, and follow-through), when you want extra distance, concentrate on two phases: (1) bracing or pushing with legs, and (2) good wrist action at right time.

e) For proper leg action, shift weight to rear leg on backswing, then to forward or left leg on downswing. Just before contact, complete shift by pushing strongly against ground with toes of right foot, giving more power from legs.

f) For proper wrist action, cock wrists on backswing. For maximum power, uncock them in the hitting area, just before actual contact with the ball.

| *Problems in Getting Distance* | *Corrections and Coaching Hints* |
| --- | --- |
| *Shifting weight to forward leg on backswing.* Causes: trying to keep head too steady; moving body forward as club goes backward. | Shift weight and turn in same direction as club moves on backswing; rear or right foot should "press" against ground as you shift weight. |
| *Body sways slightly.* Cause: improper body turn of shoulder and hips. Results: less than maximum use of muscles in back and left side. | Maintain address position, but backswing should result in a coil or turn of the body. This turning should stretch muscles of the left side. In practicing, turn back to sun and watch shadow to see if body sways as you make backswing. |
| *Left arm bent, right arm not cocked at start of downswing.* Results: poor use of muscles on left side of body; straightening of arm on start of downswing, which may lead to uncocking of wrists before getting to hitting area. | Shift body weight to forward foot immediately at start of downswing; move right elbow in close to side. Keep left arm firm and straight. Strengthen left arm by practicing backswing with club in left hand only. |
| *Lifting up in hitting area.* Cause: improper weight shift; uncocking wrists too soon; straightening legs. | Weight shift must come on downswing; do not uncock wrists until they enter hitting area; hit down and through the ball; flex legs until the follow-through. |

3. Hitting the slice

   a) Slices are caused by: (1) hitting ball with an "open" club face, and (2) hitting ball on an outside-to-inside path.

   b) For deliberate slice, change grip. This "weak" grip consists of turning one or both hands too far to the left of the shaft. Usually, in a normal grip, you can see two or three knuckles of left hand, and one on right hand. However, in slicer's grip, only one knuckle shows on left hand and two or more on right hand. (See Fig. 9–14 for slice grip.)

   c) In slicer's grip, the "V" of right hand points toward chin, or even toward left shoulder (in normal grip, it usually points toward right shoulder).

   d) As result of this grip, wrists turn to right at start of backswing, opening club face; almost impossible to turn club face to a square position for the hit.

**Fig. 9-14.** Slicer's grip and normal grip. (a) Weak position of hands, which leads to slice. (b) Grip corrected to eliminate slice.

e) Stance is open; right foot is approximately three inches ahead of left foot; this forces club head to start back outside line of flight, helping to produce spin needed for slice.

f) Sometimes people slice unintentionally; see helpful hints below.

| *Problems in Eliminating Slice* | *Corrections and Coaching Hints* |
|---|---|
| *Slice as result of weak grip.* Causes: incorrect grip; hands too far to left on shaft. | You should be able to see 2 or 3 knuckles on left hand, and 1 on right hand. "V" should point toward right shoulder. Make grip stronger by turning hands more to right of shaft. |
| *Slice as result of open stance.* Result: club face goes back outside intended line of flight. | Use a square stance, with shoulders and hips square and on line with target. |

*Slice as result of swaying.* Causes: too much weight shift to right foot, making it almost impossible to return weight to left foot on downswing. Results: an open club face or an outside-in swing.

Keep right leg firm, and turn hips on backswing; transfer weight to left leg on downswing.

*Hands too far ahead of club face before contact.* Causes: hips leading too much; failure to uncock wrists soon enough. Result: open club face at impact.

When hands have passed shoulder height on downswing, accelerate club head; un-cock wrists immediately before contact. Shift weight properly to get right hip movement.

**Fig. 9-15.** Grip to perform a hook shot.

4. Hitting the hook

   a) Use hooks to get ball around dog-leg or other obstacle on left.

   b) Hooks are caused by: (1) hitting ball with closed club face, and (2) hitting ball on inside-to-outside path.

   c) For deliberate hook, change hands to "strong" position on shaft. Move hands more to right. You should see three or more knuckles on left hand, while back of right hand may be turned so far that no knuckles can be seen. (See Fig. 9-15 for hook grip.)

   d) In hook grip, the "V" of right hand will point to right shoulder or even beyond. As result of this grip, club face is closed at top of backswing and at impact.

e) Use closed stance, with right foot about 3 inches behind left foot, forcing club face to start back inside line of flight.

f) On the hit, the wrists pronate; on the follow-through, left palm faces up and right palm down.

g) The hints given below offer some help in getting rid of an unintentional hook.

| Problems in Eliminating Hook | Corrections and Coaching Hints |
|---|---|
| *Grip too "strong."* Cause: hands turned too far to right of shaft. | Turn hands more to left, and grip shaft in palm and fingers. V of right and left hands will point between chin and right shoulder. |
| *Standing too far from ball.* Results: hook, as player has to reach out to hit ball, causing club head to go back on an inside path. | Move closer to ball; stand in more upright position. Take club head straight back. |
| *Compensating for hook.* Player anticipates hook and aims to right of target. Results: closed stance; club head forced back inside target line. | Use a square stance, with feet, hips, and shoulders parallel with target line; take club head straight back. Practice by placing piece of tape or yardstick on ground lined up with target. Then place feet in line with tape, and make club head follow tape back in straight line. |
| *Lack of firmness with left hand at top of backswing.* Results: too much domination of swing by right hand; club face turned to left. | Keep grip firm with left hand; may be necessary to use a shorter backswing. Strengthen left hand by squeezing tennis balls and by isometric exercises. |

5. Pushing the ball

a) Pushing causes ball to go to right of target.

b) Pushed ball does not have a spin or slice, but is usually result of: (1) incorrect alignment when addressing the ball, (2) club face closed at address or during downswing, (3) lack of hip turn, and (4) overemphasis on keeping head down [7].

c) After ball has been hit with a fairly square club face, swing is usually inside-out rather than straight.

| Problems Causing Pushing of Ball | Corrections and Coaching Hints |
|---|---|
| *Incorrect alignment and aim.* Causes: shoulders, hips, and feet are on line to right of target, forcing hands and arms to swing on a path to right of target. | Open stance from previous address, allowing shoulders, hips, and feet to line up with target. Place club down on ground to line up address position if necessary. |

| | |
|---|---|
| *Closing club face at address or early in backswing.* Causes: golfer "feels" this incorrect club face position during swing. Tries to compensate by opening club face at top of backswing; ends up pushing ball to right. | Be sure club face is square to ball at address, then carry club straight back. |
| *Incomplete body turn.* Causes: hip rotation is incorrect. Results: it blocks movement of hands and arms, causing swing to go to right. | Coil hips when turning to left; this allows arms to swing along target line. |
| *Keeping head down too much during follow-through.* Result: may force restricted turn of hips and shoulders. | Allow head to move and turn naturally during follow-through. This will let hips and shoulders make a natural turn. |

6. Pulling the ball

    a) Causes ball to go to left of target.

    b) Pulled ball goes on a fairly straight line, and is caused by: (1) incorrect coil of body on the backswing, (2) incorrect weight shift, and (3) uncocking of wrists too soon on downswing [7].

    c) After ball has been hit with a fairly square club face, swing is usually outside-in rather than straight.

| *Problems Causing Pulling of Ball* | *Corrections and Coaching Hints* |
|---|---|
| *Swaying to right on backswing.* Possible result: forcing club head outside of target line. | Maintain a fixed point around which you coil body, keeping right leg firm. |
| *Weight does not shift to right side on backswing.* Possible result: forces player to fall back on right foot on downswing, causing club head to go outside target line. | Shift weight to right foot on backswing in order to allow proper weight shift to left foot on downswing. |
| *Uncocking wrists too early on downswing.* Results: breaks up natural shift of weight to left side, forcing club head outside target line. | Don't rush hit; allow wrists to uncock naturally as they enter hitting area. |

7. Hitting effectively from poor lies

    a) *From sand traps:* Most effective means is explosion shot. Wedge is best club for this shot. Plant feet firmly in sand in an open stance, with ball off left heel. Use swing similar to pitch shot; hit sand one to two inches behind ball. Club head must not touch sand, should be open for best results in cutting through sand, and squared with target line. Concentrate on spot club will hit sand, and continue motion of club until it has cut through sand. Follow-through is important to prevent club head from stopping in sand and leaving ball in trap due to lack of force. If too little sand is taken, ball will go too far. If ball is not buried in sand, regular shot may be used instead of explosion shot.

| *Problems of Hitting from Sand Traps* | *Corrections and Coaching Hints* |
| --- | --- |
| *Ball still in sand after shot.* Causes: taking too much sand; lack of follow-through. | Hit closer to ball; be sure club head comes out of sand on follow-through. |
| *Ball goes too far.* Cause: taking too little sand. | Hit at least an inch behind the ball; watch *spot* you are going to hit, rather than ball. If sand is wet, decrease distance between ball and spot of contact with sand. |
| *Ball is topped and knocked deeper into sand.* Causes: looking at ball rather than spot behind ball; lifting up on hit. | Concentrate on spot one to two inches behind ball; keep knees flexed; hit down through sand. |
| *Poor balance.* Cause: not getting good foothold in sand. Results: club can hit too far behind ball; can hit on top of ball if weight isn't shifted properly. | Move feet around in sand until they are planted firmly. |

b) *From uphill lie:* Ball should be opposite left foot with weight on downhill leg. Club should follow slope of hill on backswing and follow-through. Hook or pull usually results from weight being concentrated on rear foot, so aim ball to right of target. More height and less distance will also result, so use a lower-numbered club than usual. If you cannot shift weight normally, choke up slightly on grip, take a shorter backswing, and pivot less than usual.

c) *From downhill lie:* Ball should be opposite uphill or right foot, with weight on downhill foot. Slice or push shot usually results from weight shift to downhill foot too early in swing, so aim ball to left of target. Open stance slightly, with swing following slope of hill. If possible, shift some weight to uphill foot on backswing. Ball will fly lower than usual and roll farther, so higher-numbered club should be used to get more height on ball.

d) *From side-hill lie:* Swing depends on whether ball is lower or higher than feet. In either case, ball is usually positioned in center of stance, so use a square stance. If ball is above feet, flex knees slightly, keep weight on balls of feet, and choke up on club (ball is closer to body than usual). Hook usually results, so aim to right of target. If ball is below feet, flex knees and keep weight more on heels to prevent too much lean forward. You may need to widen stance to help balance. Use lower-numbered club and three-quarter swing to compensate for need to reach more for ball. Slice or push usually results, so aim to left of target.

8. Putting

  a) Method of putting varies according to personal preference and comfort.

  b) You can use hinge swing (wrist action) or pendulum swing (arm action).

  c) Bring club face back with left hand square to putting line; keep club face as low and close to ground as possible. Then bring club face straight through ball and follow predetermined line of putt.

  d) When you stroke a putt, you keep club face in contact with ball longer than you do when you tap a ball, so this usually gives you greater accuracy.

  e) Place ball off toe of forward foot with head over ball. Ball placement, stance, and head and body position vary greatly with different golfers. Consistency is the key.

  f) Reading the green is an important part of putting. (See Strategy for information on this.)

STRATEGY

The golfer does not have to counteract his opponent's moves, as one does in team sports, but must be able to react to the golf course, environment, and opponents' shots in a confident and a controlled manner.

*Reaction to Pressure.* Many golfers, although they do well during practice rounds, score higher in a tournament because they can't handle pressure. Strategy in golf demands control of the emotions.

  On the tee, in the rough, and on the putting green: these are three places where pressure becomes particularly intense, usually because the player lacks confidence in his or her ability to hit the ball to a specific area (such as down a narrow fairway), or feels anxiety when faced with an unusual situation, such as a bad lie in the rough.

  Relating the unusual situation to a common one can often relieve the tension. For instance, a golfer can form a mental picture of a green in the middle of a narrow fairway and aim for the middle of the "green," rather than thinking about the hazards of the fairway. It also gives the player more confidence to select a club she knows she can control even though she may not get as much distance on the shot with this club as with another.

  On the green, the same principle can be applied if the golfer forms a mental image of the hole as being the center of a larger area about the size of a bucket. Aiming for the "bucket" rather than for a small hole gives the player confidence, and takes her close enough to the hole to make the second putt effective even if the first does not go in. Another image frequently used by golfers is an imaginary line or path about an inch wide that goes from the ball to the cup; the player tries to roll the ball down this imagined line.

*Hitting from the Rough.* When playing the ball from the rough, a person's first objective should be to get out of the rough and back on the fairway. The second objective is as much *distance* as possible. The player should select a club that she knows will take the ball out of the rough, regardless of the distance that must be sacrificed. In thick rough, a lofted club should be used. If there are overhead obstacles such as tree limbs, a lower-numbered club should be used to keep the flight low.

When playing the ball, the player should take everything into consideration: the wind, the terrain, the hazards, the distance, the best position to land if a second shot must be taken, the skill of the player making the shot, etc. The player should take risks only when the circumstances justify it.

*Placement of Shots.* The golfer should cultivate the habit of thinking positively, and of visualizing the shot she wants to make. On long shots, she has a better chance if she aims for the center of the green rather than for the pin, since a slight error can result in the golfer missing the green if the pin has been placed to the side. On close shots, she should aim for the pin, but play toward the low side of the hole if the green is not level.

She should aim the ball short if the hazards are behind the green, and long if the hazards are in front of the green. She should select a club that will give the desired distance without her having to overswing.

Hazards present a special problem, not only in concentration and confidence, but in club selection. If the hazard is close, players should select a club that will give adequate distance and enough loaf to send the ball over safely. If the player is not sure she can hit the ball far enough to clear the hazard, she should play the first shot to the front of the hazard so that the second shot can clear it.

When a golfer is approaching a green which has no hazards in front of it, she should use a lower-numbered iron for a pitch-and-run shot. She should aim the ball at the edge of the green and allow it to roll toward the cup. The wetness of the green determines the amount of roll obtained; a dry green gives the ball a faster and longer roll than a wet one.

*Playing the Grain and Slopes.* The speed of the roll for pitch shots and putts is also determined by the type of grass growing on the green. Most courses in the southern and southwestern states use Bermuda grass, which gives a very slow-rolling surface. Courses in the east, midwest, and along the west coast mainly use bent grass. Bent grass allows the ball to roll fairly fast, since its blades are narrow [31].

Another factor in the roll of the ball is the direction of the grain of the grass. If the grain goes toward the cup, the ball rolls faster than it does when the grain is going away from the cup.

You should stroke the ball with less force when you are putting with the grain, and stroke it harder when you are putting against the grain. To determine the grain: (1) look at the edge of the cup, (2) look at the fringe of the green, and/or (3) look at the reflection of the sun on the green. Inspect the cup for an area that is ragged-looking, and then stand on that side and look across the cup. You will then be looking into the grain. You may also rub your hand over the grass at the fringe of the green to determine the grain, since all the grain on the green usually runs in the same direction. The easiest method is probably to look for a reflection of the sun off the grass. You can detect more of a sparkle or a shine when the grain is running in the same direction you are facing.

Before you putt, look at the ground and try to determine whether there are any rough spots or divots that need to be repaired. Also check the cup for any rough edges. If there are spots that can't be repaired, stroke the ball a little harder than usual to prevent it from being bumped out of line by these spots.

Get a good picture of the slopes on the green by stepping back from the ball and looking at the entire green. Some golfers prefer to look at the ball from the opposite side of the cup also. As it gets closer to the hole, the ball tends to break more because of its slower speed. When you are putting uphill or up a slope, tap the ball firmly. When putting downhill, stroke the ball gently.

*Stance.* In the fairway, positioning of the ball in relation to the feet depends on the distance to be covered and the type of shot to be executed. Usually, when hitting the ball hard, a player uses the square or slightly closed stance (with the ball placed off the left heel). For shorter shots, such as chipping and pitching, she uses an open stance. An open stance is usually also used for trouble shots, such as shots from traps and from the rough. For chips and pitch shots, the ball is usually more toward the right foot, while for trap shots the ball is off the left heel.

*Playing the Wind.* A golfer must always consider the wind when making a shot. She should keep the ball as low as possible to reduce the effects of the wind, except in a tee shot, when the wind is coming from behind her. In such a shot, the objective is to get the ball high into the air so that the wind can carry it a greater distance. She can achieve this by: (1) teeing the ball up higher than usual, or by (2) playing the ball more toward the forward foot.

If the wind is blowing toward the golfer, she should: (1) use an iron that is 2 or 3 numbers lower than usual, (2) move the ball back slightly toward the right foot, and (3) choke up about an inch on the grip. These factors help keep the ball low.

If the golfer is using an iron and has the wind to her back, she should again keep the ball low, to keep the wind from affecting its flight. However, the wind will usually add some distance to the hit even when the ball is kept low, so she should use a higher-numbered club or less swing.

If the player is hitting the ball into the wind from the tee, she can keep it low by moving it more toward the center of her stance or by teeing it lower.

When a player is hitting the ball into a crosswind, she should apply the same principle of keeping the ball low. If the wind is coming from her left, she should aim the ball to the left of the pin; if the wind is coming from her right, she should aim the ball more to the right of the target.

*Adjusting to Climate.* When a golfer is playing on a cold day, she should keep both her hands and the ball as warm as possible (a cold ball won't travel as far as a warm one). She can keep her hands warm by wearing gloves in between shots or by keeping her hands in her pockets. When the ball is not in use, it will stay warm if she puts it in her pocket.

On hot days, a golfer should take salt pills before the round. If water is not available on the course, she should carry a thermos of water in her bag. She should try to maintain a leisurely pace to prevent fatigue from the heat, and if she perspires freely, she should carry an extra glove or a rosin bag so that she will always be able to get a firm grip on the club.

*Competing.* In medal play, the golfer shouldn't gamble, but should take the safest shots to get out of a trap or the rough. In match play, she can afford to take chances on a hole. Of course, even in medal play, there are situations in which the player must play boldly if she is to win. For instance, if she is down one stroke on the last hole and her opponent is in good position to chip on, she may have to gamble everything on her second shot.

A golfer should warm up properly before playing an actual round. She should sharpen up her timing in putting, use her irons to increase her accuracy, and hit a few balls from the tee. During these practice shots, she should concentrate and aim at something specific; this enables her to make last-minute adjustments before the round starts.

**GYMNASTICS\***

COACHING EMPHASIS

1. Rhythm, beauty, poise, expression, and variety of gymnastic and ballet moves for floor exercises.

2. Composition of steps, runs, jumps, turns, rolls, acrobatic stunts, balance positions, etc., for balance beam, with a mount and a dismount.

3. Strengthening program for upper trunk and abdomen, development of routine involving swings with changes in hand grips, and fluid patterns of movement from one bar to the other in work on uneven parallel bars.

4. Development of leg strength and timing for long flight, perfection in execution of specific vaults, and complete control of body during performance in vaulting.

MECHANICS

1. Floor exercises

a) Composition consists of exercises performed within 1 to $1\frac{1}{2}$ minutes.

---

\* Most of this section is based on materials and techniques obtained from a workshop conducted by Carolyn Osborn Bowers at the University of Utah, in the summer of 1963; used by permission.

b) Music should complement all movements.

c) Composition should cover entire area (12 meters by 12 meters or 39′4.44″ by 39′4.44″ at the minimum).

d) Composition usually starts with sequence of tumbling, followed by the main part of the routine, consisting of ballet jumps, turns, spins, balancing movements integrated with additional tumbling, and ends with another tumbling sequence.

e) The skilled competitor must blend tumbling and dance, and exhibit back flexion, forward flexibility and extension, support movements, balance, agility, and coordination.

f) When one is composing a floor exercise routine the possibilities are unlimited. A few moves that might be utilized are: the yogi handstand, front walkover, back walkover, Swedish fall, back somersault, and shoot-through. These moves are elementary in a sense, with the exception of the back somersault and the yogi handstand.

g) The *yogi handstand* demands excellent balance and body control, as well as arm strength. The prerequisite is a regular handstand, since the performer goes from this position into the yogi handstand by dropping the hips backward while jack-knifing the legs forward. The head is brought forward slightly, allowing the legs to counteract the angle of the back (which remains stiff). See Fig. 9–16.

| *Problems with Yogi Handstand* | *Corrections and Coaching Hints* |
| --- | --- |
| *Body falls backward.* Causes: dropping hips back too far; bringing head toward chest too much. | Let legs form approximate right angle to hips; don't tuck chin; contract stomach muscles and pull down with legs and toes. |
| *Body falls forward.* Causes: hips not going back far enough; head arched back too far. | Shoot hips back more; pull head forward slightly, and look at abdomen. |
| *Hands give way under body.* Cause: lack of arm strength. Results: inability to hold position for 3 seconds; extreme trembling. | Do program of exercises to strengthen arm and shoulder muscles; "push" with hands and fingers to ensure balance. |

h) The *front walkover* requires flexibility as well as strength. Start in standing position; lift arms over head as right leg is lifted, and step **forward** on right foot, placing hands on floor as for a handstand. The head should be up and the eyes focused forward, while the first leg is "kicked" over and the second leg pushed. The kicking leg should lead, while the arms and fingers help with the push. As the first foot lands, the other leg should be out and stretching forward to help pull the upper body up to its original position.

**Fig. 9-16.** Yogi handstand.

| *Problems with Front Walkover* | *Corrections and Coaching Hints* |
| --- | --- |
| *Inability to get completely over.* Causes: not enough "kick" with leading leg and push with second leg; not enough strength in abdominal muscles. | Kicking leg should lead throughout; second leg pushes against floor; muscles should be kept tight, especially those in the abdomen. |
| *Jerky movements.* Causes: poor timing; not enough muscle control. | Motion should be fluid, with one leg following other leg; do not hesitate; strengthen muscles in hands, arms, legs, and abdomen. Use spotters to help with feel of timing. |
| *Inability to come up to standing position.* Causes: not enough push with arms and fingers; second leg not stretching forward; abdominal muscles not contracting enough. | Use muscles of hands and fingers to aid in pushing body up; stretch out second leg to help lift upper body; keep abdominal muscles firm; contract abdominal muscles as hands and fingers push from floor; use spotters. |

i) On the *back walkover*, start in a standing stride position (one leg forward and one back), bend backward, and reach with the arms. The right leg should be kicked up and over while the extended hands are placed on the mat, and the left one follows. Land with right foot and then left, and end up in a standing position. The performer should have a spotter or a safety belt until she has perfected the movement. See Fig. 9-17.

| *Problems with Back Walkover* | *Corrections and Coaching Hints* |
| --- | --- |
| *Inability to get over.* Causes: not enough lead with head and extended arms; not enough kick with leading leg and push with second leg; not enough upper back arch or abdominal strength. | Lead with head and look back; try to arch upper back; reach with the arms; use "kick" on lead leg; push with second foot. Use spotter or belt to give added lift. Contract stomach muscles as lead leg goes over. |
| *Inability to stand up.* Causes: not enough push with hands and fingers; feet spaced too far apart or too close together when they hit floor. | As legs go over, push hard with hands and fingers; place feet in comfortable stride position. |

j) On the *Swedish fall* or forward drop, the performer goes into arabesque position, falling forward while keeping the back arched. The arms reach out, catching the body weight and lowering the chest to the floor by flexing the elbows. The free leg should be lifted, with toes pointed, as the fall is executed. See Fig. 9-18.

**Fig. 9-17.** Back walkover.

Fig. 9–18. Swedish fall.

| *Problems with Swedish Fall* | *Corrections and Coaching Hints* |
|---|---|
| *Lack of smooth motion as body is lowered to floor.* Cause: not enough strength in arms. | Use exercise program, including push-ups, to strengthen arms and shoulders. |
| *Incorrect body line.* Causes: sagging of stomach; not enough extension of free leg; head may be dropped or lifted too much. | Keep stomach muscles firm; extend free leg as fall starts; point toes; keep head up slightly. |

k) *Back somersault* should be performed with the help of two spotters with a belt. Spotters hold belt close to performer's waist and *lift*, as she does somersault. Spotters may use "on" hand to help her rotate. Progression for learning back somersault: (1) Jump high into air, tuck legs, return to original standing position. (2) Jump high into air, bring knees to chest, with arms extended straight up over head. (3) Attempt somersault, with help of spotters and belt. Complete movement involves jumping into air, lifting arms straight up, looking back and bringing knees to chest, rotating body until one can see the floor, opening up the tuck, and landing on the feet.

| *Problems with Back Somersault* | *Corrections and Coaching Hints* |
|---|---|
| *Jump not high enough.* Leads to inability to make the complete turn. Causes: not enough leg strength; incorrect pushoff; not enough arm extension. | Work on trampoline to build up leg strength and to get feel of arm extension. Flex knees and *push* hard on jump from floor, extending knees and ankles, and throwing arms upward. Jump should be vertical and not backward. |
| *Incomplete turn.* Causes: improper head position; jump not high enough; coming out of tuck too soon. | Look back and try to see the floor; person must be able to jump well before trying this stunt; hold tuck a second longer. |
| *Turn too far.* Cause: holding tuck too long; this results in off-balance landing. | Come out of tuck when you can see the floor. Don't keep head thrown back too long. |

l) The *shoot-through* requires flexibility, plus strength in arms, abdomen, and hips. Extend body with weight on arms, flex hips and shoot legs quickly through arms. End up in a sitting position, with legs and feet together and toes pointed. Body should be tilted backward, with hands behind the shoulder line and supporting the body as it leans. See Fig. 9–19.

(a)

(b)

Fig. 9-19. Shoot-through.

| *Problems with Shoot-Through* | *Corrections and Coaching Hints* |
|---|---|
| *Inability to get legs through arms without bending of knees.* Causes: hips not lifted high enough; too little flexion in hip area; not enough abdominal strength. | Push with toes and hands; work on flexibility of hips and strength in abdominal muscles. |
| *Lack of smoothness as body goes into sitting position.* Causes: not enough strength; failure to extend legs far enough forward; hands too close to hips in sitting position. | Use exercises to strengthen arms; slide legs forward with heels on floor and toes pointed; don't stop motion until hips are past hands. |

2. Balance Beam

  a) Composition consists of basic locomotor movements, sitting and lying positions, rolls and acrobatic stunts, some balance positions (maximum of 3 held positions may be used), and some dance techniques.

  b) Mount and dismount should be perfected.

  c) Balance positions are usually held for 3 seconds.

  d) Composition should run from one minute and 20 seconds to one minute and 45 seconds.

  e) *Straddle mount.* Progression for learning straddle mount is: (1) squat mount, (2) squat mount with feet placed outside of hands, and (3) straddle mount. Complete movement for straddle mount includes starting from a side stand frontways, running and jumping, lifting hips high, and keeping the legs straight. Feet are placed on beam outside hands in a wide straddle. Head should be up. Practice first on low beam.

  f) *Straddle hold* is accomplished by lowering the hips from the straddle mount, bringing legs forward, and supporting body in a balanced position by using a straight arm support. (See Fig. 9–20.) Practice on low beam.

| *Problems with Straddle Mount* | *Corrections and Coaching Hints* |
|---|---|
| *Legs bent.* Causes: not enough flexibility; feet too close to hands; performer's fear that she cannot balance. | Increase flexibility in legs and hips; place feet as far from hands as possible; practice straddle on floor first, and then on low beam. Be sure adequate spotting is done to eliminate fear of falls. |
| *Lack of balance.* Causes: not enough grip with hands and toes; too much or too little forward motion; head too far down. | Grasp beam firmly with hands and toes; judge approach so that jump motion is basically upward; let shoulders end up forward of the beam; keep head up. |

Fig. 9-20. Straddle mount, with gymnast going into a straddle hold.

Fig. 9-21. Forward roll.

g) *Forward shoulder roll.* Start in kneeling position, lower head and one shoulder to beam with head to side while hands grip beam underneath. Bring hips slowly up and forward as roll is executed. Hands help regulate speed of the turnover. Stomach muscles help control movement of legs as they come over head and then lower to the beam. Legs remain extended as they are brought up and over the head, with toes pointed. (See Fig. 9-21.) To come out of this roll, drop legs down on each side of the beam and let body come up into a sitting position; or go to a single-leg squat, pose, and then to a stand.

| *Problems with Forward Shoulder Roll* | *Corrections and Coaching Hints* |
|---|---|
| *Inability to get over.* Causes: insufficient pull with hands; insufficient push with toes; failure to move hips forward to start roll. | "Squeeze" beam with hands; push toes against beam; move hips over head. |
| *Lack of balance.* Causes: body not aligned with beam; going over too fast; not enough abdominal strength to control movements of legs. | Be sure roll is in a straight line. Start hips up slowly; allow body to roll over slowly, keeping hips and legs under control by contracting abdominal muscles. Use spotter to guide hips and body in a straight line. |

h) *Backward shoulder roll.* Start in back-lying position, dropping head to one side of beam, and gripping beam with hands. (Hand on head side should have heel of hand on top and fingers on side of beam; hand on opposite side from head should grasp under side of beam.) "Squeeze" beam and pull forcefully with hand under beam while contracting abdominal muscles to lift hips and legs over shoulder. Place one knee on beam, while extending other leg fully. Lower hips; use hands to push shoulders up in order to come up to a knee scale [4]. See Fig. 9-22.

i) To go from backward shoulder roll into a stand, place hands on top of beam at the neck. Bring legs up and "kick" left leg upward while pushing with hands to get head through. Bend right knee and place right foot on beam behind hands. Continue to swing left leg straight forward; flex left knee to allow placement of left foot on beam in front of right foot. Push with hands to help body go into the stand.

| *Problems with Backward Shoulder Roll* | *Corrections and Coaching Hints* |
|---|---|
| *Inability to pull body over.* Causes: improper hold with hands; not enough arm strength; not enough abdominal strength. | Place one hand on top of beam and other hand under it. "Squeeze" with hands. Use exercises to build up strength in arms and abdomen; may need to tuck legs in close to chest to start roll until strength is increased. Have spotter help start hip lift. |

(a)

(b)

(c)

Fig. 9-22. Backward shoulder roll, to knee scale.

*Inability to come out of roll to knee scale.* Causes: incorrect positioning of legs and feet after roll; failure to lower hips and to push shoulders up by pushing with hands.

Place one knee on beam close to body; extend second leg with toes on beam; lower hips; push with hands to lift shoulders up.

3. Uneven Parallel Bars

a) Routine is primarily swings, with grasps and regrasps in maneuvers from bar to bar.

b) Movements should be continuous.

c) *Back hip pullover mount.* Stand between bars, with body turned toward low bar. Place hands on low bar in an over-grip, with arms bent, and then swing one leg outward and upward (**leg** straight in piked position) while pushing off with the other to bring both legs up and around the bar. At same time, pull with arms, which are still bent, keeping body in close to bar. As legs swing over bar, arms should be extended to complete the move to a straight-arm support. Point toes. Lift head. (See Fig. 9–23.)

*Problems with Back Hip Pullover Mount*

*Corrections and Coaching Hints*

*Inability to get hips and legs up and over bar.* Causes: allowing body to drift too far out from bar; too little swing with legs; too little pull with arms.

Arms should remain flexed to keep body in close; swing leg up forcefully (keeping it straight) while other leg pushes hard from floor to aid swing; *pull* with hands and arms. Use spotters.

*Inability to end up in straight-arm support.* Causes: not enough strength in arms and shoulders; incorrect hand position.

Work on even parallel bars to build up strength in arms and shoulders; concentrate on straightening arms when legs go over bar; use over-grip.

d) *Double-leg stem rise.* Start with feet on low bar, hands in an over-grip on high bar. Flex knees and then extend legs in order to push hips out. As hips ride out, pull up and then press downward with arms to bring body to a front support. (See Fig. 9–24.)

e) *Single-leg stem rise.* Use same grip (the over-grip) as for the stem rise. Hang from high bar, and face toward low bar. Swing up, placing one foot on low bar. (We'll use the right foot in this example.) Then extend free (left) leg up in a tight pike, push with the right leg on the low bar, and pull up with the arms. Kip the extended (left) leg down to complete the move to a front support on the high bar. Keep chest and head up during support.

(a)

(b)

(c)

(d)

Fig. 9-23. Back hip pullover.

Fig. 9–24. Stem rise.

| *Problems with Stem Rise* | *Corrections and Coaching Hints* |
|---|---|
| *Inability to get body up for straight-arm support.* Causes: failure to get hips out far enough because of lack of push from lower bar; push off in wrong direction. | Flex legs; then feet can be pushed forcefully against low bar. The push is *out*, and up, rather than just up. |
| *Inability to go into straight-arm support when there has been sufficient push with legs.* Cause: weakness in the shoulders and arms. | Do work on even parallel bars to build up strength in arms and shoulders. Remember to rotate grip during move. |

f) *Kip from low to high bar.* From sitting position on low bar (rear support), use forward grip on high bar. Look at high bar or at point back of high bar until kip is almost completed; then focus eyes over high bar. In a piked position, bring ankles up to high bar; then force legs upward and outward, extending hips and completing a kipping action. As you force your legs upward, pull with your hands on the high bar. Rotate grip, extend arms, and let body go into front support.

g) *Straddle support.* From the straight-arm support, swing one leg through the arms into a stride leg support on the high bar. From this position, go into the straddle support on the high bar. This is done by moving the hand outside the forward leg to an inside grip. To maintain balance as the grip change is made, shift the weight to the other side and place it on the stationary hand. Then shift weight back; this brings the other leg around the bar, so that one ends up in a straddle seat with both hands supporting the weight. See Fig. 9–25.

| *Problems with Straddle Support* | *Corrections and Coaching Hints* |
|---|---|
| *Trouble in changing outside hand to inside grip.* Causes: not enough weight shift to other hand; other hand too close to forward leg. | Shift weight to other side before taking outside hand off bar; move other hand away from forward leg before weight shift. Practice on low bar first. |
| *Trouble in bringing second leg over bar and maintaining balance.* Causes: not enough weight shift to other side; failure to keep arms and hands firm and legs extended once both legs are over the bar. | Shift weight to other hand as second leg is swung over bar; lift hips; once leg is over, shift weight evenly to both hands, extend legs and point toes. Use adequate spotting. |

h) The *back hip circle.* Start with a straight-arm support, on the low bar, with hands in the over-grip. Swing legs back and up to build momentum. As legs swing back down toward bar, bring hips in; let bar press against upper thigh as legs go into a pike position. As you pull from the shoulders (arms bent slightly), let the movement be continuous around the bar, until you go up and over, to end again in a straight-arm support.

(a)

(b)

(c)

**Fig. 9-25.** (a)-(c) Double-leg bounce to a straight-arm support, then to (d) a single-leg swing-up, and from there (e)-(f) to a straddle seat.

| *Problems with the Back Hip Circle* | *Corrections and Coaching Hints* |
|---|---|
| *Inability to build up enough motion to make turn over bar.* Cause: not getting enough backward swing with legs on cast-away. | Make a slight "forward press" with hips and legs before swinging backward; contract back muscles. |
| *Inability to go over bar.* Causes: too little backward swing with legs; not keeping body in close to bar; not enough pull with shoulders. | Swing legs up as high as possible; bring body in close to bar, pressing it with upper thighs; (pike should be made as hips contract bar); pull with shoulders as legs go over. |
| *Inability to end up in straight-arm support.* Causes: arms bend too much on circle around bar; not enough arm strength. | Keep arms slightly bent as legs circle bar; pull with shoulders when body is below bar; rotate grip and push with arms as body comes upright. |

4. Side Horse Vaulting

   a) The scoring is based on length of flight, execution of vault, and general control of body throughout the vault.

   b) *Handspring vault.* The prerequisite of the handspring vault is to be able to do a handspring from the floor well before one tries it on the horse. Take a regular approach, and as you spring from the board, reach out and upward during vertical lift and go into a handstand position on the horse, with straight arms supporting body during contact of hands with horse. Keep your head up, with back arched and legs extended. Point toes. Let legs continue over as hands push off quickly from horse, allowing you to land on mat with both feet. (Body remains arched until landing and arms stay extended over head during afterflight.) See Fig. 9–26.

| *Problems with Handspring Vault* | *Corrections and Coaching Hints* |
|---|---|
| *Inability to get over on handspring.* Causes: incorrect takeoff or not enough arch in back; failure to push off horse with hands. | Don't slow down run before takeoff. Push hard with toes, balls of feet, and ankles against takeoff board. Swing arms up on takeoff and reach out; let hands touch horse when shoulders are almost directly above it; push-off with hands should be forceful. |
| *Landing off-balance.* Causes: too little or too much turn as body goes over horse; lack of flexion in knees and failure to use arms to aid balance when landing on floor. | Practice timing; let knees give when touching floor. Bend slightly forward at hips; arms should be approximately shoulder high and outstretched to help balance when landing. |

**Fig. 9-26.** Handspring vault.

*Body ascent not straight.* Cause: incorrect takeoff.

Do not arch body during preflight.

## STRATEGY

Strategy in gymnastics is defined by one's physical conditioning and mental preparedness. The girl who practices her routine enough to be confident in her ability to execute it has prepared herself to perform well. A gymnast should not attempt a new stunt during competition, or include one in her routine that she has not perfected during practice. The competitive situation fosters tension and anxiety, if there is a lack of confidence; this can lead to a poor performance.

The gymnast, for her protection, should have adequate mats and spotters. A warm-up period should precede any strenuous work on the equipment. If her hands tend to perspire, she should use a powdered magnesia chalk. She should adjust the uneven parallel bars, within the limits of the rules. Since she is allowed a take-off board for mounting the uneven parallel bars and the balance beam, and for vaulting, she should take advantage of this added height and bounce when she needs it.

When the gymnast is doing a difficult stunt on the bars, beam, or horse, she should have a spotter who knows the timing involved and who can handle her full weight if anything goes wrong. Knowing that she will be saved from a bad fall if she has a mishap will add to her confidence in performing.

## FIELD HOCKEY

### COACHING EMPHASIS

1. Conditioning for the fast pace of the game.
2. Practicing of fielding, dribbling, passing, and driving.
3. Perfecting straight tackle, circular tackle, and left-handed lunge.
4. Increasing skill for the flick, the scoop, and the dodge.
5. Teamwork and strategy.

### MECHANICS

1. The Flick

   a) The flick is valuable as a pass or a shot.

   b) The flick does not lift as high from ground as the scoop, and has spin to it.

   c) To deceive the opponent, the girl executing the flick should let her body position be the same for the flick as for the push pass or the dribble.

   d) Let one foot be forward, with weight on the forward foot; flex knees and reach out for ball which is slightly ahead of and well to the outside of forward foot.

   e) Put blade against ball; do not use backswing; left hand should be at top of handle, right hand several inches below.

f) Use strong arm movement; force stick toward body with left hand while pushing away with the right hand, creating a snapping action with the wrists.

g) Let weight move forward with pass; follow-through should be low and in direction of pass.

h) The flick is effective when opponent tries to intercept ball with her stick down.

| *Problems with Flick* | *Corrections and Coaching Hints* |
|---|---|
| *Lack of distance even though ball is lifted.* Cause: ball is scooped and has too much lift. | Blade should not be angled as much, use wrists to create force as it strokes ball, push and pull with arms should be simultaneously. |
| *Ball not lifted; too little distance with stroke.* Causes: ball too close to feet; body too erect; left arm movement weak; weight not shifted properly to forward leg. | Reach out for ball; lower body by bending legs; pull left arm back; carry ball with stick and keep motion of blade low; all of weight should be forward and concentrated over forward foot. |

2. The Scoop

a) The scoop is usually used to get by a tackle, but is effective for short passes and sometimes for a shot at the goal.

b) Its disadvantage is that, because of the blade angle necessary to execute it, it is not a deceptive shot.

c) To evade opponent's stick, scoop is usually made to dribbler's left.

d) Do not lift too high; this allows opponent time to recover.

e) Left hand should be at top of stick; right hand two or three inches below left.

f) Ball should be about two feet in front of body and to right of forward foot.

g) Tilt blade backward at a sharp angle (approximately 50 degrees).

h) Lift ball by pushing stick upward and forward with right hand and downward with left. At completion of stroke, the blade should be about knee-high.

i) Shift weight almost entirely to forward foot as you make scoop.

j) The lower the right hand is on the stick, the more leverage and height on the scoop.

k) The greater the angle of the blade, the more vertical the ball's rise from the ground.

| *Problems with Scoop* | *Corrections and Coaching Hints* |
|---|---|
| *Ball does not rise into air.* Causes: blade moves forward rather than upward; blade does not have enough angle to get lift; not enough force from hands. | Tilt stick backward more; put blade under edge of ball; use force that is upward rather than directly forward. Use leverage. |

| | |
|---|---|
| *Ball goes too high into air.* Causes: too much power from hands; body too erect on follow-through; blade has too great an angle. | Lift ball upward with hands, firmly but not powerfully; concentrate weight over forward foot; bend knees; decrease angle of blade; keep follow-through low. |

3. The Dodge

a) The dodge requires that the player be able to control both body and ball.

b) Since the dodge slows up an attack, use it only if pass to teammate is impossible.

c) *Dodge to non-stick side:* (1) Ball goes to non-stick side (dodger's right) of an opponent who is attempting head-on or straight tackle. (2) To avoid collision, player making dodge goes to stick side of opponent. To regain possession of ball quickly so that you can continue your dribble, aim pass just beyond opponent's left foot. Timing is the key: A dodge too soon will give opponent time to recover; a dodge too late may mean ball will be deflected off opponent's stick.

d) *Pull to left dodge:* (1) Keep ball in contact with stick during dribble as an opponent attempts a tackle. (2) Quickly pull ball few inches to left to avoid opponent's stick. (3) Continue dribble. Footwork for pull to left: Just before opponent attempts tackle, step to left with left foot and then move right foot to left also; shift weight to right foot to allow left foot to step forward. Movement of ball follows movement of left foot. Pull of ball to the left should not be diagonally forward; if it is, it may hit opponent's stick.

e) *Scoop dodge:* (1) As tackler rushes, tilt stick back. (2) Lift ball just beyond opponent's stick. (3) Continue dribble.

f) *Pass-and-go dodge:* (1) When you are dribbling and about to be tackled, pass ball to teammate. (2) Run quickly by tackler. (3) When teammate passes ball back, continue dribble.

g) *Stop dodge* (or reverse-to-the-right dodge): (1) When opponent tries to steal ball with left-hand lunge, stop quickly. (2) Reverse stick. (3) Move ball to right or backward. (4) Pass or continue dribble.

| *Problems with Dodge* | *Corrections and Coaching Hints* |
|---|---|
| *On dodge to non-stick side, player loses ball.* Causes: ball hit too far; dodge made too soon and opponent deflects ball. | Push ball beyond tackler rather than hitting it; time dodge for the last possible second, pushing ball just barely out of reach of tackler. |
| *On pull-to-left dodge, player loses ball.* Causes: ball intercepted, deflected, or hit into stick of opponent, usually because of poor timing, or hitting ball diagonally forward rather than directly left. | Step to left before opponent is close enough to reach ball; pull ball directly left rather than diagonally; be deceptive until last possible moment. Practice footwork both with and without ball. |

*On scoop pass, player loses ball.* Causes: pass too high, giving opponent too much time to recover; pass too low to clear opponent's stick.

Scoop-pass just high enough to clear stick. Tilt blade angle quickly to add to deception; when pass doesn't leave ground, blade is not angled enough or is not placed right up against, and under, the ball.

## STRATEGY

Because of the number of players involved in a hockey game, many different combinations of moves are possible. Players must use their heads and be deceptive on offense and aggressive on defense. They must react according to the situation rather than becoming sterotyped in their method of play.

In selecting players for specific positions, the coach should look for skill in areas that complement those positions. For instance, the right halfback should be able to execute the right drive, left-hand lunge, and left-handed roll-in. The center forward should be able to bully, pass to either side, make long drives to the wings, dribble well, and be deceptive. The right and left fullbacks should be able to mark, cover, tackle, and drive. And so forth.

*Offense.* Forwards should stay spaced and in line with each other (usually about a yard behind the ball) on the offensive half of the field. At times, the distance varies because of the defense, but usually forwards stay about 12–15 yards from each other until they reach the striking circle, at which time they angle in toward the goal, reducing the space between the players.

When a team gains possession of the ball, the wings usually move the ball downfield to about the 25-yard line, where they may pass it into the center of the field so that there is a better chance of scoring. Players should work on moving the ball well down *both* sides of the field, or the opponents' defense will learn to play the stronger side, eliminating the effectiveness of an attack.

Offensive movement is usually more effective if players use a variety of passes. A well-executed dodge can give a team the advantage if it results in outnumbering the defense, but dodges should not be used often because it slows down the attack. As they are moving the ball down the field, offensive players should learn to draw their opponents away from the ball in order to open up the defense.

Through passes (hits into space rather than to specific individuals) that are long and hard-hit are more effective against a team that is marking (or guarding) closely, while short, quick, deceptive passes are better against a covering defense (one which is "sagging" or playing deep on side away from ball). If the ball is passed from the left side of the field to the right side, the pass should be timed to lead the receiver so that she can take it on her stick side without breaking her pace. A pass from right side of field to left side is hard to field because the receiver must turn the blade of her stick to play the ball legally, while at the same time a pass from the left side to the right side is also hard because the stick must be turned to hit the ball.

The dribbler must be aware of the best time to use a square pass (a hit to a team-mate who is on line with the ball) or a through pass. In general, a through pass is more effective if the receiver is being marked, and a square or flat pass is better if the receiver is being covered. Once the dribbler has passed the ball, she should move away from the receiver of the pass to give her more area in which to move.

Passing is particularly important for the wing who has taken the ball down to the 25-yard line and who wishes to center it. If the defensive team is covering deep, the wing should send a flat or square pass to the inner or center forward. If the offensive players are being marked by the defense, a hard through pass that goes behind the defense is more effective and enables a forward to move in quickly for it. Players should choose a particular spot or person to hit to, rather than just hitting the ball into a general area.

Since the defense usually marks the offensive players when the ball is on that side of the field and covers when the ball is on the opposite side of the field, there is usually one attacking player who is free. One defensive method leaves an inner forward free because it is based on the principle that one fullback will mark when the ball is on her side of the field, while the other fullback covers to prevent an unchallenged dribble to the goal. The other defensive method is run on the principle that the two inner forwards should be marked all the time, so the side halfback on the side away from the ball must pull in to mark the inner forward, leaving her own wing unmarked [3].

The attacking team must determine which type of defense the opposing team is using, and plan their offense accordingly. Regardless of the specific offensive tactics they use, the attacking team's objective is to force the defense to move rapidly, and to open up holes and spaces that the offense can use to advantage.

*Scoring Goals.* Once the wing has centered the ball and the scoring area has been entered, the attacking team must concentrate on scoring a goal, following up missed shots, and preventing the defensive team from clearing the ball.

The forward who makes the drive for the goal from the edge of the circle should usually follow her own shot in. Those rushing should keep their sticks down in order to get another shot at any ball that has rebounded off the goalkeeper's pads or the goal posts. One other forward, generally the left inner, should rush the goal to support the forward making the shot. The left inner is usually the one to help because she is on the non-stick side of her forward line. The other three forwards remain at the edge of the circle to intercept any balls that might be cleared. (Many teams prefer to have the center forward and both inners rush all shots.) If a wing bringing the ball down or waiting on the edge of the circle should have a shot for the goal and rushes her own shot, the inner forward on her side must interchange positions temporarily and take the wing's place at the edge of the striking circle. If a goal is not scored, to prevent a call of offside, those who have rushed the ball must move back quickly before another shot is taken by a teammate [18].

If the left inner makes the drive and follows her shot in, the right inner usually rushes the goal. This covers the right and left side of the goal in case of a clear. The center forward may rush or stay back for an interception. If the right wing makes the shot from the edge of the circle, the right inner may rush the shot (left inner also rushes; this supports right inner on non-stick side), while the right and left wings remain back to cut off clears. The center forward may also choose to rush.

The attacking team must get a shot at the goal quickly once they have entered the striking circle, or the defense may recover and prevent a score. A player can save time if she remembers that her feet do not have to be in the striking circle in order for her to shoot for a goal, but that once the ball has crossed the boundary line of the circle it may be hit. If the attacking forward drives the ball hard at the goal and rushes with her stick down, she may be able to deflect the ball into the goal while the defense is trying to clear it.

Scoring within the striking circle depends largely on: (1) good spacing between the forwards, (2) continuous movement to open up defensive holes, and (3) aggressiveness on the rush after the shot.

Offensive strategy demands that a team be able to pick out the weaknesses of the opponents. For example, the forwards should watch to see whether the goalkeeper is weak in covering one side, or usually tends to stop the ball with the same foot, or clears consistently to the same side. A team that thinks on its feet can put this kind of information to good use.

The attacking team, when it is shooting for the goal, must use a variety of shots. When they are coming into the circle, hard drives are effective. Close to the goal, flicks and pushes can be gotten off quicker and are more easily executed. The forwards should aim for the open spaces of the goal cage, concentrating on their shots rather than watching the movements of the defensive players.


*Defense.* Basically, defensive play involves marking, covering, backing up, clearing and interchanging.

*Marking* is like man-to-man defense in basketball, with the defensive player playing within reach of the offensive player, but always slightly to the side of the ball and between the offense and the goal. Each attacking forward is marked or guarded by one defensive player. The left halfback marks the offensive right wing, the left fullback is responsible for the right inner, the center halfback marks the center forward, the right fullback takes the left inner, and the right halfback marks the left wing. Usually teams do not use a straight marking defense, but combine it with covering so that marking is done when the ball is on the defensive player's side of the field. If the ball is on the opposite side of the field, the defensive players cover (play deep toward the goal). Because of the difficulty involved in the fullback coming up from the covering position to mark the inner forward when the ball changes sides of the field, some coaches prefer to have the side halfback mark this inner forward when the ball is on the opposite side; if this system is used, the fullbacks and halfbacks must understand it completely.

*Covering.* When a team is covering, the center halfback marks the center forward continually. The right and left halfbacks never cover as deep in the field as the fullbacks. When the defense is marking and covering, the fullback who is covering is always approximately 25 yards deeper than any other defensive player (with the exception of the goalie), until the ball is brought down the field and closer to the striking circle, at which time the defensive players pull in closer together. As the fullback covers and plays deep, she tries to play toward the center of the field. This gives her a better chance to intercept long passes and to tackle any forward who has gotten around her defensive player on a dribble into the striking circle.

If the ball is in possession of the center forward in the middle of the field, the left fullback covers while the right fullback marks. The left fullback is then responsible for the center forward if she gets around the center halfback. It is easier for the left fullback to take care of her, because of the stick side.

One danger in defensive play is having both fullbacks on a line with each other. In this situation, a hard through pass can give the attacking team a chance to get the ball without challenge from a defensive player. As the ball changes sides of the field, the covering fullback must hold her position just long enough for the marking fullback to get back to the covering position, and then she should go up to mark.

*Clearing.* When players go from defense to offense, clearing the ball is very important. If the ball is intercepted in the striking circle, the clear should always be to the sides and never to the center of the field, because an interception at this point would let the opponents have another scoring opportunity. The coach should keep this in mind when working on drills, and emphasize the importance of the left fullback and left halfback clearing to the left wing or left inner, the right fullback and halfback clearing to the right, while the center halfback may clear to either side.

Once the ball has been cleared out of the circle and is being moved down the field, it is usually kept on the side of the field it has been cleared to, to avoid an interception on a long pass across the field. If the ball must be passed across the field, it is easier for the players on the right side of the field to pass to the left, although it is harder for the receiver to field the ball.

*Backing Up.* Although marking, covering, and clearing are important defensive skills, backing up must not be neglected. The defensive players (usually three halfbacks and one fullback) must follow closely behind their forwards and help intercept clears or passes out by the opponents. They must then feed the ball back to their attacking team, in order to keep the offense moving. These players who back up the forwards usually play approximately 5–10 yards behind them. If the ball should get past them, they must quickly drop back into their defensive positions. See Fig. 9–27 for positioning when backing up.

*Interchanging.* Positions must be interchanged when one of the defensive players has been left behind on a play. The covering fullback must pick up the dangerous free forward, while the halfback on the same side of the field must take over the fullback's position. (See Fig. 9–28.) Players should stay in their changed positions until: (1) play has moved to another part of the field, (2) their team has gotten the ball and gone on offense, or (3) a goal has been scored.

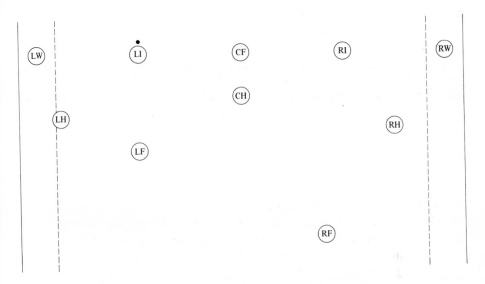

Fig. 9-27. Positions of players backing up forward line.

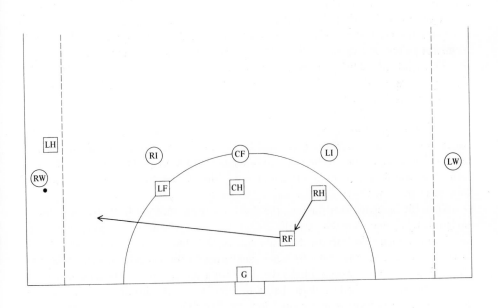

Fig. 9-28. Interchange of positions when left halfback has been passed by right wing.

*Free Hit.* The free hit must be taken immediately to be effective, and is usually taken by the back who is closest to the ball at the time (halfback when possible). When the attacking team gets a free hit at the side edge of the striking circle, it is usually quicker to have the wing take the hit. When the free hit is awarded near the player's own goal, she should hit it toward the sideline and as far down the field as possible. When the free hit is given near the opponent's goal, the player should try to center the ball. Players on the attack must position themselves to open up spaces for the hit. If the forward or halfback of the attacking team takes a free hit right outside the striking circle, the right and left inners should pull away from the center. This should draw the defense away and leave two openings for a pass: (1) a short pass behind the defense, or (2) a direct or flat pass to a cutting teammate.

On free hits, the defensive forwards should mark the opposing forwards, trying to cover all possible passes; the defensive backs are then free to mark or cover the spaces which might lead to a score. Another possibility is for the three close, defensive forwards to form a blockade in front of the ball about to be hit. Setting up about 5 yards from the ball and within about five yards of each other eliminates most of the angles for the hit. It is good strategy at times for the player taking the free hit to pass it to one of her backs. The defensive team must be alert to this possibility.

*Roll-In.* The roll-in is usually taken by the right or left halfback, unless it is near the striking circle of the opponent's goal, at which time the wing should take it. The offensive team, by their movements, must try to open up spaces. The most likely receivers are the wing, the inner, or—as a surprise tactic—the fullback. If a halfback is taking the roll-in, it is usually rolled to the wing, provided she can move quickly enough to elude the defense marking her. The inner forward on the side of the roll-in should cut toward the alley as the roll-in is taken. If she gets the ball, she should pass it quickly and then return to her correct position in relation to the other forwards.

There is an exception to this when the roll-in is near the opponent's goal. Then the inner forward should not go out, but should stay closer to the middle of the field, nearer to the scoring area. The player rolling the ball in must be deceptive. If the roll-in is being taken close to her own goal, she should try to send the ball way downfield. The defensive team naturally tries to keep the offensive team from getting a good roll-in.

When the ball goes over the line, the defensive team must get to its positions immediately. The opposing wing usually stands in front of the attacking wing, while the opposing halfback moves to the defensive side of this wing to cut off the pass to the most likely receiver. The opposing inner usually marks the attacking inner, while the fullback of the defensive team marks the space for a possible pass. The defensive forwards position themselves to block spaces and to cover all possible angles of passes. If the roll-in is taken near the opponent's goal, the ball should be rolled to the best possible position in the center of the field, to give the offensive team a chance to score by rushing the ball. In the defensive end of the field, it is usually best to roll the ball up the alley and close to the sideline.

*Tackling Back.* If a defensive player misses a tackle or is passed, she must quickly turn around and try to get back into position to regain the ball. If a forward has the ball stolen from her, she must tackle back immediately. A tackle back on the right wing should be a circular tackle (a missed left-hand lunge would give the wing a clear path to the goal). The circular tackle in this situation also helps keep the ball away from the center of the field as the scoring area is approached.

The defensive player backing up the bully must be prepared to tackle the opponent if she gets the ball. If the defensive player gets the ball after the bully, she should be ready to clear the ball to the side.

*Corner Hit.* When a corner hit is being taken, each defensive player must pull out quickly to either mark her opposing offensive player or to cover. Usually, possible receivers are marked (if hit is taken by right wing, then left halfback, left fullback, and center halfback go out to mark opponents), while the right fullback and right halfback stay in a covering position. The players must be marked closely while in the striking circle.

The offensive wing takes the hit, and should place the ball hard to the stick side of one of her forwards (usually the closest inner). The dodge is a valuable weapon during a corner, since a poorly hit or fielded ball may cause congestion in which an immediate drive for the goal is impossible.

Since a ball that has been hit hard moves faster than a person can run, the forwards should wait for the ball to come to them. This gives them added time to make the stop and then the shot for the goal. On a slow or a poorly hit ball, however, the forwards must more quickly toward the ball.

*Goalkeeper's Responsibilities.* The goalkeeper must be a specialist in defensive maneuvers. She must be able to clear the ball to one of her teammates with her feet or stick. Any time an unmarked forward is approaching the goal, the goalkeeper must come out and try to tackle her before she gets an unchallenged shot at the goal. If the goalie can reach the ball before the opponent can, she must do so without hesitation. She should never come out if there are two forwards free in the circle, but as she waits for the offense to make their move, she must try to cut off the best angles for shots. Her best stop is with her pads. She should learn to "give" with the ball as it hits her legs, and then clear the ball immediately with her instep to a back or a side halfback at the nearest side of the field. She must never clear across her goal, and she must be able to clear with either foot. She should use the instep in preference to the toe because it gives more accuracy and does not tend to lift the ball into the air. The goalie should not run into the ball, since the force of her body may cause it to rebound beyond her reach, although there are times when she will have to kick the ball while on the run.

The goalie must be taught to stop the ball with her hand without advancing it. She must also be adept at clearing the ball with her stick when it is beyond the reach of her feet. Only practice will help her judge how far she may pull out and what movements she must make to prevent the offensive team from having the best angles for making shots. See Fig. 9-29.

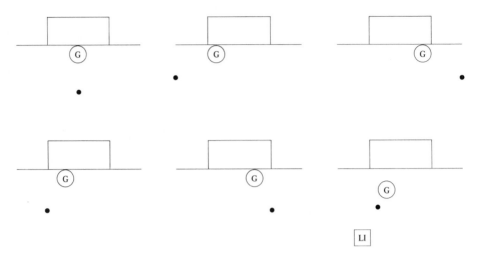

**Fig. 9–29.** Positions of goalkeeper in relation to ball. Last diagram shows goalkeeper coming out to clear ball before opponent can reach it.

## SKIING

### COACHING EMPHASIS

1. Strengthening program for legs, feet, ankles, and arms.
2. Encouraging players to participate in off-season and pre-season activities that build up endurance and balance, such as soccer, water skiing, rope skipping, etc.
3. Practicing skiing movements basic to downhill, slalom, and giant slalom.
4. Emphasizing speed, rhythm, and body control.

### MECHANICS

1. Waxing skis [10] (Laminated skis usually need wax only when it is raining, snowing, or the temperature changes suddenly.)

   a) Wax comes in solid form, but may be applied as solid or liquid.

   b) Liquid stays on longer, but takes longer to apply.

   c) To apply liquid wax: (1) melt solid wax, (2) apply with small brush applicator, and (3) allow to dry.

   d) To apply solid wax, rub solid bar of wax over skis. If wax is too hard to go on evenly, use it inside warm building.

   e) Apply from heel of ski toward the tip, rubbing into groove also.

   f) Use hard wax when there is a sudden drop in temperature or when snow is dry and nonsnowballing; use medium wax when temperature is near freezing or when snow conditions are changing while you are skiing; use soft wax when snow is thawing or sticky.

**Fig. 9-30.** Slide-slipping. (a) Knees are swung away from hill to allow skis to slide. (b) When knees are swung back toward hill, the ski edges stop slide.

g) Carry a piece of graphite or paraffin wax in pocket to use when your skis do not move smoothly.

2. Sideslipping

a) Used in skiing turns; allows skier to slow down on turn, or to stop if necessary.

b) When in traverse position with weight on downhill ski, edge skis by flexing knees forward and toward the hill. Upper body faces downhill ski.

c) Keep knees and skis together with weight on downhill ski.

d) Swing knees slowly away from hill, releasing the edges and flattening the skis to allow a drift down the hill in a sideways motion. See Fig. 9-30.

e) To slow down, swing knees back toward hill to re-edge skis.

**(a)**

**(b)**

**(c)**

Fig. 9-31. Parallel turn.

f) To make sure that *both* skis flatten out for the sideslipping motion, press the uphill knee into the downhill knee.

| *Problems in Sideslipping* | *Corrections and Coaching Hints* |
|---|---|
| *Inability to slow down while sideslipping.* Cause: failure to edge skis properly, because of incorrect knee action or poor weight concentration. | Knees should move back toward the hill *together;* try to feel edges cutting into the snow; keep weight on downhill ski. |
| *Loss of balance when executing sideslipping motion.* Causes: knee swing away from hill too extreme; body leaning too much downhill. | Knee movement should be a gentle one; don't let body lean downhill, although weight is concentrated on downhill ski. |

3. Parallel Turn from Traverse Position (see Fig. 9–31).

(d)

a) While in a transverse position, weight is on downhill ski, which is edged to prevent slipping.

b) Uphill ski is placed ahead about four inches to help lead the downhill ski on turn.

c) Shift body weight from downhill ski to uphill ski by: (1) leading with shoulders and hips facing slightly uphill (head should be facing toward tip of uphill ski), (2) pushing on downhill ski to send weight to uphill ski, (3) flexing uphill knee to accept change in weight, (4) turning uphill knee in (downhill) to get slight edge.

d) The flexing and the turning in of the uphill knee will cause foot to twist in a counterclockwise direction, forcing ski across fall line in downhill direction.

e) When downhill ski (which was uphill ski before turn) begins to edge because of weight concentration over ball of downhill foot, bring uphill ski parallel and about four inches ahead of downhill ski, and repeat movements for another turn.

| *Problems in Parallel Turn* | *Corrections and Coaching Hints* |
|---|---|
| *Loss of balance during turn.* Cause: head, hips, and shoulders in wrong position, causing weight to shift to wrong foot (uphill). | Hold head diagonally forward toward tip of uphill ski; let hips and shoulders face downhill ski. |
| *Inability to make turn.* Causes: improper weight shift; failure to edge uphill ski; upper body facing wrong way. | Shift weight from downhill to uphill ski, bending uphill knee and turning it in to slightly edge the ski. To start turn, aim head toward tip of uphill ski, let hips and shoulders slightly face direction of weight shift (uphill). During turn, head, shoulders, and hips maintain this position as uphill ski becomes downhill ski. |

4. Stopping from Parallel Turn

a) Turn shoulders and hips quickly in the direction opposite to that which skis are traveling.

b) Lean out with knees bent forward and in at an angle.

c) The movements force skis to edge and dig into snow deeply, bringing you to a quick stop.

5. *Wedeln* (consecutive parallel christies without traverse)

a) Practice a series of quick parallel turns using poles (commonly called "fishtailing").

b) Keep skis almost flat.

c) Let chest face downhill; let heels of skis shift from side to side. (Practice this at a slow speed by lifting tails of skis off snow about 3 to 4 inches in a down-up-down motion. Let poles touch snow on down motion.)

d) Allow skis to edge slightly as you make turns going downhill.

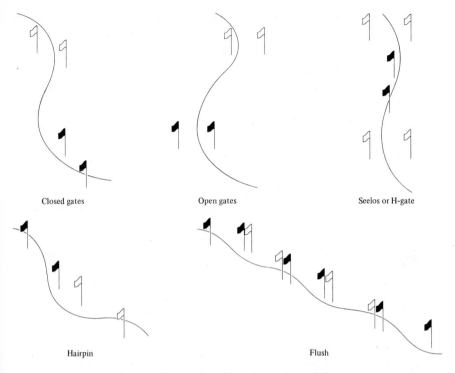

**Fig. 9–32.** Positioning of flags for racing variation.

e) Place pole at exact moment you shift weight to other foot, and allow tail of skis to slide about 6 inches on each turn.

*Strategy.* In alpine racing (downhill, the slalom, and the giant slalom), try to eliminate errors in judgment while maintaining as much speed as possible. Even a slight error can lose the race, since time differences are usually only fractions of seconds.

The order in which contestants go down the hill can make a big difference, since snow conditions change. With a competitor leaving the gate every 60 seconds, you don't have much time to get mentally prepared while waiting at the gate. You must be ready before the race starts.

In the downhill race, speed is the main objective. In this event, the gates cannot be set any closer than 33 feet from each other, which means that the turns are long enough to be taken at a fast clip. Since the event is run at maximum speed, it demands endurance and daring.

Slalom racing requires agility, quick reflexes, and the ability to make turns quickly as you go through gates. In slalom racing, the poles of each gate are spaced at least 10 feet apart, with at least $1\frac{1}{2}$ feet between each set of gates [33]. Most slalom courses are so set up that they force skiers to make a turn every second, with the race taking about a minute. For slalom gates, see Fig. 9–32.

In the giant slalom, the poles are set a minimum of 16 feet from each other. Since the gates are farther apart than those in the slalom, this race is a little faster, forcing the racer to combine speed with the ability to make turns.

The good competitor must be able to read the slopes and snow conditions, and adjust her skiing accordingly. At times she must be willing to gamble and at other times she must play it safe. If she is behind in time and it is her last run, she may have to gamble with her speed and her turns. If she is ahead in time, she must try to get down the hill in good time without taking chances on a fall or an error which would cost her her lead.

The skier must learn to take the turns tight and to anticipate the gates ahead in order to time her movements so that she will be in the best position for the next turn. Many top racers are using the step turn in slalom racing, and are finding it very effective in cutting down time. To execute a step turn while racing, move the unweighted uphill ski lightly over the snow into a stemmed position. (Maintain contact between the inside edge of ski and the snow; this will give you a continuous "feel" of the snow and the terrain.) Then place your weight firmly on the uphill ski while at the same moment starting the turn. (To start the turn, unweight the uphill ski less than you normally would in a parallel turn, with a greater weight shift from one leg to the other.) Turn the uphill ski into the fall line while bringing the lower ski in close. Then pass the inside pole in the conventional position. [47]

Although a racer shouldn't be overcautious if she wants to end up with a good time, she also shouldn't be over-daring, since a fall could eliminate her from the race.

The racer must learn to concentrate as she whips down the course at speeds of 25–45 miles per hour, and to react strictly by reflex as her skis move over different terrain. The real competitor must be a fearless and determined person, capable of precise body movements and mental awareness at top speeds. Practice on different types of slopes and under different ski conditions helps condition skiers to make sound decisions in competitive situations.

Some techniques are especially helpful to the racer. For a fast start out of the gate: (1) Plant both poles in front of the starting gate. (2) Place toe of one boot up to starting line with other about 12 inches back (feet should be about a foot apart to aid in push-off). (3) Keep body low, with bend at hips, knees, and ankles. (4) Keep weight forward on balls of feet rather than back on heels. (5) Push off hard with poles and legs. (6) Bend your knees to absorb bumps.

On sharp, steep slopes or slalom courses, using two poles to start a turn enables the racer to unweight skis more easily.

To accelerate from flat starts and in slower areas of racing course, use the skating step. Push with one leg and then the other, using the inside edge to create a more powerful thrust against the snow and to control body movement forward.

When making a turn, keep 12–18 inches away from the pole. Complete your turn before you enter the gate line.

Bend your knees to absorb bumps.

If you take a fall, and have any control at all, try to fall to the side of your skis and slightly backward. Relax as much as possible. Check safety bindings each day to be sure they release properly.

# SOFTBALL

## COACHING EMPHASIS

1. Working on fundamentals of throwing, catching, batting, and pitching.
2. Doing special work on sidearm throw, bunting, pitching, place-hitting, fielding, and base-running.
3. Strategy.

## MECHANICS

1. Sidearm Throw

a) The sidearm throw is used when the fielder does not have time to come up into an erect position for throw, or when the baseman catches a low ball and must release it quickly for a double play.

b) Grip is same as for overarm throw.

c) While body is in low position, swing arm back below shoulder level and then forward almost parallel to ground; finally extend arm and snap wrist for force. When you release the ball, your thumb should be on top, your first and second fingers should grip the under side of the ball, and your third and fourth fingers rest on the side of the ball.

d) Body movement: (1) Lift up with throw while rotating forward; (2) shift weight from rear to forward foot; (3) extend arm about waist high and in the direction of the throw.

| *Problems with Sidearm Throw* | *Corrections and Coaching Hints* |
|---|---|
| *Throw goes to right of intended target.* Cause: ball released too early in throw. | For accuracy, wrist snap and release must be consistent. Hold wrist flexion and release a second later. Hang a tire or a hula hoop up and practice throwing through it. |
| *Ball goes to left of intended target.* Cause: ball released too late in the throw. | Snap wrist and extend elbow a second or so sooner. |
| *Ball goes too high or too low.* Cause: arm swing and follow-through not parallel to ground. If hand drops down, arm swing is upward, causing ball to go too high. If hand comes back too high, swing is down, causing ball to go too low. | Bring hand back no lower than hip and no higher than shoulder. |

**2.** Batting

a) Grip: (1) The hand about an inch from end of bat is the usual grip for power and control. (2) For accuracy in placement, and for times when pitcher is very fast, keep hands 3 or 4 inches above end of bat (choke grip). (3) When power is more important than control, use the long grip (hand at end of bat).

b) Relax hands while waiting for ball; just before hit, tighten grip.

c) Stance: (1) Face plate, a bat's length from outside edge. (2) Vary position according to pitcher, by moving back or forward in box. (3) For fast balls and curves, move back in box to allow break and time to react; or you may prefer to move forward to hit curve or drop ball before curve or drop develops. (4) For bunts or hit-away situations, stand forward in box so you are closer to first base. (5) Keep feet about shoulder width apart. (6) Point rear foot toward plate and turn forward foot at about a 45-degree angle to allow good weight shift.

d) To hit ball: (1) Bend knees and place weight evenly on both feet. (2) Bring bat back at about shoulder level, while rotating shoulders and hips away from pitcher (3) Keep arms out and away from body. (4) Cock wrists and watch pitcher over left shoulder. (5) Watch ball all the way.

e) Just before release, shift weight to rear foot. Start swing by shifting weight to forward foot (or even step with forward foot). Rotate hips and shoulders toward ball, and swing bat forward and parallel to ground.

f) Arm action: (1) Let left arm pull bat forward while right arm pushes; (2) snap wrist on contact. (3) Follow-through: wrists about shoulder high, palm of left hand faces up, and palm of right hand faces down.

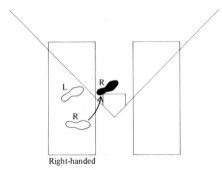

Right-handed

**Fig. 9–33.** Batting stance, with right foot taking first step toward first base.

g) Push off with forward foot. For run to first base, take first step with rear foot. See Fig. 9–33.

3. Place Hitting

a) Change direction of hit by swinging bat faster or slower, using extreme wrist action, or changing position of feet at plate.

b) To hit to left field, swing more quickly; to hit to right field, swing late.

c) Remember that change in wrist action is hard to control.

d) Since change in position of feet lacks deception, move forward foot at last possible second.

e) To hit to left field, use an open stance (pull forward foot back 2 or 3 inches). To hit to right field, use a closed stance (move forward foot farther toward the plate). See Fig. 9–34.

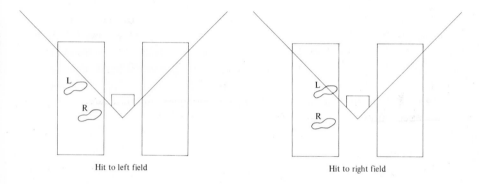

Hit to left field

Hit to right field

**Fig. 9–34.** Open stance to hit to left field; closed stance to hit to right field.

4. Bunting

a) Bunting is used to advance runner on base, or to get fast runner to first.

b) For deception, use regular batting stance.

c) Hit ball down first- or third-base line, preferably halfway.

d) To bunt: (1) Use regular stance; pivot and face pitcher at last moment. (2) On pivot, keep body low. (3) Slide right hand up bat to about trade mark. (4) Hold bat loosely by thumb and index finger of right hand. (5) Hold bat firmly with left hand at end of bat. (6) Let bat "give" when contact is made.

e) Pivot on forward foot, stepping up with rear foot. Be careful not to step out of batter's box.

f) Get bat over plate and parallel to ground before ball reaches plate.

g) Slant bat in direction of desired hit.

h) To drop ball close to the plate, hit it on top, "giving" on contact for slow roll. Hitting below center will result in "pop-up."

i) Don't try to bunt high pitched ball.

j) If runner is on second or third, don't bunt to third-base line.

| Problems in Batting | Corrections and Coaching Hints |
|---|---|
| *Lack of power.* Causes: wrong grip; incorrect stance; failure to shift weight; lack of wrist action. | Use regular or long grip (long grip for most power); use open stance; shift weight from rear to forward foot; uncock wrists as contact is made. |
| *Lack of control.* Causes: wrong grip; failure to watch ball; lack of timing on swing. | Choke up on bat with hands three or four inches from end; keep eyes on ball until ball is actually hit. Concentrate on hitting to a particular area during practice. |
| *Poor balance.* Causes: poor stance; batter too far from plate; batter too close to plate; feet too close or too far apart. | Move closer to plate to prevent lunging at balls on outside corners; move back slightly to prevent falling back on inside balls. Place feet approximately shoulder width apart. Players who step toward the ball when they hit should not use as wide a stance (usually feet should be about 6 inches closer together). |
| *Ball hit too far to right.* Causes: stance closed; swing late; wrists not uncocked soon enough. | Keep stance square to plate; swing a fraction sooner; uncock wrists just before contact. |
| *Ball hit too far to left.* Causes: stance open; swing too early; wrists uncocked too soon. | Keep feet parallel, but forward foot turned at about a 45-degree angle; swing fraction later than usual; delay uncocking of wrists. |
| *On bunt, ball rolls too fast.* Causes: right hand does not "give" to allow bat to move backward as ball hits it; because of incorrect positioning, bat is moved toward ball before ball gets to plate. | Allow right hand to be relaxed and to recoil slightly as ball hits bat; get bat into position over plate before ball gets there. |
| *On bunt, ball goes into the air.* Cause: ball hit below center. | Keep eye on ball; try to hit on top of ball; don't bunt high inside balls. |
| *On bunt, ball rolls toward pitcher rather than down base line.* Cause: bat not angled toward base line as it is held in position over plate. | To get the correct angle for hit toward third base line, push tip of bat forward; for bunt down first-base line, push handle out slightly and pull end of bat back. |

5. Pitching

    a) Two common wind-ups are the figure-eight and the windmill.

    b) For figure-eight wind-up, ball is brought to chest with pitching hand holding ball and with other hand covering back of pitching hand. All motion must stop for at least one second. For deception, let the ball follow a figure-eight path as the swing goes sideward, then let it move back and behind the body, upward slightly, then continue downward and forward to complete the delivery. During the movement of the swing behind the back, the hips should rotate away from the batter, then toward the batter on the forward and downward motion of the arm [50]. The left foot steps toward the plate, and the ball is released with a snap of the wrist. Both backswing and forward swing should be on line with the pitch. Follow-through consists of bringing right foot up parallel with left foot, with fingers pointing at the plate.

c) In the windmill wind-up, the arm makes almost a complete circle before release of the ball. Bring ball to chest in both hands; let pitching arm go forward and then upward, with weight shifting to right foot. Let arm continue up and back as left foot steps toward plate. On downward swing, wrist is cocked back. This arm rotation builds up momentum, which adds to the speed of the ball. During circling motion, keep the arm almost straight, and snap the wrist at the last moment to release the ball. After the release, take a step forward with right foot to put yourself in position to field any balls hit your way.

d) Another method used by some skilled pitchers is to lean backward by arching the back before the wind-up; this means that the stomach muscles help snap the body forward, which adds power to the ball. This method is very hard on the back, and in most cases is too difficult for the pitcher to maintain throughout the game.

| *Problems in Pitching* | *Corrections and Coaching Hints* |
|---|---|
| *Ball too high.* Causes: release too late; step forward shorter than usual. | Snap wrist and release ball sooner; take same-length step each time. Mark spot on ground for first step if necessary. |
| *Ball too low.* Causes: too-early release; first step too long. | Delay release fraction of second longer; be consistent in first step. |
| *Illegal delivery.* Causes: both pitcher's feet not on rubber at start; throw side-armed; pitcher takes too many steps before release; incorrect position of pitcher before wind-up; pitcher not at full stop before wind-up. | Some part of both feet must be on rubber; hand must be below hip and wrist not out beyond elbow. Take only one step during delivery. Face batter and keep shoulders square with plate. Stop and hold position from 1 to 20 seconds before wind-up. |
| *Poor control or loss of balance.* Causes: first step taken with wrong foot; weight shifted incorrectly; body not rotated back to face batter on the release; arc not flattened; release too early or too late. | Take first step and shift weight to left foot as arm swings downward. To start forward swing, rotate trunk toward batter. After release, bring right foot up parallel with left foot, and let fingers follow through toward batter. Determine best point of release by practice. |

**Fig. 9-35.** Grips for pitching softball. Top left: In-curve and fast ball. Top right: Rise ball. Lower left: Drop ball. Lower right: Out-curve ball.

6. Types of Pitches

    a) Pitch is determined by grip, spin on ball, and delivery.

    b) Types of pitches are: curve, drop, rise, fast ball, change of pace, and slant. (For grips, see Fig. 9–35.)

    c) Fast ball: (1) grip ball between thumb and first and second finger, (2) let ball leave from tips of fingers, and (3) turn palm slightly to left.

d) Change of pace: (1) hold ball in palm of hand, (2) keep thumb and all four fingers on ball (knuckles may be bent under), (3) release ball from hand rather than fingertips (this prevents spin).

e) Drop ball: (1) place thumb on right of ball, (2) place first three fingers close together, (3) bend little finger, (4) bring hand forward so that palm faces batter, and (5) let ball roll off fingers with top spin.

f) Out-curve: (1) position thumb and first and second fingers in triangle on ball, (2) turn palm slightly to left, (3) pull second finger away from ball and snap wrist to left to create right-to-left spin. (Ball leaves little-finger side of hand.)

g) In-curve: (1) use same grip as that for fast ball, (2) snap wrist to right to create left-to-right spin, (3) let ball leave from between thumb and first finger, creating a clockwise spin which makes ball curve toward the batter.

h) Rise ball: (1) hold ball with thumb pointing down, (2) place first and second fingers on top of ball, (3) place third and fourth fingers slightly to right, (4) let knuckles face batter as hand comes forward, (5) snap wrist upward to create back spin (push with thumb and pull upward with fingers).

i) Slant: (1) stand on extreme corner of rubber (to hit outside corner of plate, stand to extreme right of rubber—to hit inside corner, stand to extreme left), and (2) pitch ball diagonally to opposite corner of home plate. Vary by releasing ball from a low position (without spin), so that ball goes upward to cross plate at about level of batter's shoulder.

## 6 Fielding the Ball

a) Wait in a crouched position for batter to hit ball.

b) Move quickly to get in line with ball.

c) Keep eyes on ball all the way as it comes toward you.

d) On balls that are hit high, allow ball to drop slightly in front of head; for grounders, move toward ball and stop it immediately after bounce if possible.

e) Learn to get rid of ball as soon as possible after you make catch. This can be done by: (1) catching ball with arms flexed, (2) taking ball out of glove as hand begins to move back into throwing position, (3) taking step in direction of throw as you cock your arm and wrist, and (4) snapping arm and wrist forward quickly.

f) Save time by looking the situation over before the ball is hit to determine which base the ball should be thrown to.

g) If ball is hit over your head, turn and run as fast as possible to point you think ball will come down; then look over shoulder to locate ball before making turn for catch.

h) If in doubt, let ball bounce in front of you rather than taking chance of overrunning ball or letting it go over your head.

i) When fielding fast low balls and grounders, go down on one knee with body low and in position to block ball if you miss catch with glove. On slow and medium balls, bend body forward, letting legs and feet remain positioned for a quick throw after the catch.

8. Base-Running

a) If you are a right-handed batter, when you start run to first base, take first step with right foot.

b) Keep motion low at start of run, using short strides to build up speed.

c) When going to first base, run out every hit at full speed.

d) To determine whether to continue run to second, watch base coach. If hit is only a single, go across first without changing stride and slow down only after you have passed the base. If you are going on to second, swing out to the right when you are about 10 to 12 feet from first base, touching inside of bag with the foot as you turn back toward the next base. (Left foot is usually used to make turn easier.)

e) Once you are on base, threaten to steal or go for the next base on a hit. You can't leave the base until the pitcher releases the ball, but you can get set for a fast start by waiting with your left foot on the corner of the base and your right foot about a foot behind your left. This enables you to start your body in motion by pushing with your right foot as the pitcher's arm starts the downswing, and yet keeps your left foot on the base for the legal lead at the release of the ball. Bend your body forward and keep low while waiting.

f) Unless it is a hit-and-run situation, change your movements to a side slide about 10 feet down the base line, with your body facing the batter to see whether you can proceed to the next base or must move back quickly to the base you have just left.

g) If the catcher fumbles the ball or can't get to a wild pitch, go immediately to the next base; if it is a high fly, go back and tag up and be ready to grab any chance to go to the next base. On a ground ball, if a runner is behind you, don't hesitate to break for the next base immediately.

h) If the baseman is playing tight, don't lead off farther than your ability to beat the throw back in a pick-off situation.

9. Base Coaching

a) Two coaches—one on first and one on third—should be used to help the runners. The most experienced person should be stationed at third base because of the chances to score from this position.

b) The first-base coach controls the movements of the runner approaching and leaving first base; the third-base coach controls the runner approaching or leaving second or third base. The third-base coach also gives signals to the batter.

c) The purpose of batting signals is to help the batter and runner know when to take the pitch, steal, bunt, or hit and run. To throw off the opponents, batting signals can be very complex and contain useless devices. The coach gives many signals that the batter and runner ignore; then the coach gives the cut-off signal (a signal predetermined by the team, such as coach touching ear). The next signal after the cut-off sign is the one the players follow. The cut-off signal may be changed each game, to prevent the opponents from reading the signals.

d) Running signals are sometimes given with the hands, sometimes verbally. Some common coaches' signals are: (1) circling arm high over head (keep running), (2) both arms held high over the head with palms facing runner (stop), (3) quick downward movement with hands (slide), and (4) circling left arm over head with right arm held high, palm facing runner (continue to next base, make turn, and stop to locate ball and determine whether to continue).

10. Reading Batters and Signals

a) The catcher signals for the type of pitch; however, the pitcher must also be aware of the batter's weaknesses. The pitcher has the final say on the type of ball to be thrown.

b) The catcher signals by showing the pitcher a prearranged number of fingers on her bare hand. (For instance, one finger means a fast ball, two an in-curve, etc.) While the catcher is in the crouched position, she hides this hand from the opponents with her legs and her glove.

c) Once the pitcher has agreed to type of ball to be thrown, the catcher goes into a semi-crouched position, with feet about shoulder width apart (left foot usually slightly forward). The catcher holds up her glove to give the pitcher something to aim at, and maintains balance by keeping her weight on the balls of her feet. This enables her to push off quickly to stop any stray balls, or to make the throw to a base.

d) Pitcher and catcher can pick out a batter's weaknesses by looking at: (1) her grip, (2) her stance, (3) her position in the box in relation to the plate, (4) her preliminary swings, and (5) her attitude.

e) Generally, a batter likes to swing her bat back and forth in her strongest hitting area as she waits for the pitch.

f) If the batter is choking up on the bat, curves to the outside corner are effective because of her limited reach. A good change of pace is a high inside ball.

g) If the batter is using the power grip at the end of the handle, balls thrown to the inside corner usually cause her to hit with the weak part of the bat.

h) If the batter takes a long step forward as she swings at the ball or tends to swing upward, high balls usually result in pop-ups.

i) If the batter steps toward the plate on her swing rather than toward the pitcher, inside balls are effective.

j) If the batter's position is away from the plate, or if she tends to steps away from the ball on her swing, place the balls to the outside corner.

k) If the batter seems to be nervous or crowds the plate, inside balls usually increase her nervousness or cause her to hit balls off the weaker part of the bat.

l) If a batter seems to be impatient or eager to hit the ball, pitcher and catcher should take their time between deliveries. A bad pitch usually draws the batter into a swing, while a slow ball may catch her off balance and throw her timing off.

m) When you're pitching to a power hitter, keep the ball away from the center of the plate, and vary the pitches. Don't use the fast ball, since this speed plus her own power usually results in a long hit ball when the batter does make contact.

n) When the situation calls for a bunt, place the ball high and inside. The fast ball is usually best because it's hard for the batter to eliminate the speed for an effective bunt.

o) If the count is two strikes and no balls, throw a ball slightly outside the hitting area. The batter will probably swing at anything that's close.

p) Pitchers and catchers should file away all the information they can get about batters. In a crucial situation, a good memory can win the ball game.

## STRATEGY

The best way to win a softball game is to keep the opponents from getting hits, because hits are what give them the chance to score. Preventing hits is mainly the pitcher's job. Here are some general things to remember about pitching: (1) Against the player who chokes up on the bat, use outside curve or high, inside ball. (2) Against the power hitter, or the hitter using the long grip, use inside curves or inside slants. (3) In bunting situations, use high, inside, fast balls. (4) Against the hitter who crowds the plate, use inside pitches. (5) Against players who stand back from the plate, use outside balls. (6) Against hitters who swing hard, use change of pace. (7) When you are pitching to a good hitter and want to determine her weakness, aim for corners and use several different types of ball.

When the count is at two strikes and no balls, or two strikes and one ball, throw close to the corners of the plate, to tempt the batter to swing at a bad pitch. When there are runners on base, keep balls low to increase the likelihood of a ground ball and a chance at a double play.

## THINKING AHEAD AND MAKING CALLS

Every player on the team should at all times know: (1) the exact score and the number of outs, strikes, etc., (2) positions of the base-runners, and (3) the best place to play the ball when a player catches it. If there are two outs, try for the easiest out. When the ball is hit to the outfield, the person who catches it should throw it immediately to the infield, aiming it one base ahead of the runner. When the ball is hit between an outfielder and an infielder, the outfielder should be the one to call for the ball, since she is in a better position to move into it and make the throw after the catch. A call for the ball should be made any time it is hit between two positions, with the player going from right to left making the catch when possible; this allows an easier throw-in.

On infield flies, the pitcher and the catcher should let another player take the catch whenever possible. If a runner or runners are on base, a player who does not have to cover a base should catch the ball; otherwise the infielder might be pulled too much out of position to make a play if she needs to. When a catch is being made by a baseman, however, other players should always be prepared to cover her base. On ground balls, the player closest to the ball should try to field it in order to save time in making the throw. If there is doubt as to who should take the ball, the person in the best position to throw to a base after the catch should call for the ball. If the sun makes it hard for players to see, a player who can turn partly or completely away from the glare should play the ball. High flies over first and third bases should be taken by the second baseman and the shortstop, respectively, since they have a better view of the ball than other players.

On a force-out play, the ball should be thrown about chest high. On a tag-out, it should be aimed about a foot above the ground. On tags, the person on base should touch the runner with the back of her glove to prevent losing the ball on the tag.

## POSITIONING OF PLAYERS

A team plays deep (infielders move almost back to grass of outfield) when a strong hitter is at bat or when there are no outs. A team plays tight, or "in" (infielders come in several feet from base paths), when a weak batter is up, or when a runner threatens to score. A ground ball is more likely to get by the infield that has pulled in, so this formation is not used when a strong hitter is up at bat, unless there is a runner in position to score.

## PITCHER'S RESPONSIBILITIES

Ordinarily, the pitcher fields all balls hit toward her and any bunts along the base lines. If she can't stop a ball going to her left, she should move over quickly to cover first base, since the first baseman will be drawn off the base to field the ball. On out-field hits with runners on base, the pitcher covers behind the third baseman or the catcher to cut off any overthrow. She also backs up the third baseman when a runner is on first, and the catcher when a runner is on second. If the catcher loses a pitched ball, and there is a runner on base, the pitcher moves in quickly to cover home plate.

## CATCHER'S RESPONSIBILITIES

The catcher's responsibilities include: (1) fielding hits and bunts close to the plate, (2) getting rid of her mask quickly to catch pop-ups at the plate, (3) calling for curves, fast balls, etc., (4) throwing to side of base away from runner, (5) picking off players attempting to steal, (6) backing up first baseman if there are no runners on base, (7) blocking home plate on scoring plays, and (8) helping run down player caught between third and home.

## FIRST BASEMAN

The first baseman's position is about 10 feet toward second base and about 8–10 feet behind the base path if there are no runners on base. If a ball is hit to her, she must make the stop and then throw to the pitcher covering the base. With a runner on first, the first baseman plays tighter for a possible pick-off. If pulled off base to stop the ball on a possible double-play situation, she throws to second and moves back to first for the return throw. If the pitcher has come in to cover her base, she moves out of the path of the ball from second to first. On a throw-in from right field, the first baseman moves into position to intercept the throw, if necessary, and relay it on to home. If the runner has already crossed the plate, she may be able to make a play at one of the other bases.

## SECOND BASEMAN

The second baseman usually plays about 15 feet to the left of second base (second baseman's left) and about 8 feet behind the base path. Balls to the right of second base are fielded by the second baseman and thrown to the shortstop, who should be covering the base. Balls to the left of the base are fielded by the shortstop, while the second baseman covers the base. With a runner on first, the second baseman watches for a possible steal.

## SHORTSTOP

The shortstop plays about 18 feet to the right of second base and about 15 feet behind the base path. She covers the left side of the infield, backs up the second baseman, relays balls thrown in from left field, covers third base when the third baseman is pulled off, and helps with run-down plays.

## THIRD BASEMAN

Third baseman must field all balls hit down her baseline, takes pop-ups in area between third base and home and those near the pitcher, and helps with run-downs between third and home. Her position is usually about 8 feet to her left of third base and about 5 feet behind it.

## FIELDERS

The left fielder backs up the center-fielder, shortstop, and third baseman. The center-fielder backs up the right and left fielders, the shortstop, and second baseman. She also backs up second base on an attempted steal, pick-off, run-down play, or force-out. The right fielder backs up the center-fielder and the second and first baseman.

## BATTING ORDER

The first batter in the batting order should be the one most likely to get on base. The second batter is usually chosen on her ability to bunt or to hit behind the runner, while the third, fourth, and fifth batters should be consistent or power hitters. The fourth player should be the strongest hitter on the team. The other batters are usually the weaker hitters, with the pitcher batting last.

HIT-AND-RUN

The hit-and-run is initiated by the third-base coach, who signals the play to the batter and the runner. As the ball is pitched, the runner breaks for second to draw the second baseman in, and the batter tries to hit the ball through the hole between second and first. When there is a runner on first, or runners on first and third, the hit-and-run can be used. The signal for the hit-and-run should be given only on a count that forces the pitcher to give the batter a fairly good ball. This play is hard to execute, and often ends up with the batter hitting into a double play.

SQUEEZE PLAY

In a squeeze play, the objective is to get a runner home from third by a sacrifice bunt. It can be executed two ways: (1) The player on third starts for home as soon as the pitch is released. (2) The player on third waits until the ball has actually been bunted.

If there is a runner on first base, the batter usually lets the first ball go by, to give the runner a chance to steal second. The batter should try to hit behind the runner to right field, or attempt a bunt down the third-base line to force a long throw to first.

## SWIMMING AND DIVING

COACHING EMPHASIS FOR SWIMMING

1. Practicing strokes for speed events, with special work on butterfly stroke.
2. Developing efficient starts and turns.
3. Working on endurance.

MECHANICS

1. Start for front crawl, breast stroke, and butterfly:

   a) Two variations are given here. Select the variation that seems to be the most effective, and then work hard to perfect it. (One well-known coach [49] believes that the circular arm swing is more effective. This variation is discussed in subsection (g).)

   b) Racing start [2] : (1) Place feet three to six inches apart, or in comfortable position. (2) Curl toes over edge of pool or starting block. (3) On "take your mark," bend forward from trunk, with weight concentrated on balls of feet, knees flexed, and arms back. (4) Keep head up, with eyes on far end of pool. (Some people prefer to focus on a point about halfway down the pool.) (5) Take 2 or 3 deep breaths and hold until the gun. (6) On starting signal, throw your weight for-

**Fig. 9-36.** The start.

ward by moving your arms back even more, then reversing their swing force-fully to throw them straight out ahead of body, and by flexing and extending knees and ankles with a final push by the toes. (7) Go as far out as possible, and as parallel to water. (8) To increase buoyancy, take deep breath before hitting water. (See Fig. 9-36.)

c) As your body is in the air, place head between arms and keep body extended in as straight a line as possible. Your hands should touch the water first, then the rest of your body.

d) Let your body go under water slightly, to cut down water resistance on top where it is choppy.

e) Stay in glide until speed has slowed to maximum swimming speed, then start stroke. Don't turn head for 2 or 3 strokes, until rhythm has been established.

| *Problems with Start* | *Corrections and Coaching Hints* |
|---|---|
| *Start too slow.* Causes: Incorrect position before starting signal; lack of concentration on starting signal; slow reflexes. | On "take-your-mark" signal, bend knees, curl toes over side, and put arms back. Take two deep breaths and hold until starting signal, listening only for the gun. Practice starts while someone uses signals that are differently spaced, to learn to react automatically to signal rather than to movement of others around you. Experiment with the circular arm motion to see whether this gives you a faster start. |
| *Dive too shallow.* Causes: keeping head up; turning hands up at an angle toward the surface. Result: less speed, because of resistance of water on surface. | Put head between arms on dive; keep fingers and hands in straight line with arms and body. |
| *Dive too deep.* Causes: putting head down too much; bending from waist. Result: glide slowed, since swimmer must come back up to surface. | Don't duck head; try to keep body horizontal, with legs, trunk, head, arms, hands, and fingers in a straight line. After body is under water, lift head slightly and use hands as rudder to keep body from going too deep into the water. |

f) On the breast stroke, let the angle for entry be a little deeper than the angle for the crawl, in order to take your first stroke under water, to increase your speed before surfacing. In the butterfly stroke, as the glide slows down to swimming speed, your legs should begin to recover (let knees bend, bringing heels toward the surface). Your feet are then in position to make the kick downward as your arms begin to pull.

g) Variation of start. Circular arm action is used as follows: (1) Let arms hang down, with arms almost straight, and with palms facing away from pool. (2) Bend body forward at waist, but with less hip and knee flexion than in start previously described. (3) On starting signal, let arms go upward and back in circular motion, and then down and out to help take the body forward. As arms reach their peak and start downward, the heels lift from the starting block, and the bending motion at the hips and the flexion of the knees is increased. (4) When the arms reach the knees, let the legs and ankles push off.

h) A third technique is to use the standard starting position without any knee flexion. At starting signal, flex knees quickly and bring arms downward and out as your legs and ankles push forcefully.

2. Start for backstroke

a) Racing Start: (1) In water, face starting block. (2) Grip starting board or side of pool (hands about 1 to $1\frac{1}{2}$ feet apart). (3) Brace feet against side of pool (anywhere from surface to 3-5 inches under water) with legs about hip width apart. (4) On "take your mark," bring body up and out of water with head forward ("coiled" or tucked as close to wall as possible) and with knees against the chest. (5) At gun, throw arms and head backward. (6) Push legs forcefully against side trying to send body out over the water rather than pushing through it. (7) Arch back slightly so arms and head enter water first. (8) As head and shoulders hit the water, raise head to keep glide near surface (about 15-18 inches from surface).

b) When speed of glide slows to maximum swimming speed, start flutter kick, then first arm stroke. (Although any type of backstroke is permissible under the rules, all good swimmers use the back crawl for competitive swimming.)

c) Take breath during push-away and hold through most of glide (some swimmers prefer to exhale through the nose slowly on glide to keep water out of nose).

| *Problems with Backstroke Start* | *Corrections and Coaching Hints* |
| --- | --- |
| *Hips and legs hit water first.* Result: poor glide. Causes: lack of arch in back; throwing arms and head back weakly. | Fling head and arms back forcefully; arch back slightly. Throw body up and out, rather than just out. |
| *Glide too deep.* Result: slowing-down of movement. Causes: wrist hyperextension; keeping head back too long. | Keep wrists and hands in line with forearm; when head and shoulders enter water, bring head up. |
| *Glide on surface.* Results: friction and slow glide. Causes: lifting head too soon; not throwing head and arms back enough. | See to it that head and shoulders are under water before head is lifted; throw head and arms back forcefully at start of race. |

3. Turn for Front Crawl

   a) Learn to make turn with either arm; look at wall when about 10 feet out to judge which hand will be leading at turn. (A more advanced turn used by top swimmers today does not use the hand reach to the wall, but consists of throwing the head downward, bending at the waist, kicking downward with the feet in a "fishtail" action, and pushing downward with the hands as in a surface dive.)

   b) To execute somersault or flip turn:* (1) As you reach out with your hand, duck your head with chin against chest (turn head toward armpit opposite that of reaching arm). Hand must touch wall near the surface. (2) Tuck knees close to body. (Many feel that making the turnover in a pike position is faster.) (3) During somersault, body does a quarter twist (results from turning of head). (4) Extend knees to about 90-degree angle, then straighten forcefully as feet touch side of pool. (5) As feet push off against wall, let body take another quarter turn; end up in glide on face. (See Fig. 9-37.)

   c) To get an effective somersault, duck head quickly when hand touches wall; make the somersault, turn and push off all in one motion.

| Problems with Flip Turn | Corrections and Coaching Hints |
|---|---|
| *Getting too close to wall before making somersault.* Result: shoulders and back hit wall and push-off is poor. Causes: Delay in ducking head; poor timing. | When you use hand reach, duck head just before or just as you touch wall. Extend arm when touch is made; for maximum strength, let hips be about two feet from wall on push-off. Touch with hand just below the surface. If hand reach is not used, begin flip turn a second or two sooner than usual. (Last arm pull is usually made when swimmer's head is about 4–7 feet from the end of the pool.) |
| *Lack of sense of direction on turn.* Causes: closing eyes; taking reaching hand off wall too soon; lack of practice. | Keep eyes open; keep hand in contact with wall until turn is almost completed; practice turns until movement is done naturally. |
| *Lack of power on push-off.* Causes: too far from or too close to wall; too little extension of ankles following extension of knees. | Make turn close to wall to allow knee flexion before the push, but not so close that heels remain tight against hips (knee flexion should be about a right angle); straighten legs and then extend ankles forcefully. |

* Developed by Dave Armbruster in 1936.

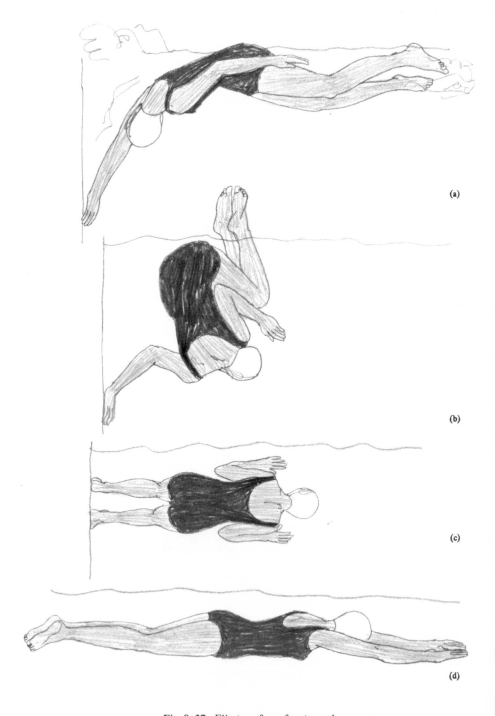

(a)

(b)

(c)

(d)

Fig. 9–37. Flip turn from front crawl.

**Fig. 9-38.** Tumble turn from backstroke.

4. Turn for Backstroke

  a) For tumble turn: (1) Reach for wall. (2) Take breath. (3) Let the other hand continue its pull as hand touches wall. (Fingers are pointing inward.) (4) Bend arm to allow head to come close to wall. (5) Tuck legs tightly and turn over shoulder of arm reaching for wall (on turn, let legs, from knees down, come out of water and swing to side). (6) Push feet against wall. (Usually place feet about 14–18 inches below the surface of the water.) (7) As you push, extend arms over head for glide. (8) When glide slows to maximum swimming speed, start stroke. (See Fig. 9–38.)

  b) To help with turn, use free hand, with palm inverted, to scull, and use hand touching wall to help exert leverage. Remember: This turn is a spinning or pivoting action on the back rather than a somersault.

| *Problems with Tumble Turn* | *Corrections and Coaching Hints* |
| --- | --- |
| *Body stays on surface during turn.* Result: turn slows down. Cause: failure to lift knees and lower part of legs out of the water on the swing to the side; hand placed too high on the wall. | Lift legs from knees down out of water to make the pivoting action; touch wall with hand in a line directly over head (some prefer to touch from 6–10 inches beneath the surface). |
| *Making complete somersault.* Result: person ends up on face or side rather than back. Cause: legs turned over head rather than swung to side and around shoulder of touching hand. | Swing legs to side, up and over water as they turn over the shoulder of the arm touching the wall. Remember: The motion is a spinning action on the back. |
| *Lack of force on push-off.* Cause: too much flexion in arm, causing hips to be too close to wall; pushing off with hand before turn, forcing hips too far from wall. | Extend arm as hand reaches out, but, for maximum push-off power, allow hips to come in close for about a 90-degree knee flexion. Maintain contact with wall with reaching hand during spinning action, but as you throw your legs sideward let your touching arm begin to straighten to push the upper part of your body away from the wall. Use free hand to scull. |

5. Turn for Breast Stroke and Butterfly

  a) To execute: (1) Make contact with wall during arm recovery. (2) Touch wall with both hands (hands 4–8 inches apart, fingers slightly above surface of water). Grasp gutter, or place both hands against wall about water level. (3) Bend arms to allow head to come in close to wall, and bring legs into tight tuck. (4) Push hands against wall to help turn hips to side. (5) Let hand on side of turn come away

**(a)**

**(b)**

**(c)**

**(d)**

Fig. 9-39. Turn for breast or butterfly stroke.

from wall and pull water across chest to help with turning action (turn head in direction of spin and keep legs tightly tucked until turn is made). (6) For glide on stomach, place feet against wall and push. (Feet usually placed against wall about 2 feet below the surface.) Before feet begin push, take breath and submerge for the glide beneath surface of water. Since the breaststroker is allowed one stroke under water, angle the push-off on the breaststroke turn downward slightly to keep yourself deep enough to take advantage of this stroke under water. See Fig. 9-39.

| *Problems with Breast Stroke and Butterfly Turn* | *Corrections and Coaching Hints* |
| --- | --- |
| *Glide to side rather than straight ahead.* Cause: pushing off before complete turn has been made. | Be sure head is completely turned around and both feet are against side of pool before pushing. |
| *Lack of power.* Causes: too far from wall on turn, resulting in legs being extended too much when feet touch wall; failure to extend ankles on push-off. | Bend elbows; let head almost touch wall before turn; after extending knees, extend ankles and push with balls of feet and toes. |
| *Glide too deep.* Causes: hands placed too low; head lowered too much or too soon; feet too far below surface of water. | Let tips of fingers be just above surface; lower head just before touch, but either lift head for air on the turn, or let it remain under water. Place feet about 2 feet below surface; submerge head to allow glide about 2 feet beneath surface. |
| *Glide too much on surface.* Causes: hands placed too high; head not lowered before contact with hands on wall; head and shoulders lifted high out of water on the turn; head lifted too quickly on push-off; feet placed too high on wall. | Place hands properly, fingertips barely at surface; lower head just before touch with hands; keep shoulders in water, and don't let mouth get more than a few inches above the surface of the water; don't lift head on push-off, but submerge it after taking breath of air. Be sure feet make contact with wall about 24 inches below surface. |

6. The butterfly stroke (see Fig. 9-40)

   a) This stroke demands strong abdominal and shoulder muscles, as well as good ankle flexibility.

   b) You must synchronize leg action (dolphin kick) with arm stroke to conserve energy and get the most power possible.

   c) Dolphin kick: (1) To start upward beat, lift hips; as legs pass line of body, begin to bend knees. (2) As feet near surface of water, start downstroke, with knees flexed about 90 degrees at last part of downbeat, then straighten out knees force-

**Fig. 9-40.** The butterfly stroke.

fully. (3) On upbeat, point toes back. (4) On downbeat, hyperextend feet, with toes turned slightly in. Keep knees and ankles flexible for the up-and-down motion while the whole body weaves in an undulating motion.

d) Raise your hips upward on the downward kick and drop them slightly on the upbeat as your legs propel your body by a fishlike or whipping action.

e) Let your legs go up and down twice during one complete arm motion. Do first kick (legs going down) just after hands have entered the water. Do second kick when arms start their recovery. The first kick is usually the most forceful of the two.

f) Arm motion: (1) Start with arms over head, with palms turned downward and slightly outward (keep arms and fingers relaxed). Hands should enter water before arms. (2) As arms hit water, start stroke immediately. (3) Pull arms obliquely downward and outward. After the press outward, let hands begin to come closer together, but then move apart again as stroke continues outward and backward. (Arm pull pattern has been described as an hourglass or double-S pull [49].) (4) Lift arms out of water and shoot forward (keep few inches above surface to decrease water resistance). Use straight-arm recovery (start with elbows bent slightly). (5) Let arms go back into water in front of shoulders. (6) Repeat stroke.

g) Lift head for breath of air either at end of arm pull backward or during the recovery. You should complete your breath before your arms move by your shoulders on the recovery. Most swimmers breathe only every other stroke, although timing of breathing depends on the distance of the race. In short races, take a breath after every three strokes. When you are swimming long distances, you may have to take a breath with every stroke. Don't lift your head any higher than you have to to get your mouth clear of the water.

i) Timing of arms and legs is big factor in speed.

j) To start butterfly stroke after glide: (1) Bend legs at knees to start upbeat. (2) Let arms start pull backward and legs go into downbeat. (3) As arms continue pull to hips, let legs start back up on second upbeat. (4) As arms come out of water for recovery, let legs start second downbeat. (5) When arms are about halfway through recovery, legs are moving up for second upbeat of the cycle.

| *Problems with Butterfly* | *Corrections and Coaching Hints* |
|---|---|
| *Lack of timing.* Causes: arms too slow on pull or recovery; leg motion has too great a range. | Increase speed of arm pull and recovery; decrease distance covered by legs by stopping upbeat sooner. Body and leg movements should be relaxed. |
| *Lack of power.* Causes: poor timing; failure to get full thrust with legs be- | Work on timing to get arms and legs synchronized; start upbeat with legs |

cause of incorrect kick or lack of stomach and leg strength; weak pull with arms.

straight, bending them after legs have passed line of body, point toes, then on downbeat turn toes inward slightly, straighten knees forcefully. Use hourglass pattern on pull, with fingers relaxed but together. Build up strength by sit-ups, leg lifts, etc.

*Inability to breathe.* Cause: lifting head at wrong time in stroke.

Your head will automatically be lifted partially by the pull back and the downbeat of arms and legs during recovery; lift head slightly at completion of arm pull and as arms fly through the air during recovery.

## STRATEGY

Speed swimming or competitive swimming is a matter of speed in the short events and speed and endurance in the longer events. Therefore you should plan your strategy accordingly. In short races, strategy involves getting a good start and swimming at top speed for the entire race. In the longer events, strategy involves a good start, quick turns, and the ability to conserve energy if you cannot cover the entire distance at maximum speed.

Work on establishing the best rhythm, the rhythm that will enable you to swim at top speed without wasting effort and energy. Sticking with an established rhythm during a race enables you to turn in your best possible time. Don't look around during the race because that throws your rhythm off and cuts down your speed. If it's a close race and you need to know how close the competition is, glance to the side during the normal breathing action.

In many cases, poor performance is a result of improper breathing. During competition, many people tighten up too much and begin to breathe differently from the way they ordinarily would during practice; this causes them to tire more quickly. Take 2 or 3 deep breaths before you start, and then try to breathe normally.

If you are entering endurance events, there is no substitute for conditioning. In order to perform at top efficiency, you have to build up to the event by practicing your start and turns until they are as perfect as you can make them. Only then will you achieve the best strategy: performance at maximum speed.

In some competitions, you may have a choice of lanes. If so, choose one of the two middle lanes, since the water is not as choppy and it gives you a better view of your opponents during the race. Before the race, check to see whether your lane has a warning mark 4 feet from the turning wall, and whether the lane markers are on the bottom of the pool or on the surface of the water.

When swimming middle and long distances, learn to pace yourself in order to save enough energy to finish strong. Decide whether you want to expend extra energy to take the lead at the start, or to swim at a consistent pace in hopes that your opponent will not be able to match the pace. Avoid building up a high oxygen debt at the beginning of the race.

In swimming against others of similar skill, never let an opponent get more than a length or a length and a half ahead of you; preferably less than that. If you're behind in the last part of the race, you may decide to pass the opponent and then try to hold this lead for the rest of the race. You can take the lead by trying faster turns, by increasing the speed of your strokes, or by holding to a pace that will tire the opponent.

Decide on your strategy before the race, but be able to adjust this plan according to the way the race is going. Sometimes a race is won by strategy; oftentimes, it is won by pure heart and determination.

In the 400-meter medley, one has to swim the backstroke the first 100 meters, the breast stroke the second 100, the butterfly the third 100, and freestyle the last 100 meters. Anyone training for the individual medley should be proficient in at least three strokes and have exceptional endurance. In the medley relay, the same order is used. Team members should be selected according to their strengths in the specific areas.

COACHING EMPHASIS IN DIVING

1. Practicing of approach, take-off, execution of movement in air, and entry into the water, with special emphasis on the three basic diving positions in the air: the layout, the pike, and the tuck.
2. Developing skill in doing a somersault in a tuck or pike position (forward, backward, inward, and reverse), in combining a twist for various combinations, and in executing a "save" when body is at wrong angle for the entry.

MECHANICS

1. Somersaults

   a) Keep in mind that the body rotates faster in tuck position than in pike or lay-out position, and that the head largely controls the movement of the body.
   b) To come out of somersault correctly when timing is off: (1) if turn is too slow, tuck body even more, and (2) if turn is too fast, straighten out body to slow turn down.
   c) When you are combining multiple twists with multiple somersaults, use the pike position rather than the tuck position, to enable yourself to go from one move to another.
   d) The forward somersault and the inward somersault are executed in the same way, except that the take-off for the inward one is backward (facing board). To execute forward somersault or inward one: (1) Start movement after feet have left board. (2) Bend knees and bring heels in close to hips, meanwhile throwing arms,

Fig. 9-41. Inward somersault.

head, and upper body downward. (3) Grip legs about halfway between knees and ankles to help tighten tuck. (4) Hold position until desired rotation has been accomplished. (5) For entry into water, come out of tuck position (straighten legs and lift chest and head up to come out of tuck).

e) If you are entering water feet first, straighten arms, place hands against thighs, and point toes; if entering head first, extend hands over head (toes pointed).

f) To avoid hitting diving board on the inward somersault, use same take-off as for the inward header, completing the press (spring) before starting the spin. (See Fig. 9-41.)

g) To do a backward somersault: (1) Start movement during thrust from board. (2) Lift arms, chest, and head upward. (As you move your arms above your head, tilt your head backward.) (3) Bring legs up close into tuck position. (4) Grasp legs with hands. (5) Hold tuck until you reach desired position. To help keep entry straight, keep your eyes on the end of the board.

h) To gain more rotation for a move such as the one-and-a-half, use more force in throwing upper body backward, or use a tighter tuck. (See Fig. 9-42.)

| *Problems with Somersaults* | *Corrections and Coaching Hints* |
|---|---|
| *Going too far over.* Cause: waiting too long to open tuck, which results in poor entry. | Extend legs sooner; lift head. Open tuck usually when you have completed three-quarters of a turn. |
| *Not going over far enough.* Causes: lack of spinning action; opening tuck too soon. Results in poor entry. | On forward somersault, bring arms, head, and upper body forward forcefully. On backward somersault, throw arms, head, and chest back more. Pull legs in with hands for tighter tuck; hold tuck longer before opening up. |
| *On one-and-a-half, going too far over.* Causes: tuck opened too late; arms extended over head at same time legs are straightened out. | Straighten legs by kicking out, pull head back before bringing arms over head (backward one-and-a-half). If entry is still long, open tuck sooner. |
| *On one-and-a-half, not going far enough over.* Causes: coming out of tuck too soon; poor spinning action. May also happen if tuck is too loose. | Hold tuck longer; on backward somersault, swing arms over head at same time you extend legs and throw head backward. On forward somersault, bring tuck in tighter, throwing arms, head, and upper body down forcefully to start spin; hold tuck longer. Tighten arms around legs to make tuck more compact. |

**Fig. 9–42.** Backward one-and-a-half.

**Fig. 9-43.** Reverse one-and-a-half.

i) Reverse somersault: (1) Execute in same way you execute back somersault, except that direction of take-off is forward rather than backward. (2) To avoid hitting board, complete press *before* executing spin. (3) Open tuck when body is about three-fourths of the way around. (See Fig. 9–43.)

| *Problems with Reverse Somersault* | *Corrections and Coaching Hints* |
|---|---|
| *Inability to get over quickly enough.* Causes: too little arm, head, and chest movement; too loose a tuck; leaning too far forward when leaving the board. | *After* complete press, and after the arms have reached upward, tilt your head and chest backward; tuck legs close to body. Don't lean too far forward out of fear of hitting board. |
| *Going over too fast.* Causes: throwing arms, head and chest backward too forcefully; staying in tuck too long. | Don't use as much force in throwing upper body backward; come out of tuck sooner; delay arm reach over head until after you extend legs. |
| *Coming down too close to board.* Cause: starting movements for spin before full press is completed. | Wait until you have completed press and body is well into the air before executing backward spin. |

2. Pike Dives

   a) Remember that abdominal strength and hip flexibility are very important.

   b) Develop flexibility in ankles especially, for graceful line when pointing toes.

   c) To execute pike dives: (1) Use more force than in tuck position. (2) Keep legs straight. (3) Place hands behind the knees. (4) For deeper pike, relax hips. (5) Point toes and extend ankles. (See Fig. 9–44.)

3. Twists

   a) For more difficult dive, combine twist with somersault, pike, or lay-out.

   b) Control speed of twist by: (1) extending arms (for slower turn), (2) bringing arms in closer to body (for faster turn).

   c) To execute twist: (1) Move both arms at same time in direction of turn. (2) Bring one arm up and behind head (for twist to left, use left arm). (3) Let other arm "reach" across chest (for twist to left, right arm does this). (4) Keep the arm that goes up over head close to the head. (You may bend elbow.)

   d) To execute forward dive lay-out with one-half twist to the left: (1) Use same take-off as for swan dive. (2) On the lift, let arms begin the turn. (3) As body leaves board, swing arms up over head. (4) Move right arm into position as for a swan dive. (5) Move left arm into same position, but pulled backward. (6) To continue twisting movement, keep left arm back. (7) Just before entry, let right hand join left hand. (See Fig. 9–45.)

Fig. 9-44. Somersault in pike position.

**Fig. 9-45.** Forward dive layout with one-half twist.

| Problems with Twist | Corrections and Coaching Hints |
|---|---|
| *Body hits water sideways rather than vertically.* Cause: pressing laterally from the board. | As you leave board, twist slightly but smoothly. |
| *Inability to make complete half-twist.* Result: body ends up turned to the side rather than with back to board on entry. Cause: too little motion to start twist as arms swing overhead on leaving the board. | Pull left arm backward from swan position as body leaves board, resulting in first quarter of twist. Hold arm behind head to continue twisting movement before entry. |

4. Saves [24]

   a) Use a save to correct the angle of entry, to eliminate excessive splashing.

   b) To execute reverse save: (1) Use reverse save when timing is off on backward-spinning dive. (2) Keep same arch until body is in water to waist. (3) Then increase arch of back (by raising head and using arms to make entry shallow). (4) Bend knees to allow lower legs to enter on a vertical plane. (See Fig. 9–46a.)

   c) To execute forward save: (1) Use forward save when spinning action is forward and timing is off for entry. (2) Start correction movements when lower legs are still above water. (3) Go into forward pike position by bringing head and arms forward. (4) Use arms to pull on water to deepen pike and to turn upper body toward the surface. (See Fig. 9–46b.)

STRATEGY

Strategy in diving involves both physical and mental readiness. Try to increase the flexibility in your hips and ankles by a sound training program. Strength in the abdominal region is especially needed for dives involving the pike position. You should be able to control all the muscles of your body, and they should all be *firm* muscles. This gives you poise and grace in the air and strength and control upon entry into the water.

Practice under competitive situations. Before you use a particular dive in competition, work on it until you feel you have it really under control; confidence plays a big role in competitive diving. To help your timing, use a trampoline, or a diving board with an air mattress underneath, during off-seasons. It may help you, while you are practicing feet-first entries into the water, to use a nose clip; this may prevent nasal and sinus congestion. Avoid excessive bouncing on the board, since this may lead to shin splints. Try to develop courage, since advanced dives require daring and the ability to take occasional hard smacks on the water.

While in the starting position, concentrate on the dive you're about to execute; visualize it in your mind and picture yourself doing it perfectly. To relax, take two or three deep breaths before the approach.

**Fig. 9-46(a).** Reverse save.

**Fig. 9-46(b).** Forward save.

Before a meet, practice as much as possible on the board you're going to use, so that you can make any needed adjustments in spring, space perception, etc.

Strive to analyze your mistakes so that you won't repeat them the next time you attempt the same dive, or a similar one. In diving, performance depends on the individual alone. Therefore strategy in diving means being at your best, both physically and mentally.

## TENNIS

COACHING EMPHASIS

1. Controlling forehand and backhand.
2. Placement and variety of serve.
3. Developing strong overhead and volley, and "touch" on the drop shot.
4. Practicing the lob as a defensive stroke.
5. Strategy.

MECHANICS

1. Twist serve

   a) The twist serve requires much back and abdominal strength; for some girls, it may create too much strain on the back.

   b) To execute American twist: (1) Use backhand grip. (2) Use stance slightly more parallel to base line than stance in slice serve. (3) Toss ball behind head and a little more to left than for slice or flat serve. (4) Bend body backward, with knees bent. (5) Keep weight on balls of feet (concentrate weight on rear foot during toss-up; shift it to forward foot during hit). (6) Snap body, arm, wrist, and racket up and out, in that order. (7) Let racket face go up and slightly over top of ball to create top spin. (8) Let follow-through go to right side of body. (See Fig. 9-47.)

| Problems with American Twist | Corrections and Coaching Hints |
|---|---|
| *Poor toss.* Cause: ball does not go high enough or far enough behind head. | Let arm action be slightly backward; make toss slightly higher than one can reach with racket. |
| *Poor balance.* Causes: weight on heels; lack of knee flexion; improper spacing of feet. | Keep weight on balls of feet; on toss-up, shift weight to rear foot; on hit, shift it to forward foot. Bend knees on toss-up, straighten them on hit; space feet comfortably. |

**Fig. 9–47.** American twist service.

*Lack of top spin.* Cause: incorrect wrist action. Result: inadequate bounce or "kick" when ball hits ground.

Immediately on contact with ball, roll face of racket over ball, snapping wrist and whipping racket out to right.

*Lack of power.* Cause: incorrect body and wrist action.

Cock wrist and then snap it forcefully. You get more power if you snap body and arm forward before contact.

*Lack of accuracy.* Cause: inconsistency in stance, toss-up, or shoulder rotation.

Take same stance each time; practice toss-up to get it in same place each time; keep left shoulder toward net as long as possible.

2. Volley

   a) Use modified Eastern or Continental grip, because fast play at net does not allow time for change in grips. (In this grip, the hand is placed in a way that is halfway between a forehand and a backhand grip, with fingers slightly closer together than in the regular grip.)

   b) To execute volley: (1) Keep weight low and knees bent. (2) Keep racket head above wrist. (3) Rotate upper body to get shoulder toward net if possible. (4) Watch ball. (5) Keep wrist firm. (6) Block ball and use short follow-through.

   c) Keep body weight in motion by bouncing slightly on balls of feet as you wait for ball at net.

   d) Make contact with ball slightly in front of the body.

   e) If ball drops below net before hit, angle racket face up slightly to clear net on volley.

   f) Work on deep placements and angled shots on the volley.

| *Problems with Volley* | *Corrections and Coaching Hints* |
| --- | --- |
| *Lack of confidence.* Cause: inadequate practice. Results: unsure and weak hits. | Get someone to hit soft volleys to you until you feel confident in your ability to volley. Practice volleying against a wall which has a line drawn on it at net height. |
| *Too much swing.* Results: lack of control and inability to get ready for next ball. | Just block ball and then "push" it back; if you have a firm wrist, this will give the ball enough power so that the rebound will go back over the net. |
| *Too much wrist action.* Results: inaccuracy, caused by cocking and uncocking of wrist. | Don't allow wrist to break back; keep wrist locked and firm; let wrist act as an extension of the arm. |

(a)

(b)

(c)

**Fig. 9-48.** Overhead smash.

*Too much spin on ball.* Results: ball goes into net; ball bounces too high. Cause: racket head dropped on contact.

Keep ball on strings as long as possible; lock wrist and make contact with ball slightly in front of body, pushing forward about a foot on the follow-through. Keep racket head above wrist. Don't cut under ball by angling racket face back unless ball has dropped below the net and the angled face is necessary for clearing the net.

*Lack of power and accuracy.* Causes: no follow-through at all; wrist "gives" with ball; ball hit behind body; lack of strength.

Take short follow-through; keep wrist firm; contact ball in front of body. Build up arm and wrist strength by practicing backhand and forehand strokes, swinging *slowly* with the press on the racket.

*Ball hits wood.* Causes: lack of concentration; moving in too close to ball.

Watch ball all the way; position body to allow room for volley without too much crowding of arm.

*Poor positioning at the net.* Results: balls hit at feet of player; player can't reach balls.

Practice stroking ball from base line, then move in to net on strong returns for the volley; go beyond service line; set up position on side of center line, as previous placement, to cut off the shortest return.*

*Poor reactions.* Causes: inertia of the body; lack of knee flexion; inability to anticipate.

Bounce lightly on toes; keep body moving while waiting; keep weight low with knees bent; try to anticipate opponent's best possible return.

3. Smash or Overhead Stroke

  a) Use motion similar to that used in slice or flat serve.

  b) To execute smash or overhead stroke: (1) Get in position under ball (let ball drop slightly in front of right shoulder). (2) Bring racket back behind head, cocking wrist. (3) Shift weight to rear foot as you bring racket back. (4) Time swing to hit ball at height of reach. (5) Extend arm and snap wrist through ball while shifting weight forward. (6) Let follow-through be to left side of body. (See Fig. 9–48.)

  c) Turn left side slightly toward net while waiting for ball.

---

* For example of cutting off the shortest return, see Fig. 9–8.

d) If you're having trouble with timing, try two things: (1) Wait for ball with racket on shoulder rather than taking full swing. (2) If lob is high, let it bounce before smashing it.

e) Practice positioning by tossing balls high into the air, then moving under ball for hit.

| *Problems with Smash* | *Corrections and Coaching Hints* |
|---|---|
| *Poor timing.* Result: ball not hit solidly. Cause: ball too high or too low on hit. | Move into position quickly; let ball bounce if lob is high; reach up to hit ball so that arm is extended as you make contact with ball. |
| *Poor positioning.* Result: ball hit into net or out of court. Causes: player not getting in line with ball; player hitting in an off-balance position. | Hustle into position; get in direct line with ball and allow it to drop in front of right shoulder. If ball goes into net, you may have let it drop too low or may need to get more directly under it before contact. If ball goes out of court, body is too far under ball or wrist snap is too late. |
| *Lack of power.* Result: weak hit. Cause: incorrect wrist and body action. | Cock wrist and snap it through ball; shift weight from rear to forward foot before hit, and follow through across left side of body. |

4. Drop Shot

   a) This shot requires soft touch and "feel."

   b) You can execute a drop shot by allowing racket face to give slightly on contact with ball; this is even more effective when you apply spin.

   c) Try to place ball just over net.

   d) Use the drop shot when: (1) opponent plays deep at baseline, (2) opponent's movement has previously been away from net, and (3) you want to pull opponent up to net for a passing shot.

   e) To execute the drop shot, use the same movement you use for any other stroke, except at the last moment, stop forward stroke and let racket "give" or recoil slightly as you hit the ball. For spin, angle racket face and move down or across ball gently.

5. Spins

   a) Top spin: (1) You are using top spin when your racket face moves up and over the ball, with the movement starting behind the ball. (2) To keep ball in court more easily, use top spin on forehand and backhand drives. (3) The top spin gives a lower line of flight. (4) The top spin causes faster and lower bounce.

b) Side spin: (1) Use side spin for change of pace, or on service, to achieve a slice. (2) To make ball have a side spin, let racket face move down and to the side of ball. (3) Note that bounce is sideways and higher than usual. (4) To execute a side spin, you must snap wrist toward ground.

c) Back spin: (1) Use back spin to create a chop; this is very effective on drop shots. (2) To execute a back spin, let racket face move downward and slightly under ball from the back. (3) Note that bounce is higher than usual, and almost vertical.

## STRATEGY

Work continually on perfecting your strokes and on obtaining endurance. Set up your practice sessions with the aim of achieving accuracy on specific strokes. For example, if you're weak in hitting the backhand cross-court shot, practice this two ways: (1) Stand in the left-hand corner of the court and stroke balls across the net into the right-hand corner (preferably by hitting with another player, but you could use a bucket of balls). (2) Run across the court to take the backhand and stroke it to the opposite corner; then move back to the center of the court to repeat the movement. Or take a bucket of balls and practice your slice service by aiming at specific areas marked out in the service box.

Practice against another good player is a must. Hitting a thrown ball is not the same as stroking a ball hit at you by a racket. In tennis as in everything else, there's no substitute for real live people and gamelike situations.

## PLAYING THE OPPONENT

Everybody plays a different game of tennis. Within certain limits, you must adjust your game to cope with a specific type of game.

To beat the steady player, either play more steadily than she does or play very aggressively to get the sure put-away shots. When you're playing against a girl who likes to rush the net, keep her off-balance by keeping the drives deep. If the net player does come up to the net, use lobs to force her away from it, or try to pass her down the sideline. If the opponent hits the ball hard, use soft returns to prevent her from increasing her power by combining her force with a hard-hit return; drop shots, chops, and soft angled shots are good against this type of player. You may even lob the ball back continually, provided you keep it deep to prevent a smash. This again prevents her from combining her power with your power on regular strokes.

## SURFACE

The type of surface you compete on can make quite a difference in the type of game you play. On hard surfaces, the player who has a strong game with a fast serve and a good volley has the advantage, because of the fast bounce on the court. On clay and other soft-surface courts, the ball bounces more slowly. Drop shots, chops, and slice or twist serves are effective on this type of court because the spin takes hold better. Slow-moving players have an advantage on clay and soft-surface courts (the bounce gives more time to get to the ball) such courts are a disadvantage to the power hitter.

Grass courts give the edge to the aggressive player because of the low bounce and skid. It is almost impossible to get to a hard-hit ball on grass courts because of the speed of the ball as it rebounds off the court. Here the advantage definitely belongs to the player with a hard serve, strong strokes, and an accurate volley. Drop shots can be effective at times, since a person has trouble starting or stopping quickly because of the footing on the grass.

WIND

Wind can also affect a person's game. If the wind is blowing toward you, you should: (1) Keep lobs to a minimum. (2) Hit ground strokes harder than usual. (3) Use drop shots if opponent is playing deep. (4) On passing shots at the net, keep ball low and to opponent's weak side.

If wind is coming from behind you, you should: (1) Keep lobs to a minimum. (2) Use top spin to keep balls in court. (3) Keep drop shots to a minimum. (4) Let high lobs bounce before smashing them. (5) Move in closer to receive service. (6) Keep ball in play until opponent hits weak shot into the wind; then be aggressive for put-away.

When hitting into a cross wind: (1) Allow a margin for error. (2) Get in position quickly, allowing for movement of ball toward or away from you, according to direction of wind. (3) Keep ball in play. (4) Try to let wind carry ball away from opponent rather than toward her. (5) Don't rush net indiscriminately.

SUN

When you're facing the sun and serving, throw balls up more to the side, so that you won't have to look directly up into the sun on the service. On overheads, position yourself with the same idea in mind. If you're serving and the sun is to your right, the toss for the twist serve may be easier to see. If the sun is directly over your head, the toss for the slice or the flat serve is better. If you do have to look into the sun when you're serving, don't follow your serve up to the net. If your opponent is having a sun problem when she is serving, hit the serve to a corner and follow it to the net. A lob over the net player's head when she is facing the sun is also an effective shot.

GENERAL STRATEGY

The subject of strategy in tennis can be divided into factors applicable to singles and factors applicable to doubles; but individual readiness is basic to both. Learn not to choke up under pressure (this usually comes only with experience and confidence). Learn to concentrate, and watch the ball until you have actually hit it. (Some coaches tell their players to try to read the name printed on the ball as it comes to the racket.) Another thing you must be able to do if you are to play well is to relax. If you're too tense, and your play is tight as a result, you have what is commonly called "the elbow." Remind yourself constantly to go ahead and stroke the ball rather than playing too cautiously.

If you're winning, stay with the strategy that has put you ahead. If you're losing, change your strategy, in hopes that your opponent will not be able to cope with your new tactics.

The skilled player should be able to hold her serve, since a well-placed serve gives anyone a definite advantage. Therefore she should concentrate on breaking the opponent's serve. If you return the service down the sidelines and deep in the court, this keeps the opponent from taking advantage of a rush to the net behind her serve, and may help in breaking the serve.

When the score is 4-3, this is probably the most crucial point in a set. At this point, a service break or a service win can throw the game either way. Another critical time in a game occurs when the score is 30-5. Winning the point can give the receiver a fighting chance. Losing the point can put the score at 40-5, which is quite an advantage for the server. However, don't forget that *every* point is important. It gives you a psychological advantage if you can win the first two points of a game; you should therefore work especially hard at the beginning.

Try to hit the ball to the opponent's weaknesses, and play the percentage shots. If you know that one type of play is giving you more points and less losses than another, stick to this type of play. Don't get upset when you miss a shot; learn to take each point as it comes.

STRATEGY FOR SINGLES

1. *When Serving*

   a) Vary your serves. The slice and twist give greater control and are effective as second serves.

   b) If your serve is hard and effective, follow it to the net.

   c) Place serves deep and to the corners.

   d) If receiver is overplaying, hit serves away from her.

2. *When Receiving*

   a) Position yourself according to the power and spin on the serve. Move in closer for: (1) weak serves, and (2) serves with spin.

   b) If server rushes net, hit return low and deep, preferably down the sideline. Use lobs to force her away from the net.

   c) Hit weak serves deep to backhand corner and go to the net.

   d) Keep weight on balls of feet; for most effective return of serve, keep weight in motion.

   e) When serve is angled toward sideline, best return is high lob or shot back down sideline.

   f) On a fast, hard serve, if you cannot stroke ball, keep wrist firm and attempt to just "block" shot.

### 3. *Ground Strokes*

a) Place ball deep and to opponent's weak side.

b) For better control of forehand, use top spin on ball.

c) Run opponent as much as possible; when she is running fast to get back into position, hit ball behind her.

d) Use drop shots, chops, and angled volleys to make drives more effective.

e) If opponent is slow, hit one drive deep and then on the next one drop the ball right over the net.

f) Always get racket back *before* the ball gets into hitting position.

### 4. *Net Play*

a) When opponent hits the ball short, hit return deep and go to net.

b) Stop forward body motion before volleying.

c) To prevent balls hitting at feet, go beyond service line.

d) Be aggressive; keep opponent on defense.

e) When ball drops below level of net, angle racket face up slightly.

f) When hitting toward sideline or baseline, allow 2–3 inches for error.

g) To come to net on a ground stroke, hit ball deep to middle of court or to deep backhand corner; then move up.

h) When the opponent angles balls to one side, move slightly in that direction to cut off the shortest return back down the sideline, but be ready for cross-court shots.

i) Keep weight low, racket head above wrist, and be firm.

### 5. *Overheads*

a) When you hit an overhead from a position close to the net, angle it as much as possible; when you hit ball from area close to baseline, smash ball deep and go up to net.

b) If ball is too far over head for safe smash, put racket up and hit ball as deep as possible, with a soft but firm blocking action.

c) If opponent hits a high lob to your backhand side, if possible run around the ball for the smash after it bounces.

d) When you can, let lobs bounce before you smash them; this helps your timing (provided lob will take high-enough bounce).

e) Allow for wind; keep eye on ball; get into position quickly.

### 6. *Lobs*

a) Lob over opponent's head when she is at net, to force her back.

b) Use lob when you are out of position, or when you need extra time before next stroke.

c) Place lobs as deep as possible and to the backhand corner.

d) Don't lob often when you are up against a player with a good overhead.

e) As a defensive stroke, lob high. As an offensive stroke, send lob barely over opponent's reach.

f) When opponent is off-balance and must hurry back to return a lob, go to net.

g) When wind is blowing, keep lobs at a minimum.

7. *Other Strategy*

a) Return to middle of court (behind baseline) after each stroke.

b) Don't get caught between baseline and service line ("no man's land").

c) Play balls that hit close to a line.

d) Don't give up on a point; don't relax until ball has been put away.

e) When you are distracted while your opponent is serving because of a ball rolling across court, or other uncontrollable factors, call for a "let" immediately.

f) When you return a serve, or go in to the net to volley, follow angle of ball to cut off shortest return.

STRATEGY FOR DOUBLES

1. *When Serving*

a) The best server of the team should serve first game of each set.

b) Follow first serve in, but stay back on second, unless it is also a strong serve.

c) Move to net immediately; try not to get caught between baseline and service line.

d) If you serve with a lot of spin rather than power only (flat serve), this gives you more time to go to the net.

e) Server coming in to net must be ready to reverse direction and take a lob placed over partner's head.

f) Try to get to net at first possible chance, since in doubles there is a definite advantage in net play.

2. *When Receiving*

a) If both players are right-handed, the best backhand player should take the left court.

b) If possible, return ball deep or at an angle and go to net.

c) Best shots are: (1) lob over head of net player, (2) ball hit at feet of server coming in to net, or (3) sharply angled shot away from net player.

d) To allow faster move to net, play as close to service line as possible.

3. *General Strategy*

    a) Work as a unit; when one player moves to the side, other one should too. This prevents opening up a large hole between the two players.

    b) Be aggressive at the net; keep balls low and angle off when possible.

    c) Poach on signals or when there is a sure put-away shot.

    d) Player with best forehand should take all shots in middle of court.

    e) Hit between players; when players pull into middle, hit to alley.

    f) When out of position, lob ball to allow time for yourself and your partner to get set up.

    g) When ball is lobbed over you at net, change sides with partner.

## TRACK AND FIELD

### COACHING EMPHASIS

1. General conditioning.
2. Specializing in skills and conditioning for specific events.
3. Working on starts, running, hurdling, jumping, and throwing.

### MECHANICS

1. Starts

    a) The object is to start body from "set" position in fastest possible time.

    b) To start effectively, body must be in an unstable position (obtained by moving center of gravity forward so that body must move quickly to regain balance).

    c) To execute start from blocks: (1) On "get set," move hips upward and forward, forcing most of body weight to fingertips. (Shoulders usually move 2-3 inches beyond hands.) (2) Head position should be a relaxed one, with eyes focused about 3 feet ahead of the starting line. (3) On "go" signal, push hard against blocks with both feet to start motion forward (forward foot gives most power). (4) Keep body low when coming out of blocks. Arms move in opposition to legs. (See Fig. 9-49.)

    d) Spacing of blocks varies. Stance usually used is the medium-elongated, with first block about 6-12 inches (about two hand spans) from starting line, and rear block about 12-16 inches from front block. (Knee of rear leg is usually opposite arch of front foot.) In bunch start, feet are close together; in elongated stance, feet are spaced wider than in medium-elongated stance. Although the medium start is thought to allow the runner to go into her running stride more quickly, the bunch start gets her out of the starting position the fastest. However, this fast start out

(a)

(b)

Fig. 9-49. The start.

of the blocks by use of the bunch start forces the runner to lose valuable time in regaining balance before hitting her running stride.

e) Forward leg should be strongest leg.

| *Problems with Starts* | *Corrections and Coaching Hints* |
|---|---|
| *Lack of balance when going into the "set" position.* Causes: center of gravity moved too far forward for hands to support weight; placing blocks too close to starting line. | Experiment with spacing of blocks; find best position for concentrating weight over hands and forward foot without losing balance. |
| *Difficulty in holding "set" position comfortably until "go" signal.* Causes: incorrect arm and hand positioning; lack of strength in arms and hands. | Place hands slightly farther apart than shoulders; let fingers support most of weight, as thumb and fingers form an inverted V; lock wrists; keep arms straight (elbows locked). Build up strength in hands and arms with finger-tip pushups and isometric exercises. |
| *Too little power or push coming out of blocks.* Causes: blocks spaced too close or too far apart for maximum push; weaker leg placed in front position; push made with only one leg. | Experiment with spacing of blocks to get maximum push. Exchange lead legs to see if this increases speed coming out of blocks. Push against blocks with both feet. |

f) After push out of blocks: (1) Keep leaning forward and keep body low, gradually coming up to normal running position (body lean should still be about 20–25 degrees). (2) Make first steps out of block as long as possible, while maintaining good balance. (3) Increase stride as you pick up speed (length of stride should become progressively greater until full speed has been reached). (4) Swing arms alternately (elbows bent at about a 90-degree angle, and hands relaxed). (5) Point feet straight ahead.

g) Speed depends on: (1) distance between feet on stride, and (2) number of strides per second.

h) Standing start is usually used for distance running.

| *Problems after Leaving Blocks* | *Corrections and Coaching Hints* |
|---|---|
| *Swaying of body during run.* Results: loss of speed; body does not move on straight line. Causes: incorrect steps; failure to swing arms properly. | Point feet straight ahead. If body sways, concentrate on swinging arms in straight line. Arms may swing toward the middle of the body but should not cross the midline of the body. Hands should not go above the shoulder or beyond the back of the hip on the swing. |

*Coming up into an erect position too soon after start.* Results: runner loses power in leg drive forward. Causes: taking too-long steps; not having head in correct position; body lean inadequate.

Shorten first 2 or 3 steps when coming out of blocks; don't lift head when coming out, but keep head in line with body; body lean should be as great as balance will allow, with approximately 20-degree lean when top speed is reached.

*Lack of speed and smoothness during stride.* Causes: too little knee lift by front leg; head sways from side to side; exaggerated arm swing; not enough push on ground; too-short strides.

Lift knee of forward leg high; keep head steady, with eyes focused straight ahead; arm swing should be synchronized with leg movement; push should be result of leg and ankle extension, with greatest push against ground coming during first 7–8 strides. Increase length of strides.

2. Hurdling (see Fig. 9–50)

a) Adjust running stride just enough to allow hips and legs to clear hurdle without spending an unnecessarily long time in air.

b) To execute a hurdle: (1) Leave ground far enough from hurdle to allow good stretch between legs. (2) Increase body lean as lead leg starts over. (3) Let lead leg skim hurdle (lead leg should lift toward chest until heel is slightly above level of top of hurdle). (4) Snap lead foot down. (5) Let trailing leg come over hurdle in sideward motion (inside of leg is next to hurdle). (6) Turn foot outward to avoid hitting hurdle. (7) When lead leg hits ground (about 2 feet from hurdle), bring trailing leg forward quickly with knee high (reach forward and out to gain full stride). (8) Take three strides. (9) Repeat movement.

c) Let opposite arm reach out at same time as lead leg, while other arm goes back about hip level. Arm action between hurdles is same as for other running action, following opposition pattern.

|  |  |
|---|---|
| *Problems in Hurdling* | *Corrections and Coaching Hints* |

*Too much clearance between runner and hurdle.* Causes: take-off too close to hurdle; too much push-off from take-off foot; lack of body lean. Result: loss of speed.

Distance between take-off and hurdle depends on individual, but usually about 5–6 feet; push-off is *forward* and across hurdle rather than up; lean forward with body. "Skim" hurdle with legs.

*Runner hits hurdle with lead leg.* Causes: take-off too far from hurdle; too little lift on lead leg.

Be consistent in steps taken between hurdles; let take-off be closer to hurdle; lift forward leg to clear hurdle.

*Runner hits hurdle with trailing leg.* Causes: failure to swing leg to side; failure to rotate ankle.

Flex knee, swing leg to side, rotate ankle to allow foot to turn outward.

| | |
|---|---|
| *Inadequate stride when landing.* Results: loss of speed; poor timing for next hurdle. Cause: failure to lift knee toward chest after clearing hurdle. | As leading leg hits, let trailing leg complete its swing over hurdle and lift toward chest, and then out, to give long stride for maximum speed. |

3. Jumping

    a) Jump depends on a build-up of momentum and the ability to direct this momentum in an outward or upward motion.

    b) Increase height or length of jump by: (1) swinging arms upward or forward, (2) practicing leg action on the ground and in the air, and (3) increasing speed of approach. (In high jump, increased speed on approach is valuable only if this speed can be converted into an upward motion at take-off.)

    c) For greatest distance in broad-jumping, the take-off should be at approximately a 45-degree angle. The arms and legs should be used for balance, and to gain a reaction from other parts of the body. For greatest height in high-jumping, the speed of the approach must be converted upward; leg and arm action makes this possible.

    d) *Standing Broad Jump:* (1) Space feet about width of shoulders. (2) Rock back and forth, with weight going from toes to heels and back, etc. (3) Swing arms in time with rocking movement. (4) Push with legs forcefully, swing arms forward at same time, and lean in direction of jump. (5) Give final thrust, extending ankles and toes. (6) As body is in air, pull legs up and extend them forward as arms reach out. (7) Flex knees on landing. (8) Keep body lean forward. (9) Swing arms forward and down.

| *Problems in Standing Broad Jump* | *Corrections and Coaching Hints* |
|---|---|
| *Illegal jump.* Causes: both feet not kept in contact with board; feet not behind scratch line. | If raised beat board is used, toes may be curled over edge but must not touch floor or ground; otherwise, keep feet behind line. Keep part of both feet in contact with board at all times. |
| *Lack of timing.* Cause: incorrect arm movement. | As arms swing forward, shift weight to toes; as arms swing backward, shift weight to heels. |
| *Landing off-balance.* Causes: inadequate body lean; failure to use arms. | While body is in air, and upon landing, the body leans forward. Arms are extended forward until landing and then are brought forcefully downward to keep body from falling backward. |

    e) *Long Jump:* (1) Approach take-off board at about 90 percent of top speed. (2) Shorten last stride about 6 inches. (Runner should relax during last 3–4

(a)

(b)

(c)

**Fig. 9-50.** Going over a hurdle. (a) Body leans forward as lead leg goes over. (b) Lead leg snaps down. (c) Lead leg has hit ground and trailing leg has been brought high to give long stride.

strides. This "coasting" action is not a reduction in speed, but a controlling action as runner gets ready for the take-off.) (3) Hit take-off board with knee bent. (4) Straighten leg and push hard with leg, ankle, and toes (body weight rotates from heel to ball of foot). (5) Throw arms, head, chest, and shoulders upward and outward, and lift lead leg. (6) As body goes into air, swing both legs forward. (7) Use hitch-kick for balance and to keep feet in the air as long as possible. (8) As feet hit ground (heels first), bend knees to absorb force of jump. (9) To help body continue forward motion, extend legs forward, pull head and trunk forward, and swing arms forward and then backward.

f) Speed of approach is very important for the long jump. Most girls use an approach of about 90–120 feet, although a longer distance may be used by a person who is in good condition. Check marks should be used.

g) The three main factors in a successful long jump are the sprint down the runway, the foot plant and push-off, and the leg lift.

h) To execute hitch-kick: (1) After take-off, straighten lead leg. (2) Bring lead leg back as take-off leg moves forward and upward (in flexed position). Take-off leg then straightens as it reaches out. (3) Move lead leg forward again. (4) For the landing, let the take-off leg and the lead leg meet in extended position. This leg action for the hitch-kick is like taking a step in the air.

| *Problems in Long Jump* | *Corrections and Coaching Hints* |
|---|---|
| *Poor take-off.* Causes: failure to use check marks; incorrect foot plant; not enough leg lift. | Check marks vary according to individual's stride, but are usually approximately 60 and 30 feet from take-off board. Plant foot heel first; then let weight roll from heel to toes, extending leg and pushing from the toes; lift leg up forcefully as head and shoulders also lift. |
| *Jump too short.* Causes: inability to gain enough momentum and then relax during last few strides; inability to shorten last stride; lack of flexion in take-off knee; insufficient leg lift and upward movement of head, shoulders, and arms. | Increase length of approach; relax during last few strides, but don't slow approach; shorten last step about 6 inches; plant foot and lower body by flexing knee; lift lead leg, arms, head, and shoulders as leg pushes off. |
| *Falling backward on landing.* Causes: too little body lean; failure to pull arms down; insufficient knee flexion. | Body should lean forward; arms should pull forcefully down; knees should "give" as heels hit. (If arms are carried high, they are moved forward; if carried low, they are pulled forward and then backward.) |

*Sore, bruised heels.* Cause: tremendous force of foot plant.

Insert piece of sponge in the shoe to absorb shock of foot plant.

i) *High Jump:* (1) Start approximately 7–8 strides back. (2) Build up speed gradually on approach, from a relaxed trot to a relatively slow run. (Approach should be at about a 45-degree angle to the crossbar; some prefer an approach of 30–40 degrees for a straddle roll.) (3) Quicken and lengthen last three strides. (4) Let take-off point be about an arm's length away from bar. (5) Plant heel of take-off foot and lean backward (for push-off force, bend knee). (6) Keep other leg straight as it swings upward. (7) As leg swings upward, lift arm on that side up forcefully and transfer weight from the heel to the toes of the take-off foot as it straightens for the push-off.

j) The two techniques most used for the high jump are the Western and the straddle roll. The approach and the take-off are the same for both techniques (the inside foot is used as the take-off foot), but they vary in the lay-out as you go over the bar. For the Western, you go over on your side; for the straddle roll, you go over on your stomach. Many people think that the straddle roll is the more efficient of the two.

k) To execute straddle roll (after take-off): (1) Swing lead leg up and over bar. (2) Start to turn body toward bar (body facing bar). (3) Tuck arm next to bar in close to side, with elbow bent. (4) Straighten push-off leg and rotate it outward to clear the bar. (5) Let right arm and right leg touch pit first. (6) Roll to back to absorb force of landing. (See Fig. 9–51.)

| *Problems with Straddle Roll* | *Corrections and Coaching Hints* |
|---|---|
| *Take-off forward rather than vertical.* Causes: taking off too far from bar; failure to lengthen last three strides to help backward lean. Result: jumper goes into bar rather than over it. | Move take-off point closer to bar; make last three strides the longest and fastest of the approach; lean backward after planting take-off foot. |
| *Insufficient upward motion.* Cause: poor take-off. Result: inability to clear bar. | Flex knee of take-off foot and plant heel, and then rock weight to toes; straighten other leg and lift up while arms go up to aid in lift; extend take-off leg and push hard with ankle and toes. |
| *Improper action going over bar.* Results: failure to get hips over; trailing leg hits bar. | As you straddle bar, duck head and right shoulder slightly to help lift hips; as body passes bar, straighten trailing leg; this helps trailing leg to clear. |
| *Leading leg hits bar on way up.* Causes: take-off point too close to bar; swing is toward bar rather than parallel to it. | Move take-off point back; place take-off foot in line with approach; make initial swing-up almost parallel to bar. |

**Fig. 9-51.** Straddle roll on high jump.

4. Throwing

a) The objective in a throwing event is to transfer body momentum to the object being thrown.

b) For best results in throwing events: (1) Throw object at 45-degree angle. (2) Use body rotation and/or rotation of throwing arm. (3) Shift body weight. (4) Direct force in one direction by proper sequence of weight shift, trunk rotation, elbow extension, wrist snap, etc.

c) In the shot put, strength is the biggest factor, though glide helps the shot-putter to achieve distance. In the discus throw, strength and speed of movements in the circle are important. In the javelin throw, speed on the approach, ability to stop suddenly, and strength affect distance.

d) To execute the *shot put:* (1) Start in rear of circle, facing away from direction of throw. (2) Hold shot in fingers of right hand, with hand behind and underneath shot. (3) Tuck shot under jaw and against neck just back of the ear. (4) Keep elbow close to body and pointed toward ground. (5) Bend forward and put weight on right foot. (6) Flex left leg and kick back while straightening right leg (this starts glide). (7) Keep body low and upper trunk almost parallel to ground during glide. (8) Place left foot down near toe board. (9) Begin to rotate trunk, with power coming from push by right leg, trunk rotation, arm extension, and wrist flexion. (Release shot at end of sequence of power resulting from rear leg thrust, hip rotation, shoulder, arm, hand, and finger push.) (10) Follow through by extending arm in direction of throw. (11) Reverse step (bend right knee to absorb force of body weight shift). (See Fig. 9-52.)

e) To help your balance, extend your left arm during glide.

f) In reverse step, your right foot simply trades places with your left.

g) To execute the *discus throw* with one and three-quarters turn: (1) Stand in rear of circle, facing away from direction of throw. (2) Press discus against palm with tips of fingers around edge. (3) Spread feet comfortably, flex knees, and keep head up. (4) Swing discus back parallel to ground while rotating upper trunk. (5) Repeat swinging motion once or twice to build up momentum. (6) On final backswing, shift weight to right foot. (7) Transfer weight back to left foot, which has dropped back 16-18 inches from right foot, and begin pivot (from heel to ball of foot). (8) When left toe faces front of circle, push with left leg. (9) Jump to right foot (which is placed in center of circle). (10) Continue pivot on right foot while swinging left leg around and letting it come down at front edge of circle and about 6 inches to left of center line. (11) Throwing arm is still trailing body at this point. (12) When left foot is planted at front of circle, begin body rotation from hips (keep right knee slightly bent). (13) "Explode" by forceful extension of right leg as discus reaches hip. (14) Continue swing forward at 45-degree angle while you pull your left arm back and down to help body to rotate. (15) Release discus on thumb side. (16) Follow through. (17) Reverse step. (See Fig. 9-53.)

**Fig. 9-52.** Shot put. (a) Beginning of knee bend for kick back. (b) Glide as result of kick back and extension of right leg. (c) Body almost parallel to ground. (d) Left foot set down near toe board. (e) Follow-through after release.

**(a)**

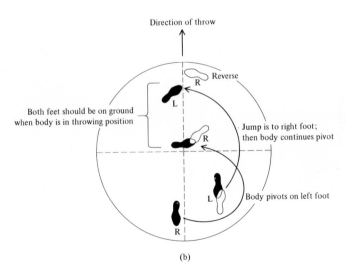

Direction of throw

Reverse

Both feet should be on ground
when body is in throwing position

Jump is to right foot;
then body continues pivot

Body pivots on left foot

(b)

**Fig. 9-53.** Discus throw. (a) Hand position, with fingers spread and tips of fingers over edge.
(b) Footwork for discus throw.

**Fig. 9-54.** (a) Last five steps of javelin throw involving crossover. (b) Feet cross over. (c) Right leg begins push for throw, (d) the throw, and (e) reverse after javelin has been released.

h) To execute *javelin throw* with front cross-over: (1) Approach should be approximately 90–100 feet (about 15–17 running strides). (2) Grip javelin in palm of hand with middle finger and thumb at back edge of cord (tip of thumb on top of binding and middle finger curled around shaft), forefinger hooked slightly around grip, and other two fingers curled naturally around the binding (Finnish grip). (3) Carry javelin above shoulder (near top of head) with elbow bent and tip slightly down. (4) Build speed up during approach. (5) Use last five steps for cross-over. (6) First step of cross-over: point right foot slightly out (about 45-degree angle to direction of throw). (7) Second step: bring left foot almost parallel to right foot (about 60 degrees to right of approach direction). (8) Take javelin back with arm extended (keep point close to face and tail just off ground). (9) Third step: cross right foot over left and place it at a right angle to the line of approach (flexing knee to allow backward lean). (10) Keep javelin as far back as possible. (11) Lift left leg and lean backward for the throw. (12) Fourth step: force left leg down to ground and push hard with right leg. (13) Bring javelin forward powerfully as right leg pushes and pull left arm downward and backward to aid the release at approximately a 45-degree angle. (14) Follow through. (15) Reverse step to stop forward momentum. (See Fig. 9-54.)

## STRATEGY

*For Sprints.* The strategy for sprints involves coming out of the blocks correctly and immediately when the gun sounds, building up maximum speed as quickly as possible, and then maintaining this speed until the end of the race. The sprinter should not slow down until she is well past the finish line. In the 220, try to reach full speed for the first 60 yards, conserve energy by maintaining a fast pace or a "floating" pace for the next 100 yards, and then go all out for the last 60 yards. The better sprinters are able to maintain their top speed for a greater distance.

*For Hurdles.* The start for the hurdles is just as important as the start for the sprints. The runner should continue to build up speed as she clears the first two or three hurdles, and then maintain her speed throughout the race. She must learn to skim over the hurdles as if they weren't there, maintaining three strides between each hurdle and sprinting all the way. When she has taken the last hurdle, she should concentrate on maintaining her rhythm until she is well past the finish line.

*Relays.* For relay races, the second-fastest runner is usually selected as the lead-off runner, unless another team member has more experience or can be depended on more not to make a false start. The third-fastest runner usually runs the second leg, while the slowest member of the team runs the third leg. For psychological reasons, the coach sometimes runs the slowest girl on the second leg and the third-fastest girl on the third leg. The fastest runner runs the last leg. This decision is usually based on the lineup of the chief opponent in the race. However, other factors should be considered in placing runners, such as ability to run straightaways and curves, psychological advantage of having fastest girl give team a good start, ability of a girl to come from behind, and efficiency in the baton exchanges.

*Middle-Distance Running.* Strategy in middle-distance running is a little more involved, since the runner must maneuver for the lead, prevent opponents from boxing her in, and pace the run so that she can challenge for the lead or maintain the lead at the end of the race. The runner's main objective should be to enter the first and last turns in a good position, either as the leader or within easy reach of the leader and to pace herself correctly. In the 440, the girl should learn to run the second half of the race at the same pace as the first half. The time between the first and second half of the race should not vary more than a couple of seconds. In the 880-yard run, a shorter stride is more economical from the standpoint of energy, but overstriding or understriding can put one at a disadvantage. In an ideal run, each 220 would be run at the same pace. In middle distances, if the girl can take the lead on the first turn and still have enough energy to run strong for the rest of the race, she definitely has the advantage.

Reaching the last turn in a good position is important because if the leader has too much of a lead the other runners won't be able to close the gap, or if the leader has not overextended herself she can hold off any challenge by other runners. If you're trailing the leader on this last turn, in order to have a chance to overcome her lead during the remaining distance of the race, you must stay within at least 9 or 10 feet of her.

When you're going into the turns, decide whether to follow the curve in the pole position, in order to travel less distance, or to expend extra energy and try to move up in the order of runners by passing on the outside. If you decide to move up, don't hesitate. Ordinarily, do your passing on the straightaway, so that you cover the shortest possible distance on the pass. When running a curve, stay on the inside of your lane, lean into the curve, and increase your speed as you go around the curve.

If you're leading and want to maintain your lead, you must anticipate the challenge from your opponent and accelerate your pace accordingly, to keep your lead and the inside position. Going into the final stretch, you must start your sprint in time to hold off any challenge while choosing a spot to open up that will allow you to finish the race. Usually, if you are leading and have not been challenged before, begin your "kick" 40 to 50 yards from the finish line. If you are challenged earlier in the straightaway or on the turn, accelerate at that point to maintain the inside position and the lead, and try to continue at the necessary pace until the end of the race.

If you're trailing the leader, don't make your move too soon in coming off the last turn, or the leader may force you to run extra distance around the curve by speeding up and keeping you on her outside shoulder. Instead, choose a pace that will keep you close behind the leader and then make your move at a point on the straightaway where you can sprint the rest of the way to the line. When you come around any of the turns, hold the inside (or pole) lane and don't swing too wide; otherwise another girl will pass you on the inside.

*Throwing and Jumping Events.* Mental readiness is especially important in the throwing and jumping events. Strategy for shot putting demands synchronization of all your body movements in order to have a total "explosion" action on the release. This involves practice, timing, balance, and strength. The shot-putter should follow a program of exercises designed to increase strength in her legs, hips, upper body, shoulder, arm, and wrist. It is also important for her to practice an efficient glide across the circle.

The javelin throw is based on the principle of coordinating your body movements to end up with a total effort to give the object thrown the most distance. This is accomplished by building up speed on the approach and stopping your body forcefully as you release the javelin. An adequate warm-up period is necessary. You must condition your muscles for the strain of the throw by weight-lifting and isometric exercises; don't overthrow during practice sessions, because this could lead to shoulder and elbow injuries.

The discus-thrower needs a continuous movement across the circle, with the upper body and the discus trailing the hips and legs until the actual delivery. Force comes from the speed of the glide and the sequence of power derived from the toes, ankles, knees, hips, upper trunk, shoulder, arm, and hand, as the body uncoils and transfers momentum to the discus.

Strategy, in high jumping, must include an approach that gives optimum force that can be converted into a vertical direction, sufficient push-off and lift, and correct turn in clearing the bar. A mental picture of the body clearing the bar seems to aid the body in accomplishing this feat.

Strategy for the running broad jump includes: building up speed on the approach, shortening the final stride, push-off and leg lift, balance in the air, and a forward motion on landing. If you miss a check mark or feel that your approach is off, abort the try and save your energy for a better run.

*General Strategy.* In most track and field events, strategy is mostly a matter of preparation and practice before the event. The good athlete learns to relax during her performance, although her muscles are working at maximum efficiency. Self-confidence, attained by means of practice and experience, contributes to this ability to relax.

Mental readiness before an event is of prime importance. The athlete must concentrate and shut out all noise and other distractions. She must know what she wants to accomplish and believe that she can do it.

In events in which three tries are allowed, an athlete who knows what she has done wrong and knows how to make the necessary corrections before the next attempt has an advantage.

The good athlete does not let the performance of another athlete "psyche" her out, but plans for her event by setting goals that are within the possibility of achievement, continually raising her goals as she improves her performance.

## VOLLEYBALL*

COACHING EMPHASIS

1. Practicing basic fundamentals, such as overhead or chest pass, net recovery, side-arm serve, etc.
2. Giving special instruction in: two-arm bounce pass ("bump" or dig), one-hand dig, effective serving (floater, overhead top-spin serve, etc.), setting for the spiker (forward, backward, and short-set), spiking, recovery techniques, individual and team blocking.
3. Offensive and defensive strategy.

MECHANICS

1. Two-arm bounce pass
   a) Use the two-arm bounce pass for hard-hit balls below the waist, to recover the ball out of the net, or to hit ball when back is to net.

**Fig. 9-55.** Two positions for hands for two-arm bounce pass.

* Based on a workshop conducted by Frances Schaafsma at the University of Utah (summer of 1966), and articles written for the Fourth National Institute for Girls' and Women's Sports. Used by permission of Frances Schaafsma, Sharon Peterson, JoAnne Thorpe, Betty Jane Trotter, and Jane Ward.

b) Two grips are commonly used: (1) Hands together with one fist in the other fist, and with thumbs together and parallel on top. (2) Hands open (palms up) with back of one hand in palm of the other, thumbs flat against the sides of the hands. (See Fig. 9–55.)

c) Execution: (1) Move in line with ball. (2) Bend knees and lean forward slightly (use forward stride). (3) Keep elbows straight and close together. (4) As ball hits forearms, straighten legs, lift body, and keep arms firm. (5) Use little arm motion for hard-hit balls, but lift upward more on slow balls. (6) Keep feet on floor.

| *Problems with Two-Arm Bounce Pass* | *Corrections and Coaching Hints* |
|---|---|
| *Inaccurate passing.* Causes: body out of line with ball; having one forearm higher than the other. | Before hit, get directly in line with ball; let arms form an even hitting surface. Practice by getting someone to throw balls at your arms, first gently and then harder, to simulate a spike or hard-hit serve. Practice against a wall. |
| *Ball hit too high.* Causes: too much arm action; in some cases, too-forceful leg extension. | Let arms remain relatively still and firm and keep elbow and wrist action to a minimum. Let leg extension be firm but not forceful. |
| *Ball hit too low.* Causes: incorrect alignment with the ball; lack of leg power; in the case of slow balls, lack of slight upward movement with the arms. | Line up with ball to prevent overreaching. Flex knees and then extend them as you hit ball; in recovering ball from the net, use a solid upward movement with the arms, as well as push with the legs. |

2. One-Handed Dig

a) Use a one-handed dig to play the ball when good positioning for a two-arm dig is impossible; this is usually used in hitting spike.

b) Objective is to get ball back up into the air to allow teammate a good hit, or to play ball back over net on last legal hit.

c) To execute: (1) React quickly, since positioning depends on reaction time. (2) Try to have left foot forward when hitting with right hand, right foot forward when hitting with left hand. (3) Bend knees and get body low. (4) Keep weight on balls of feet, with most of weight usually concentrated on forward foot. (5) Use fist or slightly cupped hand for hit. (6) Hold wrist and forearm rigid so that ball gets a good bounce just from its own force.

| *Problems with One-Handed Dig* | *Corrections and Coaching Hints* |
|---|---|
| *Ball rebounds from arm with too much force.* Cause: swinging arm into ball. | Keep arm rigid and let ball bounce off from its own force. |
| *Hit inaccurate, out of bounds, etc.* Causes: failure to hit ball squarely; not enough concentration on ball; not getting down low enough. | Keep eye on ball until you hit it; get hand and body down close to floor and try to get under center of ball. |
| *Ball goes into net or forward rather than up.* Causes: hand or forearm not under ball; on a slow ball, not giving enough upward motion with arm to give ball momentum. | Reach out and get under ball even if it means going to the floor; hit *under* the ball rather than behind it; on net recoveries and other slow "saves," hit upward with arm on follow-through. |

3. Floater Serve

    a) A floater serve has an erratic flight because of the placement of the valve on the ball before the hit.

    b) Valve usually faces forward, but you can turn it to one side or down to get a different flight.

    c) For best effect, toss-up must be done without spin.

    d) To execute: (1) Have feet behind line in a comfortable position. (2) To ensure best transfer of weight, put left foot a little ahead of right. (3) Face net, with right shoulder turned away slightly. (4) Hold ball about chest high with left hand, steadying it with right hand. (5) Toss ball high enough to hit with extended arm (usually 2–3 feet) and about 1 to $1\frac{1}{2}$ feet in front of right shoulder. (6) On toss-up, shift weight to rear foot and bring right arm up and overhead with elbow slightly bent (hand may be brought behind head with greater elbow flexion). (7) Shift weight to forward foot, reach for ball with elbow leading out. (8) Hit with flat of fist or heel of the hand, keeping wrist firm (make contact in center of ball). (9) Let the follow-through be in line of flight (sometimes arm is pulled back quickly after contact of hand with ball) and in line with right shoulder.

| *Problems with Floater Serve* | *Corrections and Coaching Hints* |
|---|---|
| *Ball goes high.* Causes: hitting ball overhead rather than in front of body; lack of wrist firmness; hitting too much under ball. | Throw ball up 1 to $1\frac{1}{2}$ feet in front of shoulder; snap wrist by bringing it from a flexed to a straight position as contact is made. (Some prefer to keep wrist firm throughout the hit, without a wrist snap.) Watch ball, and try to make contact in the center. |

*Ball doesn't float, but spins.* Causes: ball hit off-center; follow-through is incorrect.

Pick out a spot in center of ball and hit it squarely; follow-through should be toward line of desired flight.

*Ball goes into net.* Causes: ball toss too far in front of body; incorrect weight transfer; not enough arm extension on hit.

Toss ball closer to body; transfer weight from rear to forward foot before contact; throw ball higher or don't let it drop so low before hitting it; reach up for ball.

*Serve has no speed.* Causes: not enough speed on arm swing forward; failure to shift body weight.

Bring hand back behind head; shift weight forward and then bring hand forcefully "through" ball on contact. (Some skilled players prefer to use a wrist snap. )

4. Overhead Top-Spin Serve

   a) Spin makes this kind of ball hard to return.
   b) To execute: (1) Use same position at line as you use for floater serve. (2) Hit ball with heel of hand, making contact in center of lower rear part (ball should be hit at a full arm's reach). (3) Snap wrist quickly to cup hand over ball (force is from heel of hand upward and forward to create over-spin). (4) On follow-through, extend arm fully in direction of serve, with wrist flexed and slightly pronated.

*Problems with Overhead Top-Spin Serve*

*Corrections and Coaching Hints*

*Ball hard to control.* Causes: inconsistent hand and wrist action; poor toss-up.

Heel of hand should hit center of rear lower part of ball; snap through with wrist, cupping hand over ball. (Practice motion by bouncing against floor with cupped hand.) Toss-up should be slightly higher than reach, and in the same spot each time.

*Not enough power behind ball.* Causes: Failure to transfer weight; failure to use abdominal muscles, elbow, and wrist snap.

Shift weight from rear to forward foot before hit; contract muscles in abdomen, pulling upper body forward; then snap or extend elbow, and finally snap wrist.

*Ball hit too far.* Cause: hitting too high on ball; not enough wrist snap.

Contact ball lower (on lower portion of rear). Snap wrist just as heel of hand contacts ball.

*Ball goes into net.* Causes: throwing ball too far in front of body; letting ball drop too low before hitting it; failure to reach up for the ball.

Toss ball slightly higher than reach; extend arm to hit it, reaching up with arm and body to contact ball.

*Ball goes to right or left of target.*
Causes: ball tossed too far to right or
left of right shoulder; using stance with
side to net rather than front of body
facing net; hitting ball with sidearm
pattern.

Toss ball in front of right shoulder; extend arm straight upward from bent
elbow, hitting up and over ball.

5. Forward Set

  a) Use forward set in controlled play when you have time to get into position under
  the ball; also use it to set up ball for the spike.

  b) To execute: (1) Get body under ball and in line with intended pass. (2) Place side
  toward net. (3) Adopt a position that would cause the ball to hit your nose if
  you allowed it to drop. (4) Spread feet comfortably, knees bent, weight on balls
  of feet. (5) Hold hands up and in position (elbows shoulder high, wrists back,
  index fingers and thumbs forming a triangle, with thumbs about 5 inches apart).
  (6) Watch ball. (7) Extend arms and legs at same time, making contact with ball
  about 6 inches over head. (8) Hit with fingers only (last segment of each finger).
  (9) On follow-through, turn palms in direction of ball's flight.

  c) Place ball approximately 5–6 feet above net and about 12–15 inches back from it.

6. Backward Set

  a) Use the backward set for purposes of deception.

  b) To execute: (1) Use same body and hand position as for forward set, except that
  you keep your back to the intended set, your wrists are flexed back more on
  contact, and the motions of your hands and arms are upward and backward
  (back may be arched). (2) Position of body with respect to ball determines degree
  of wrist tilt and angle of arm follow-through needed.

  c) To avoid "throwing" calls, arch back and use a straight follow-through, or get
  directly under ball, tilt hands backward, and follow through in upward direction.
  (See Fig. 9-56.)

*Problems with Setting Up Ball*

*Corrections and Coaching Hints*

*Inaccuracy because of poor positioning.*
Causes: player fails to face intended direction of set, hits on the run, or doesn't
shift weight into hit.

Face direction of set (in backward set,
back is to intended flight); get under
ball; stop body movement before hit;
"step" into set by extending knees and
arms.

*Setting ball too high.* Cause: too much
knee and arm extension.

Learn, through practice, to gauge height;
aim ball so that it arches and then drops
in desired spot; don't push as hard with
arms and legs.

**Fig. 9-56.** Backward set with wrists tilted back.

*Setting ball too low.* Cause: not enough extension of arms and legs.

Bend knees before contact; then, as you make contact with ball, straighten out knees and extend arms.

*Ball goes forward instead of up.* Causes: failure to get into position; failure to hyperextend wrist or to hit under ball.

Move quickly to get under ball; lay wrist back, watch ball, and try to contact bottom of it.

*On backward set, ball goes straight up instead of backward.* Causes: not enough backward motion with arms and body; not enough back arch; not enough wrist tilt.

Let hands and arms follow through over and beyond back of head, with body weight shifting to rear foot. If back is arched, use a straight follow-through; if body is right under ball and wrists tilted back, use an upward follow-through.

7. Short Set

   a) Use short set as change of pace and to add deception to spike.

   b) The short set is very difficult because of timing and need for signal between setter and spiker.

   c) To execute: (1) Receiver of ball sends it to setter. (2) Spiker approaches net. (3) Setter places ball a few inches above net as spiker jumps. (4) Set should be timed so that ball goes into spiker's hitting hand just as she is at the peak of her jump. (5) For variety, use semi-short set, 12–18 inches above net.

8. Spiking

   a) Spiking involves two types of sets: (1) the off-hand spike, when set must cross your body to reach spiking hand, and (2) the on-hand spike, when set reaches your hitting hand without crossing body.

   b) If spiker is to left of setter, it is an on-hand spike; if spiker is to right of setter, it is an off-hand spike.

   c) To execute on-hand spike: (1) Start about 9–10 feet from net (far enough back for 3-step approach). (2) Approach net at an angle from left sideline (with left shoulder to net). (3) Lengthen last stride, lower weight, and bring second foot forward for two-foot pushoff. (4) Swing arms upward to help take-off and gain height on the jump. (5) Bring arm into hitting position (elbow bent and up, hand open or cupped, but flat and firm). (6) To achieve maximum power, rotate right shoulder toward net, contract stomach muscles, extend arm, and snap wrist, in that order. (7) After you hit ball, stop follow-through to prevent hand from hitting net. (8) Land with knees flexed, ready for next move. (See Fig. 9–57.)

   d) When ball has been set above net rather than back from net, use follow-through that is parallel to net; give ball a glancing blow to prevent hitting net with hand.

   e) If your spike is blocked by opponents, move back from net for another approach as your team sets ball; if spike gets by block, stay at net, ready to block opponent's return shot.

(a)                                                                (b)

**Fig. 9-57.** Spiking action. (a) Elbow bent and wrist cocked for hit. (b) Player hits ball with an extension of the elbow and snap of the wrist while rotating shoulder toward net.

| *Problems with On-Hand Spike* | *Corrections and Coaching Hints* |
|---|---|
| *Not enough power.* Causes: facing net on approach; not enough contraction of muscles of abdomen; failure to snap elbow and wrist. | Keep left shoulder to net; then, as you make hit, rotate right shoulder into ball; move into ball with stomach, elbow, and wrist snap. |
| *Hitting ball too long.* Causes: hitting too much under ball rather than on top; approaching too soon. | Let ball fall in front of your right shoulder and contact top of ball; don't make approach until ball leaves setter's hands. |
| *Hitting ball into net.* Causes: hitting ball after it has dropped too low; jumping off floor too far from net. | When you make the hit, reach up with fully extended arm. Practice jumping up with tennis ball in hand and throwing it over as close to top of net as possible. Jump off floor as close to net as you can without going into net after hit. |

f) To execute off-hand spike: (1) Take approach more from center of court, and turn left shoulder to net. (2) Before hit, allow ball to cross over body to point in front of right shoulder. (3) Use same method of execution and hit as for on-hand spike.

| *Problems with Off-Hand Spike* | *Corrections and Coaching Hints* |
|---|---|
| *Not enough power.* Causes: facing net or turning right shoulder to net on approach; not enough elbow extension and wrist snap. | Approach net more in center of court; keep left shoulder to net; allow ball to cross body to the hitting-arm side. Rotate right shoulder toward ball and extend elbow forcefully. Snap wrist when you hit ball. |
| *Jump too low.* Causes: push-off from only one foot; arms not used in lift; strides too short. | Let last stride be a long one; bring rear foot up and push off with both feet. Lift arms vigorously to add height. |

9. Angles on Spike

  a) Angle is obtained by hitting ball on side rather than in center.

  b) To angle the ball to the right, hit the ball off-center on the left side; to angle the ball to the left, hit it off-center on the right side.

  c) If you are the spiker, to get the most effective angle, you must be able to picture blocker's hands in relation to the ball.

10. Drop Volley or "Dink"

  a) Use "dink" on third hit to get ball over if it has fallen below net, or use it as a deceptive move to get ball by block on a spike.

b) To execute: Hit ball gently with heel of hand, closed fist, or knuckles.

c) In executing the "dink" from spike, use same movements as for power hit, but slow swing down and place ball to the side of, or just over, the block.

d) To recover ball below net height, place hand under ball and nudge it over with fist, knuckles, or heel of hand.

11. Shoulder Roll

a) Use shoulder roll in emergencies when you have to lunge or reach out to execute a save, or when force of ball drives you backward.

b) To execute: (1) Use two-arm bump if possible, and in extreme emergencies a one-handed dig. (2) Let body rock backward as ball hits arms or fist. (3) Keep arms or fist rigid; backward motion results in ball rebounding upward. (4) Continue backward movement, rolling over shoulder. (5) Come up into a standing position. (See Fig. 9-58.)

c) To prevent hard fall, bend legs and lower body as much as possible.

12. Blocking Spike

a) The blocking of a spike may be executed by one player or two.

b) To execute: (1) When opponents pass ball to their setter, move in 12-15 inches from the net. (2) Determine direction of set to spiker. (3) Slide along parallel to net, following flight of ball. (4) After spiker has left floor, jump (usually when spiker has hand cocked to hit). (5) Place hands 6-8 inches above net (about 2-3 inches back from it) with thumbs close together, fingers spread and tense, and wrists tilted slightly backward. (6) Land with knees flexed. (See Fig. 9-59.)

c) To execute two-player block: (1) Player closest to sideline "sets" block. (2) Second player moves to her side (to time jump so that you jump simultaneously, touch elbows). (3) Keep hands within 2-3 inches of hands of second player. (4) Execute as described in (b).

d) To prevent sideline spike, girl on outside tries to turn block into the court (her outside hand should be turned to face the court).

STRATEGY

In volleyball, strategy includes knowing how to set the ball, and how to cover spikes, knowing the best hitting angles to evade blocks, establishing offensive patterns geared to personnel, knowing the best defense against serves, knowing the blocking options, and knowing how to cover behind the block.

*Passing.* Ordinarily, the first pass should go to the center forward; she then makes the set to either side for the spike. As soon as the ball is on the way to the setter, the spikers should move back from the net for their approach. Whenever possible, the center forward should take the second hit, but if another player is in better position to play the ball, she should make the call for it.

(a)

(b)

Fig. 9–58.  Shoulder roll after underhand dig.

**Fig. 9-59.** Blocking with wrist tilted back.

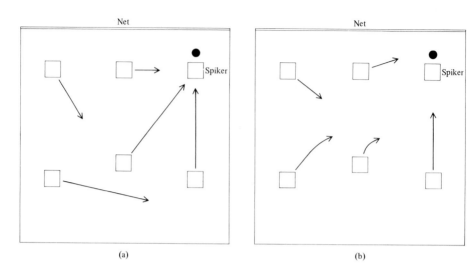

**Fig. 9-60.** Two different methods of covering court in case spike is blocked. Positioning depends on direction of ball after block.

When the pass goes to the right or left forward, a cross-court set can be used. If the ball must come from the back row on the second hit, a cross-court set should be used, since it allows the spiker more time to judge the ball's flight.

*Spiking.* Most tall players prefer to have the ball set close to the net, while a short player usually has more success in spiking from a position farther back from the net. If a short player can't make a spike, she should hit the ball with top-spin and aim deep in the court. When the opponents attempt a block, the spiker has several choices: (1) When blocker's hands are too far from the net, she may hit inside the block. (2) She may hit the ball at the blocker's sideline hand so that the ball will glance off the hand on the opponent's side of the net. (3) If the block is poorly set, she may hit around it. (4) She can use a change of pace, such as the drop shot or "dink," to throw off the defensive team's timing. (5) She can use the drop volley to place the ball over or to the side of the block.

*Covering Spike.* The spiking team must be ready to cover their court and recover the ball for another offensive attempt in case the opponents block so that the ball comes back over the net. The player covering the spike should wait with her hands up about shoulder or face level and her weight well balanced on the balls of her feet. (See Fig. 9-60 for team position when covering the spike.) If the spike clears the block but the opponents play it, players should quickly go back to their regular defensive positions. If the ball is blocked but recovered by a teammate, players should set up their offensive pattern.

**Fig. 9-61.** Four-two offensive pattern: best passer in position 6; best spiker in position 5.

**Fig. 9-62.** In four-two offensive pattern, setter (number 3) does not receive serve.

*Offensive Patterns.* Depending on the personnel the coach has available, she will set up a 3-3, a 4-2, a 5-1, or a 6-0 offensive pattern [27]. (The pattern depends on the rules used in the competition. DGWS and USVBA rules differ slightly, which means that in DGWS play some USVBA systems are ineffective.)*

The 3-3 system is built on the pass-set-spike principle with the players working in two-player units for setting and spiking purposes. This system is used when there are only three girls on the team who can spike. The players are positioned so that the setter precedes the spiker in the serve rotation. The strongest spiker should always start in the left forward position, to enable her to stay on the front row longer. If a team has a left-handed spiker or someone who can spike with either hand, the coach should start her in the right forward position.

The 4-2 offensive pattern is usually used if your team has 4 spikers and 2 setters. As it is used for competition in USVBA play,† at the beginning of the game the two setters are in the center forward and center back positions. The server, left back, left forward, and right forward are the spikers. (See Fig. 9-61.) After rotation, if the team is receiving the serve and the best setter is in the left or right forward position, as soon as the serve is hit she switches into the center forward position to take the second ball. When the setter's team is receiving, she stands near the net and does not play the serve, but remains ready to move into the setting position. (See Fig. 9-62.)

---

* DGWS systems of play have been greatly restricted by the rules concerning positioning at the time of service and the interchange of position after the service. These rules are to be changed, effective with the 1969–1971 DGWS Volleyball Guide.

† See 1969–1971 DGWS Volleyball Guide for rule changes concerning interchanging of positions.

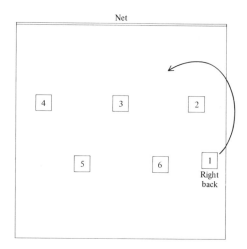

**Fig. 9-63.** Six-zero offense. Right back is shielded from serve to allow her to run up to net for the two on-hand spikers and the one off-hand spiker.

The 5-1 offense in USVBA play* is based on 5 spikers and a setter. Thus 3 spikers play at the net when the setter is in the back row, but they shift to a 4-2 when the setter is in the front row. If the setter is on the back row when she receives the serve: (1) She is shielded and does not play the serve. (2) She moves into the front court position as soon as the ball is served, so that she can set the ball. (3) The pass goes preferably to the right front side of the court for the set. (This allows her to set to the on-hand side of the spikers.)

The 6-0 offense is used when a team has 6 spikers who can also set the ball. Every center forward (regardless of number of rotations) is the setter and must be prepared to set from this position. On defense, the team tries to send the first pass to the center forward position for the set. When she is receiving the serve, the center forward plays near the net, while the rest of the team go into their receiving positions.

Under USVBA rules,* a team can use a variation for advanced players. When a team is receiving a serve, the right back player is left out of the service formation so that she can run out of the court on the right sideline. She then positions herself in the right corner to set for the on-hand spikers and the one off-hand spiker. (See Fig. 9-63.) When a team is serving, all players take defensive positions against the spike, ready to go on offense if the spike is recovered; preferably with the right back moving up into position to set the ball.

Because of the fact that under USVBA rules* the setter in the 5-1 and 6-0 offenses may shift from the back of the court after the serve, the setter from back court should not take part in blocking, but should back up her spiker until the ball is sent into the opponent's court. She then runs to the center back position for defense, while the other two back court players position themselves on either side of her.

---

* See 1969-1971 DGWS Volleyball Guide for rule changes concerning interchanging of positions.

**Fig. 9-64.** Positioning for team receiving serve. (a) Method usually used for DGWS play. (b) The half-moon formation, usually used under USVBA rules (although there are several variations of this).

*Serve Defense.* Regardless of the offensive patterns a team uses, on defense the object is to cover the defensive court effectively and to be able to execute the overhead pass, the two-arm bump, and the one-handed dig well enough to hit the serve into the air by one of these methods, so that a teammate can then control the ball. The bump and the dig should be used to play most serves, since they eliminate "throwing" and "lifting" calls.

Under USVBA rules, players may take any position so long as their serving order is maintained and the feet of the players don't overlap. Under the old DGWS rules, players had to remain in their proper areas of the court. Because of these differences, a team playing a game under USVBA rules usually used the half-moon formation, and under DGWS play they used the "fadeaway" formation (front line back from net and center back playing up). (See Fig. 9-64.) When receiving the serve, players should wait with their body weight low and their hands in position for an underhand hit. Most players find that they can react more quickly if they keep their bodies in motion while waiting for the serve by bouncing lightly on their toes. As the serve comes over, the player should try to get her body in line with the ball, stop her body movement, and then play the ball as best she can.

*Blocking.* There are two reasons for blocking: (1) to keep the spikers guessing, and (2) to block according to the spiker's weaknesses or the team's strengths in playing defense. Unless the opponents have executed a bad set, players should always be prepared to block. They can vary their blocks by: (1) blocking line hits, allowing only cross-court angles, (2) blocking cross-court angles, allowing only line hits, (3) blocking according to the spiker's ability to angle the ball, allowing line hits if the

**Fig. 9-65.** Setting the block.

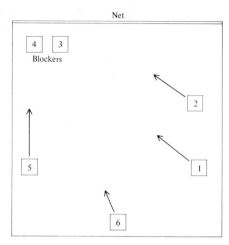

**Fig. 9-66.** Covering in case the block is successful.

spiker is weak in this area, or only cross-court angles if the spiker has trouble with this type of hit, (4) trying to block the spike regardless of the angle attempted.

Any time a team uses the block, team members must be prepared to cover all possible areas for the spike, in case it gets by the block. When the opponents set for the spiker, the two closest defensive players set the block; the third front-row player drops back into a back-court position. (See Fig. 9-65.) As the opponent gets set to spike the ball, the players move into their defensive positions, anticipating the direction of the spike. As shown in Fig. 9-66, players 2 and 5 cover spikes to their areas, as well as watch for the "dink" over the block. Player 6 covers the back-court area, and player 1 handles the cross-court spike, which is the most likely shot. When the spike is hit, the player in the area receiving the ball must move quickly and without hesitation. She has to try to hit the ball into the air to allow a teammate a controlled hit.

CONCLUSION

I regret that, because of lack of space, this chapter has necessarily been limited. However, I hope that the techniques and strategy described here will be helpful to coaches and players; and that qualified people in the different sports will broaden the resources available by contributing to the body of published material written for the skilled woman athlete and for coaches of women's athletics.

I also regret that, because of a prior commitment to another publisher, I could not include basketball in this chapter. I realize that basketball is one of the more popular sports; and therefore this omission was not a matter of choice, but of decisions beyond my control.

Finally, let me stress once again that I sincerely believe that competition for women, when *properly* controlled and supervised, is of great value. There is today an encouraging trend toward more programs for the skilled woman athlete, and I hope that the leaders will continue to make programs of this type available where they are needed. However, a note of caution: There is evidence that some would like to carry the program too fast and too far, at the expense of the average girl. Conceivably, we could swing from one extreme to another, from providing for the average girl and ignoring the highly skilled, to providing for the highly skilled and ignoring the average. There are already instances in which this is taking place. Rules and programs geared only to the highly skilled athlete and to international competition could be just as much a mistake as programs geared only to the masses. Let us hope that these factors will be considered in the future, and that our athletic programs will be a challenge and a joy to every girl.

## BIBLIOGRAPHY

1. Ainsworth, Dorothy S., *et al., Individual Sports for Women.* Philadelphia: W. B. Saunders, 1964

2. Armbruster, David A., *et al., Swimming and Diving.* St. Louis: C. V. Mosby, 1958

3. Barnes, Mildred, *et al., Sports Activities for Girls and Women.* New York: Appleton-Century-Crofts, 1966

4. Bowers, Carolyn Osborn, *Gymnastic Workshop Report.* Salt Lake City, Utah: University of Utah, June 17–28, 1963

5. Brown, Margaret, "Modern Gymnastics," *DGWS Gymnastic Guide 1963-1965.* Washington, D.C.: AAHPER, pages 14–16

6. Bunn, John W., *Scientific Principles of Coaching.* Englewood Cliffs, N.J.: Prentice-Hall, 1960

7. Burke, Jack, Jr., *et al., How to Solve Your Golf Problems.* New York: Cornerstone Library, 1963

8. Dante, Jim, and Lee Diegel, *The Nine Bad Shots of Golf and What to Do About Them.* New York: Cornerstone Library, 1963

9. Davidson, Kenneth R., and Lealand Gustavson, *Winning Badminton.* New York: A. S. Barnes, 1953

10. Day, Frank, *If You Can Walk, You Can Ski.* New York: Crowell-Collier, 1962

11. Edwards, C. B., and E. G. Heath, *In Pursuit of Archery.* London: Nicholas Kaye, 1962

12. Forslund, Ellen, *Bowling for Women.* New York: Ronald Press, 1964

13. *Golf Lessons from the Pros,* compiled by the editors of *Sports Illustrated.* Englewood Cliffs, N.J.: Prentice-Hall, 1961

14. Hochman, Lou, *The Complete Archery Book.* New York: Arco Publishing Co., 1957

15. Kentfield, John F., *Teaching and Coaching Tennis.* Dubuque, Iowa: Wm. C. Brown, 1964

16. Kidwell, Kathro, and Paul Smith, *Bowling Analyzed.* Dubuque, Iowa: Wm. C. Brown, 1960

17. Lees, Josephine T., and Betty Shellenberger, *Field Hockey for Players, Coaches, and Umpires.* New York: Ronald Press, 1957

18. Mackey, Helen T., *Field Hockey, an International Team Sport.* Englewood Cliffs, N.J.: Prentice-Hall, 1963

19. Martin, Dorothy, "Balance Beams," *DGWS Gymnastic Guide 1963-1965.* Washington, D.C.: AAHPER, pages 43-57

20. Meyer, Margaret H., and Marguerite M. Schwarz, *Team Sports for Girls and Women.* Philadelphia, Pa.: W. B. Saunders, 1965

21. Miller, Donna Mae, and Katherine Ley, *Individual and Team Sports for Women.* Englewood Cliffs, N.J.: Prentice-Hall, 1955

22. Miller, Kenneth, *Track and Field for Girls.* New York: Ronald Press, 1964

23. Mitchell, Viola, *Softball for Girls.* New York: Ronald Press, 1952

24. Moriarty, Phil, *Springboard Diving.* New York: Ronald Press, 1959

25. Neal, Patsy, *Basketball Techniques for Women.* New York: Ronald Press, 1966

26. *Olympic Sports,* prepared by United States Olympic Committee. New York: Olympic House, 57 Park Ave., New York, N.Y.

27. Peterson, Sharon, *et al., Volleyball.* Published Proceedings of Fourth National Institute on Girls' and Women's Sports, December 3-10, 1966, Indiana University

28. Robertson, David H., and Bruce Harlan, *Competitive Swimming.* Chicago: Athletic Institute

29. Sarver, Mary J., "Floor Exercise," *DGWS Gymnastic Guide 1963-1965*, pages 35-39

30. Schaafsma, Frances, *Volleyball Workshop Report.* Salt Lake City: University of Utah, summer of 1966

31. Scharff, Robert, *The Collier Quick and Easy Guide to Golf.* New York: Collier Books, 1963

32. Scott, Phebe M., and Virginia R. Crafts, *Track and Field for Girls and Women.* New York: Appleton-Century-Crofts, 1964

33. *Skiing International Yearbook, 1967.* New York: Ziff-Davis, 1966

34. Tieber, Avis Andrea, "Preparatory Work on Uneven Parallel Bars," *DGWS Gymnastic Guide 1963-1965.* Washington, D.C.: AAHPER, pages 58-62

35. Trotter, Betty Jane, *Volleyball for Girls and Women.* New York: Ronald Press, 1965

36. Vannier, Maryhelen, and Hally Beth Poindexter, *Physical Activities for College Women.* Philadelphia: Wm. B. Saunders, 1964

37. Wachtel, Erna, and Newt Loken, *How to Improve Your Gymnastics.* Chicago: Athletic Institute

38. Wilman, Joe, *Better Bowling.* New York: Ronald Press, 1953

39. Cooper, Phyllis, *Feminine Gymnastics,* Minneapolis: Burgess Publishing Company, 1968

40. Cutler, Merritt, *The Tennis Book.* New York: McGraw-Hill, 1967

41. Finsterwald, Dow, *Fundamentals of Golf.* New York: Ronald Press, 1961

42. Gabrielsen, M. Alexander, Betty Spears, and B. W. Gabrielsen, *Aquatics Handbook.* Englewood Cliffs, N.J.: Prentice-Hall, 1960

43. Hughes, Eric, *Gymnastics for Girls.* New York: Ronald Press, 1963

44. Jackson, Nell C., *Track and Field for Girls and Women.* Minneapolis: Burgess Publishing Company, 1968

45. Mortensen, Jesse P., and John M. Cooper, *Track and Field for Coach and Athlete.* Englewood Cliffs, N.J.: Prentice-Hall, 1959

46. Smith, Hope M., *Introduction to Human Movement.* Reading, Mass.: Addison-Wesley, 1968

47. *The Skier's Handbook,* by the editors of *Ski Magazine.* New York: Harper and Row, 1958

48. Thigpen, Janet, *Power Volleyball.* Dubuque, Iowa: Wm. C. Brown, 1967

49. Counsilman, James E., *The Science of Swimming.* Englewood Cliffs, N.J.: Prentice-Hall, 1968

50. Shaw, John, *et al., Selected Team Sports for Men.* Philadelphia: W. B. Saunders, 1952

ABCDE69